Factotum woodcut allegedly of John Skelton [Hodnett 2287],
uniquely found with type insert "Skylton poyet" in *Why Come Ye
Nat to Courte* [*c.* 1545], STC 22615, sig. D7. Reproduced by
express permission of the Trustees of the Henry E. Huntington
Library, San Marino, California.

JOHN SKELTON,
Early Tudor Laureate

an annotated bibliography
c. 1488-1977

A
Reference
Publication
in
Literature

Everett Emerson
Editor

JOHN SKELTON,
Early Tudor Laureate

an annotated bibliography
c. 1488-1977

ROBERT S. KINSMAN

G.K.HALL&CO.

70 LINCOLN STREET, BOSTON, MASS.

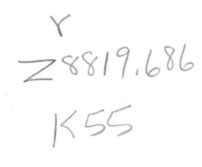

Copyright © 1979 by Robert S. Kinsman

Library of Congress Cataloging in Publication Data
Kinsman, Robert S
  John Skelton, early Tudor laureate.

  (A Reference publication in literature)
  Bibliography: p.
  Includes indexes.
  1. Skelton, John, 1460?-1529 — Bibliography.
I. Title.   II. Series.
Z8819.686.K55   [PR2348]   016.821'2   78-13239
ISBN 0-8161-8125-X

This publication is printed on permanent/durable acid-free paper
MANUFACTURED IN THE UNITED STATES OF AMERICA

Contents

Contents

Index of First Lines to Skelton's Poetry

Abstulit atra dies Astream; cana Fides sed [Second stanza in Latin of three stanza "En Parlàment à Paris" ("En Parl"), at end of Garlande of Laurell (GL), no. 1523.3]

Accipe nunc demum, doctor celeberrime Rukshaw [Envoy to "The Dolorous Dethe and Muche Lamentable Chaunce of the Mooste Honorable Erle of Northumberlande" ("DEN"), no. 1489]

Ad dominum properato meum, mea pagina, Percy [Dedicatory poem to "DEN," no. 1489--see above]

Agaynst the prowde Scottes claterynge ["Against the Scottes" ("Ag Scottes"), no. 1513.6]

Al maters wel pondred and wel to be regarded ["Against Venemous Tongues" ("AVT"), no. 1516]

All noble men, of this take hede [Prologue of Why Come Ye Nat to Courte? (WCY), no. 1522; printed as separate poem in Here after foloweth certayne bokes (CB), no. 1545 &c; occurs as separate poem in PPPW, no. 1568, sig. 16^{r-v}, and also as prologue to WCY, sig L4^{r-v}.]

Al thyngys contryvyd by mannys reason [Magnyfycence (Mag), nos. 1516.2 and 1530.3]

Alma parens O Cantabrigensis ["Eulogiam consolationis," preliminary to A Replycacion (Rep), no. 1528.2]

Arectyng my syght towarde the zodyake [opening line of English verses of Garlande of Laurell, no. 1523.3]

Aspirate meis elegis, pia turma sororum ["Elegia in serenissime principis et domine, domine Margarete" ("El Marg"), no. 1516.1]

The auncient acquaintance, madam, betwen us twayn [see Dyuers Balettys and Dyties Solacyous (DBDS), no. 1527.1]

Ay, besherewe yow, be my fay ["Manerly Margery, Mylk and Ale" ("MM"), no. 1495.1]

Calliope ["Why were ye, Calliope, embrawdred with letters of golde?" ("Calliope" Engl.), no. 1512.2]

Candida Calliope, vatum regina, coronans ["Calliope" (Lat.), no. 1512.2]

Caudatos Anglos, spurcissime Scote, quid effers? ["Vilitissimus Scotus Dundas allegat caudas contra Angligenas" (VSD), no. 1516.3]

Colinus Cloutus, "quanquam mea carmina multis" [Latin envoy to Collyn Clout (CC), nos. 1522.1 and 1531.2]

Cuncta licet cecidisse putas discrimina rerum [see DBDS, no. 1527.1]

Ebria, squalida, sordida femina, prodiga verbis [Envoy to Tunnyng of Elynour Rummyng (TER), nos. 1517 and 1521]

Excitat, en, asinus mulum (mirabile visu) ["Apostropha ad Londini cives," last of three Latin poems at end of WCY, nos. 1522 and 1545.3]

Felix qui bustum formasti, Rex, tibi cuprum ["Tetrastichon Veritatitis" (Tetr), see "Eulogium," no. 1512]

For age is a page [Introductory line, proper, to Why Come Ye Nat to Courte? WCY, nos. 1522 and 1545.3]

Fraxinus in silvis, altis in montibus ornus ["Admonet Skeltonis omnes arbores dare locum viridi lauro juxta genus suum" (first of two poems added at end of GL), no. 1523.3]

Garnyshe, gargone, gastly, gryme ["Fourth Flyting Agenst Garnesche" ("Ag Garn"), no. 1514.1]

Go, pytyous hart, rasyd with dedly wo [see DBDS, no. 1527.1]

How may I your mokery mekely tollerate ["Second Flyting Agenst Garnesche" ("Ag Garn"), no. 1514.1]

Huc, pia Calliope, propera, mea casta puella ["Eulogium pro suorum temporum conditione" ("Eulogium"), no. 1513.2]

I have your lewde letter receyved ["Third Flyting Agenst Garnesche" ("Ag Garn"), no. 1514.1]

I, liber, et propera regem tu pronus adora [Dedicatory poem in Sk's gift to Henry VIII (I, Liber), no. 1512.1]

Iam nunc pierios cantus et carmina laudis [From <u>Speculum Principis</u>
  (<u>Spec Princ</u>), nos. 1501.2 and 1511.1]

In Autumpne, whan the sonne in Vyrgyne [<u>The Bowge of Courte</u> (<u>BC</u>),
  no. 1499.2]

Ismal, ecce, Bedel, non mel, sed fel, sibi des el ["In Bedel quondam
  Belial incarnatum, devotum epitaphium" (<u>"In Bedel"</u>), no. 1518]

I wayle, I wepe, I sobbe, I sigh ful sore ["DEN," no. 1489]

Justice est morte [Beginning of first stanza in French of three stanza
  "En Parlament à Paris" ("En Parl") at end of <u>GL</u>, no. 1523.3]

Justyce now is dede [Beginning of third stanza in English of three
  stanza "En Parlament à Paris" ("En Parl") at end of <u>GL</u>, no. 1523.3]

Kynge Jamy, Jomy, your Joye is all go [<u>A Ballade of the Scottysche</u>
  <u>Kynge</u> ("BSK"), no. 1513.4]

Knolege, aquayntance, resort, favour, with grace ["Knolege," <u>see</u>
  <u>DBDS</u>, no. 1527.1]

Libertas veneranda piis concessa poetis [Second Latin poem postscript
  to <u>Ware the Hauke</u> (<u>WH</u>), no. 1505]

A lytell ragge of Rethorike [First line in English verse of <u>A Reply-</u>
  <u>cacion agaynst certayn yong scolers abjured of late etc.</u> (<u>Rep</u>),
  no. 1528.2]

My darlyng dere, my daysy floure [First line of carol with burden
  "With 'Lullay, lullay,' lyke a chylde," <u>Agaynste a Comely</u>
  <u>Coystrowne</u> (<u>ACC</u>), no. 1527]

My name ys Parott, a byrde of Paradyse [<u>Speke Parrot</u> (<u>SP</u>), no. 1521.1]

O lachrimosa lues nimis, o quam flebile fatum ["Lamentatio urbis
  Norvvicen" ("Lamentatio"), no. 1507.1]

O memoranda dies, qua, decollate Johannes [Latin poem, postscript to
  <u>WH</u>, no. 1505]

Of all nacyons under the hevyn [Title poem to <u>Skelton Laureate</u>
  <u>agaynste a comely coystrowne</u>... (<u>ACC</u>), no. 1527]

Pla-ce-bo [<u>Phyllyp Sparowe</u> (<u>PS</u>), no. 1505.1]

Porro perbelle dissimulatum ["Epitoma de morbilloso Thom": First of
  three Latin poems at end of <u>WCY</u>, nos. 1522 and 1545.3]

Preponenda meis non sunt tua plectra camenis [Latin companion poem to
"ACC," title poem of <u>Agaynst a Comely Coystrowne</u> (<u>ACC</u>), no. 1527]

Proh dolor, ecce, maris lupus, et nequissimus ursus ["Decasticon," the
second of three Latin Poems at end of <u>WCY</u>, nos. 1522 and 1545.3]

Quamvis annose est, apice et sulvate vetusto [Latin fragment preceding
"I, liber, et propera, regem tu promus adora" (<u>"I, liber"</u>), no.
1512.1]

Quamvis insanis, quamvis marcescis inanis [A distich at end of <u>TER</u>,
no. 1517]

Rejoyse, Englande [<u>The Douty Duke of Albany</u> (<u>DDA</u>), no. 1523.4]

The Rose both White and Rede ["A Lawde and Prayse made for our
Sovereigne Lord the Kyng" ("Lawde"), no. 1509.2]

Salve, festa dies, toto memorabilis evo [<u>"Chorus de Dys contra Gallos"</u>
(<u>"Chorus contra Gallas"</u>), no. 1513.3]

Salve, festa dies, toto resonabilis evo [<u>"Chorus de Dys contra
Scottos"</u> (<u>"Chorus contra Scottos"</u>), no. 1513.5]

Si quid habes, mea musa, dei resonantis amenan ["Epigramma ad tanti
principis majestatem in sua puerice," Latin elegiacs at end of
<u>Speculum Principis</u> (<u>Spec Princ</u>), no. 1501.2]

Sithe ye have me chalyngyd, Master Garnesche ["First Flyting Agenst
Garnesche" ("Ag Garn"), no. 1514.1]

Tell you I chyll [<u>The Tunnyng of Elynour Rummyng</u> (<u>TER</u>), no. 1517]

This tretise devysed it is ["A Devoute Trentale for Old John Clarke"
and "Epitaph for Adam Uddersale" (or Adam All-a-Knave) ("Dev Tr &
Ep Adam"), no. 1507]

This worke devysed is [<u>Ware the Hauke</u> (<u>WH</u>), no. 1505]

Tristia Melpomenes cogor modo plectra sonare ["Henrici septimi
epitaphium" (<u>H VII</u>), no. 1512.3]

Tu, Garnishe, fatuus, fatuus tuus est mage scriba! [Distich following
"Third Garnesche Flyting" ("Ag Garn"), no. 1514.1]

What can it avayle [<u>Collyn Clout</u> (<u>CC</u>), nos. 1522.1 and 1531.2]

With "Lullay, Lullay," lyke a chylde [Burden to "My darlyng dere" in
<u>ACC</u>, no. 1527]

Womanhod, wanton, ye want [("WW"), <u>see</u> <u>ACC</u>, no. 1527]

Youre ugly tokyn ["Uppon a Deadmans Hed" ("UDH"), in <u>ACC</u>, no. 1527]

Abbreviations and Short Titles

For compact reference to Skelton's poetry and prose; and to books, monographs, standard reference works, scholarly periodicals; and to libraries, the following abbreviations and short titles are used throughout this bibliography.

ACC	Agaynst a Comely Coystrowne (the collection)
"ACC"	"Agaynste a Comely Coystrowne" (the poem proper)
"Ag Garn"	"Agenst Garnesche" [4 flytings]
"Ag Scottes"	"Agaynst the Scottes"
AHR	American Historical Review
AIUON-SG	Annali Istituto Universitario Orientale, Napoli, Sezione Germanica
"All Noble"	"All noble men, of this take hede"
Archiv	Archiv für das Studium der Neuren Sprachen und Literaturen
ASLIB	Index to Theses Accepted for Higher Degrees by the Universities of Great Britain and Ireland and the Council for National Academic Awards
"Aunc Acq"	"The auncient acquaintance, madam, betwen us twayn"
"AVT"	"Against Venemous Tongues"
BC	The Bowge of Courte
B.L.	British Library (formerly designated B.M. = British Museum)
Bodl.	Bodleian Library
"BSK"	"A Ballade of the Scottysche Kynge"
BTF	The Boke of the Three Fooles [non-canonical]

"Calliope (Engl)"	"Why Were Ye, Calliope, Embrawdered with Letters of Golde?"
"Calliope (Lat)"	"Cur tibi contexta est aurea Calliope?"
CB	Certayne Bokes
CC	Collyn Clout
CH	The Henry E. Huntington Library, San Marino, California
"Chorus contra Gallos"	"Chorus de Dys contra Gallos"
"Chorus contra Scottos"	"Chorus de Dys contra Scottos"
"Contra asinum"	"Contra alium cantitantem et organisantem asinum"
CT	Canadian Theses (Ottawa, National Library of Canada)
CUL	Cambridge University Library
"Cuncta licet (Engl)"	"Though ye suppose all jeperdys ar paste"
"Cuncta licet (Lat)"	"Cuncta licet cecidisse putas discrimina rerum"
DA	Dissertation Abstracts
DAI	Dissertation Abstracts International (so termed with vol. xxx, 1969)
DBDS	Dyuers Balettys and Dyties Solacyous
DDA	The Douty Duke of Albany
"DEN"	"The Doulourus Dethe and Muche Lamentable Chaunce of the Most Honorable Erle of Northumberlande"
"Dev Tr & Ep Adam"	"A Devoute Trentale for Old John Clarke" and "Epitaph on Adam Uddersale (or Adam-All-a-Knave)"
"Diligo"	"Diligo rusti[cul]um cum porta[t D]is duo qu[in]tum"
DNB	Dictionary of National Biography
DS	Diodorus Siculus
Dyce	Alexander Dyce (ed.), The Poetical Works of John Skelton (London, 1843), 2 vols.
"Edw IV"	"Of the Deth of the Noble Prynce, Kynge Edwarde the Forth" [Doubtful]
Edwards, Life and Times	H. L. R. Edwards, Skelton, The Life and Times of an Early Tudor Poet (London, 1949)

EETS	Early English Text Society
EHR	English Historical Review
"El Marg"	"Elegia in serenissime principis et domine, domine Margarete"
ELN	English Language Notes
ELR	English Literary Renaissance
EngR	English Review
Engl. Studn.	Englische Studien
"En Parl"	"En Parlament à Paris"
ES	English Studies
"Eulogium"	"Eulogium pro suorum temporum conditione"
"Frax. in silvis"	"Fraxinus in silvis, altis in montibus ornus"
"Gentle Paule"	"Gentle Paule, laie down thy sweard"
GL	Garlande of Laurell
GM	Gentlemen's Magazine
"Go"	"Go, pytyous hart, rasyd with dedly wo"
Herford and Simpson	C. H. Herford, Percy and Evelyn Simpson (eds.), Ben Jonson (Oxford, 1925-52), 11 vols.
HLQ	Huntington Library Quarterly
Howard	Patsy C. Howard (comp.), Theses in English Literature 1894-1970 (Ann Arbor: The Pierian Press, 1973)
"H VII"	"Henrici septimi epitaphium"
IADD	Index to American Doctoral Dissertations
"I, liber"	"I, liber, et propera, regem tu pronus adora"
"In Bedel"	"In Bedel quondam Belial incarnatum, devotum epitaphium"
JEGP	Journal of English and Germanic Philology
"Jeperdys"	See "Cuncta licet (Engl.)"
K&Y	Robert S. Kinsman and Theodore Yonge, John Skelton: Canon and Census. (For the Renaissance Society of America, 1967)
"Knolege"	"Knolege, aquayntance, resort, favour, with grace"
"Lamentatio"	"Lamentatio urbis Norvvicen"

L&P, H VIII	Letters and Papers, Foreign and Domestic, of the Reign of Henry VIII, ed. J. S. Brewer, J. Gairdner, and R. H. Brodie (1862–1910, 1920, 1929–32), 21 vols in 33 parts; 2nd edn. vol. i in 3 parts; addenda, vol. i in 2 parts
"Lawde"	"A Lawde and Prayse Made for Our Sovereigne Lord the Kyng"
LJ	Library Journal
"Lullay"	"With lullay, lullay, lyke a chylde," burden of carol "My darlyng dere"
Mag	Magnyfycence
MAe.	Medium Aevum
"MDD"	"My Darlyng Dere" (opening line of carol)
MLN	Modern Language Notes
MLQ	Modern Language Quarterly
MLR	Modern Language Review
"MM"	"Mannerly Margery Mylk and Ale"
N/EX	= "Not Examined"
N&Q	Notes and Queries
Nelson, Laureate	William Nelson, John Skelton, Laureate (New York, 1939)
Neophil	Neophilologus
New Rep	New Republic
NYTBR	New York Times (Sunday) Book Review
PMLA	Publications of the Modern Language Association of America
PP	Piers Plowman
PPPW	Pithy, Pleasaunt and Profitable Workes, 1568
"Prayers"	"Prayers to The Father of Heaven, To the Second Parson and To the Holy Gooste" [Doubtful]
PQ	Philological Quarterly
P.R.O.	Public Records Office, London
PS	Phyllyp Sparowe
PW	Poetical Works of John Skelton (Boston, 1856 and 1864), 3 vols.
PW, S&D	The Poetical Works of Skelton and Donne, with a Memoir of Each (Boston, 1881), 4 vols. in 2
QJS	Quarterly Journal of Speech
QQ	Queen's Quarterly

QR	Quarterly Review
Rep	A Replycacion
RI	Retrospective Index to Theses of Great Britain and Ireland, 1716-1950, ed. Roger Bilboul and Francis L. Kent (1975)
RLC	Revue de littérature comparée
RN	Renaissance News (see also RQ)
RR	Romanic Review
RQ	Renaissance Quarterly
"Salve"	"Salve plus decies quam sunt momenta dierum" [Doubtful]
Sayle	C. E. Sayle (comp.), Early English Printed Books in the University Library, Cambridge
SB	Studies in Bibliography
SEL	Studies in English Literature, 1500-1900
SN	Studia Neophilologica
SP	Speke, Parrot
Spec Princ	Speculum Principis
SR	[Stationers' Register], A Transcript of the Registers of the Company of Stationers of London, 1554-1640, ed. Edward Arber (1875-77), 5 vols.
SRL	Saturday Review of Literature
STC	Short Title Catalogue of Books Printed in England, Scotland, and Ireland...1475-1640, ed. A. W. Pollard and G. R. Redgrave (1926), 2 vols.
$STC^{2.2}$	Short Title Catalogue, Second Edition, Revised and Enlarged, ed. W. A. Jackson, F. S. Ferguson, and Katharine F. Pantzer (1976), Vol. 2 "I-Z." [First volume, "A-H," here designated $STC^{2.1}$, in preparation.]
Stud. in Phil.	Studies in Philology
Tenn Studies	University of Tennessee Studies in Literature
TER	The Tunnyng of Elynour Rummyng
"Tetr."	"Tetrastichon Veritatis"
TLS	(London) Times Literary Supplement

"Tyme"	"How Every Thynge Must Have a Tyme" [Doubtful]
"UDH"	"Uppon a Deedmans Hed"
URKC	University Review (Kansas City, Mo.)
"VSD"	"Vilitissimus Scotus Dundas allegat caudas contra Angligenas" (Latin and English)
WCY	Why Come Ye Nat to Courte?
WH	Ware the Hauke
Wing	Donald Wing (comp.), Short-Title Catalogue of Books Printed in England, Scotland, Ireland, Wales, and British America... 1641-1700 (1945-51), 7 vols.
"WW"	"Womanhod, wanton ye want"
ZAA	Zeitschrift für Anglistik und Amerikanistik

Acknowledgments

I gratefully acknowledge the patience and pluck of my wife
Barbara Yates Kinsman for having bulldozed 3 x 5 index cards into a
consistent form and intelligible arrangement. Deep gratitude I freely
confess I owe to Professors Anthony Edwards of the University of Victoria, British Columbia, and William Ringler of the University of
Chicago for their generous assistance in setting mooted matters
straight and reducing stubborn problems to easy solutions. For their
promptness in reply to queries and for scholarly kindnesses, I am no
less thankful to Robert L. Collison, Head, School of Librarianship,
Ealing Technical College, London; V. A. Hinton, English Librarian,
The Brotherton Library, University of Leeds; V. H. King, Assistant
Under Librarian, Cambridge University Library; Gordon Kipling, Asso-
ciate Professor of English, UCLA; Anne MacDermaid, University Archiv-
ist, Douglas Library, Queen's University, Kingston, Ontario; Dianne
Munro, Librarian (Inter-Library Loans), Edinburgh University Library;
William Osuga, Head Inter-Library Loan Department, UCLA Library;
Katharine Pantzer, Director, Short-Title Catalogue Project, Houghton
Library, Harvard University; and Lillian Wilde, Associate Professor
of English, California State University, San Dimas, California.

To Gretchen Flesher, steadiest of research assistants, assigned
me by the Center for Medieval and Renaissance Studies, UCLA; to Ruth
Bowers and Ivy Tunick, typists extraordinary; and to the Central
Stenographic Bureau at UCLA, their gracious employer, I profess indebtedness for their patience and perception. In all instances,
mistakes made in reference or entry are mine and mine alone.

Introduction

The Need for a Skelton Bibliography

In 1960 the American poet Richard O'Connell in a "Variation on a
Theme of 'Maister Skelton, Poet Laureat,'" invoked the Tudor poet to
"Speak, parrot, poet, priest, bespeak your age."[1] His plea was very
much that of a new generation, for modern poets of the second through
fifth decades of the century, both British and American, from W. H.
Auden to John Crowe Ransom; from Robert Graves, Richard Hughes to the
Sitwells, Dame Edith and Sir Osbert, on Skelton's narrative shores;
and from Horace Gregory, Babette Deutsch and Hayden Carruth[2] on this
side of the Atlantic, had in fact already revived the spirit, sub-
stance and the very mode of Skelton's "naked, sinewy rhyme" in their
poems and in their critical essays.[3]

Twentieth century scholars and academic critics of Skelton kept
pace with their creative confreres. Indeed the morality play Magnyfycence, whose prosodic variety was praised by W. H. Auden in 1935,
had been painstakingly edited by R. L. Ramsay and published by the
Early English Text Society in 1908 (for 1906). It is true, to be
sure, that the major scholarly contributions of Nelson, Gordon and
Edwards, for example, were not in book form until 1939, 1943 and 1949
respectively, fifteen to twenty-five years behind the poets. Their
readings have nonetheless found response in younger poets of the
sixties and seventies.

The reprinting of the EETS edition of Magnyfycence in 1925 was
symbolically meaningful in terms of the growing awareness of Skelton's
significance in the long history of English letters. In the same year
the Modern Language Association of America issued photographic facsimiles of two unedited works of Skelton's: the Bibliotheca Historia,
his earliest achievement, a partial translation in English of Poggio's
fifteenth century Latin translation of the Greek of Diodorus Siculus
(written c. 60-30 B.C.); and the Speculum Principis, Skelton's moral
mirror for the young prince Henry (completed in 1501). The final
editing of these two pieces was to be proof, in one form or another,
of the truly international nature of scholarly interests in Skelton:
the Bibliotheca was edited (vol. I in 1956, vol. II in 1957) by
Frederick Salter, a Canadian-born and Chicago-trained scholar, in full

collaboration with H. L. R. Edwards, an English D.Phil. from Cambridge; the Speculum had already found Salter as its editor in 1934. One may be pardoned, I trust, for further noting the widespread interest in Skelton manifested by articles and books that were to emanate from the Netherlands (Swart 1964), France (Pollet, 1952, 1962), Italy (Schulte, 1961, 1962, 1963), New Zealand (Gordon, 1943), and Tasmania (Howarth, 1945). It is, we note further, an Australian poet, A. D. Hope, who has most recently revived the Skeltonic tone (1972).

1925 serves as a useful hinge in two other ways. In that year Ramsay's edition of Magnyfycence was reissued, and in that year appeared L. J. Lloyd's essay on "John Skelton, A Forgotten Poet" (RES, XL, 659-665), an article apparently written before the publication of Hughes' selections from Skelton in 1924. By 1926 approximately half of the items listed in this bibliography had appeared--400 of the 806 items indexed: articles, books, editions, monographs, notes, "imitations," and reviews. Or, to put it differently, half of the effort expended in manifesting an interest in Skelton, the poet so marvellously intuited by modern poets, indeed three-fourths of the formal scholarly and critical endeavor to deepen and extend our understanding and appreciation of the Tudor laureate, has been advanced in the fifty years that have since elapsed.

Skelton has had his bibliographers since the time of Bishop Bale (Index (ms.) before 1557; Catalogus 1557-59), but none, either by the passage of time or the vexatious nature of the bibliographical enterprise, was truly a "compleat" bibliograph. Bibliophiles like Ames, Herbert, Ritson and Dibdin preserved Skelton titles; memorialists like Winstanley and Wood, Skelton's name; local historians like Blomefield and Westlake unearthed documents of his life. None brought all the available materials carefully together.

By the very nature of the undertaking, that of representing the entire range of English studies both in primary and in secondary materials ("works by" and "works about"), the Cambridge Bibliography of English Literature of 1940 and its totally revised successor the New Cambridge Bibliography (volume one issued last, in 1974) have had to "aim at completeness in [their] own terms."[4] This has meant the exclusion of such materials as unpublished dissertations or their published abstracts (included in this bibliography), brief notes, some of which deal with specific passages in a particular poem (included in this bibliography), and reviews of secondary works (here noticed). These lesser matters, not always inconsequential, have necessarily been left to specialized individual bibliographies.

As for specialized bibliographies of Skelton, in 1914 Elise Bischoffberger brought forward a monograph on Der Einfluss John Skeltons auf die Englische Literatur; in 1939 Dorothy Whitmee filed for her University of London diploma a manuscript bibliography that built on Henderson (1931). Three less ambitious summaries of Skelton

scholarship have since appeared: that of R. G. Howarth in 1945, of
Margaret Schlauch in 1969, and most recently that of Burton Fishman
in 1971. The title of this last, "Recent Studies in Skelton," epito-
mizes the more or less occasional nature of the periodic reviews just
cited. Thus C. S. Lewis's complaint, advanced more than two decades
ago in his volume of the Oxford History of English Literature,[5] still
stands: for Skelton "There is [yet] no good formal bibliography."
Such a lack the bibliography contained within these covers attempts
to rectify.

The Scope of the Bibliography

In responding to C. S. Lewis's charge, as it were, I should perhaps first clarify what I am seeking to do in presenting a "formal
bibliography" of things Skeltonic. To begin with, I have spread my
net widely to haul in not only the secondary scholarship specifically
on Skelton, but also to include primary materials: his works as they
were printed, collected and edited over the centuries, and the records
of his life, sparse as they are.

Under the rubric of secondary scholarship on Skelton, I include
all known commentaries on his work (in English, French, German and
Italian), full-length studies, journal and periodical articles, monographs, master's theses (although I have examined only those in excess
of one hundred pages), and doctoral dissertations. I have incorporated as "bibliographical materials" works that include analytical
descriptions of Skelton editions as well as listings of Skelton manuscripts and printed editions, ranging from the catalogue of the Carl
H. Pforzheimer Library (no. 1940.1) to the second volume of the
second edition of the Short Title Catalogue (no. 1976.2). Under a
separate heading in the Subject Index, I have listed the reviews of
the full-length studies, and have tried to note any and all indications of Skelton's reputation as poet or personality, be they comments
on his poems, fictions involving him as a persona in "merry tales" or
dramatic scenes, or imitations of his verse.

As primary sources I have included notices of the known records
and documents of Skelton's life as originally calendared; more recently produced genealogical inquiries into his origins or biographical summaries of his known activities; and the manuscript or printed
editions of his writings as they were issued, usually individually,
then collected and finally edited. While I have listed in detail the
contents of the various collections, I have not tried to duplicate the
full bibliographical description of the editions presented in Kinsman
and Yonge, John Skelton: Canon and Census (New York: Renaissance
Society of America, 1967), but use that work as a point of reference.
In order to help assess his reputation over the years, especially in
the nineteenth century and the first six decades of the twentieth
century, I have also noticed published selections from his writings
whether printed separately or included in anthologies—until 1900, at
least, of five or more pages within the anthology—as well as musical
settings of his poems. The Skeltonic materials that I have excluded

and my reasons for so doing will be presented under a separate heading below.

Both primary and secondary sources are listed chronologically to give the user of the bibliography some notion of the ebb and flow of Skelton's reputation and influence, and some indication of the character and quality of the interest manifested in Skelton and his works. We thus range from c. 1488 when his earliest piece of canonical certainty was probably completed, a translation of Diodorus Siculus, down through 1977, four hundred and ninety years later, when the most recent pronouncement on his comico-serious, covertly ironic bio-bibliographical poem, the Garlande of Laurell, was published.

Criteria for the Exclusion of Materials

As I mentioned above, I have listed in this bibliographical guide and literary index to Skelton, as it were, selections from Skelton, published separately or included in anthologies. Thus, selections that consist of poems and pieces selected from Skelton and Skelton alone, such as Robert Graves' brief selection from the poet (no. 1927), merit inclusion, despite their incompleteness, if only to show how Skelton sits with the poets as well as to show their desire to gain him a wider audience. Yet I have chosen, defensibly, I believe, to omit the minor remarks (under 20 words) of the minor Romantic poet, Thomas Campbell, comparing Lyndsay and Skelton (Specimens of the British Poets, 1819, II, 69) but have noted Robert Southey's printing of Colin Clout and Phyllyp Sparowe (both complete) in the Select Works of the British Poets (1831). They reflect the deep and extended interest of a Romantic poet of prominence in the Tudor Laureate and are further distinguished by a perceptive introduction which, among other things, issued the call for a completely new edition of Skelton's works, a call heeded by Alexander Dyce, Skelton's great editor (1843).

Since the anthologies of the nineteenth century show popular preservers of English literature taking over the "perpetuation" of Skelton from the antiquarians and bibliophiles of the last quarter of the eighteenth century and the first two decades of the nineteenth, I have included anthology titles of the period, provided they included at least five pages of Skelton's verse within their covers, to indicate Skelton's continued existence among those who read the older poets widely if not deeply.

With the turn of the century and following the publication of William Henry Williams' Selection from the Poetical Works of John Skelton of 1902, however, I have abandoned any pretense at completeness when it comes to itemizing anthologies that include Skelton, so generally, if superficially, had Skelton become recognized. I have thus deliberately ignored a benchmark, Sir Arthur Quiller-Couch's Oxford Book of English Verse, which, in making its first appearance in 1900, included only two of the now traditional anthology pieces, "the Garlande lyrics"--those to Mistress Margery Wentworth and to Mistress Margaret Hussey. In Quiller-Couch's second edition of the

OBEV, a third lyric, but no more, was added: "Mistress Isabel Pennell." I thus do not list the names of Howard F. Lowry and Willard
Thorpe, editors of the once popular American collegiate text, An Oxford Anthology of English Poetry (1st edn., New York, 1935), for example, because they include in their choice no more than Quiller-Couch
had originally chosen.[6] When Dame Helen Gardner brought out the New
Oxford Book of English Verse in 1972, however, and included substantial passages from Phyllyp Sparowe in addition to the three lyrics,
bringing the total of pages devoted to Skelton to ten, her "Oxford"
seemed sufficiently noteworthy to be included as a significant
"Selection."

Similarly, with the general historians of English literature I
have been arbitrary. For example, when among others Skelton is mentioned in a salient way by literary men and others of the sixteenth
through nineteenth centuries, I have alluded to their observations.
While one gladly includes the "inventor," as it were, of English
literary history, Thomas Warton (1778), one can with impunity ignore
the single page of comment on Skelton by Hippolyte Taine (Histoire de
la littérature anglaise, Paris, 1863, I, 242) despite his great name,
especially when his remarks seem based on a fuller and earlier discussion of Skelton's verse by his compatriot Philarète Chasles (1842).
As a rule of thumb, I have ignored "general" histories of English
literature (as opposed to books, articles or monographs on Skelton,
specifically) if they devote less than 5 pages of space to Skelton.
Even then, as with A Literary History of England, edited by Albert C.
Baugh (1st edn. 1948, 2nd edn. 1967), when the remarks of twentieth-
century literary historians have seemed to me to be only pedestrian,
I have exercised the right of exclusion. For their special comparative quality I have, however, included Arthur Koelbing's remarks on
Skelton in the CHEL (1st edn. 1908), and for their brilliance (and
slight skewedness) those of C. S. Lewis in the OHEL (1954).

The same calculated arbitrariness has prevailed in my exclusion
of brief itemizations of Skelton manuscript or printed material.
Where they seemed of historical moment or particularly useful in fullness of illustration I have included them (see HEYWARD, no. 1947);
where not, I have excluded such brief listings of Skelton manuscript
materials as presented by Carleton Brown and Rossell Hope Robbins in
their Index of Middle English Verse (New York, 1943), in which three
of the four poems listed are doubtful to begin with. On the other
hand I have incorporated into my bibliography the Supplement to the
Index of Middle English Verse as compiled by Robbins and Cutler, no.
1965.5, for its fullness.

Skelton's Reputation and Influence

We began this introduction with a reminder that Skelton has been
as much revived in the twentieth century by poets as preserved by
scholars and critics, and with the argument that the chronological
arrangement of the bibliography would readily show the ebbs and flows
in Skelton's reputation and influence as poet and personality.

From the very outset of his career Skelton was accepted for his learning (more churchly than humanistic), his rhetorical skills, and his poetic inventiveness. At the same time he was held in bad repute by conservative authors who were suspicious of his flamboyant style and poetic daring. Such polarity of opinion will both make and mar his reputation down to the most recent times. Thus Caxton in 1490 praises Skelton for having "redde the ix. muses," and having understood "theyr musicalle syences," as evidence that "he hath dronken of Elycons well"; so in 1510 or thereabouts Skelton is remarked together with More and Cornysh as a satirist of prominence and power in the Great Chronicle of London. By 1513 Henry Bradshaw had commented on "inventive Skelton and poet laureate" as one of the "fathers of eloquens" together with Lydgate, Chaucer and "religious Barkeley [Barclay]"; yet in 1509 Skelton had been presumably censured for his excesses in Phyllyp Sparowe by the very same Barclay, probably not only for the religious parody recurrent in the "Commendations" section of the poem but also for its daring personal eroticism. Again in 1514 and 1515 Barclay lays the lash on Skelton's back for violating his laureateship by succumbing allegedly to Thais and Venus in his verse.

As a quarrelsome person and unruly poet Skelton was rebuked by the humanist and grammarian William Lily [c. 1520], the formidable opponent of Skelton's ally Robert Whittinton in the "Grammarians War" of the late 1510s and early 1520s, the same Whittinton who in 1519 had echoed Erasmus' polite praise of Skelton (in 1499) by varying the epithet to "Anglorum vatum gloria" [rather than "decus"]. It is as a bold and witty personality, no ally of those in power, that Skelton is established in Tale Forty-one of A C Mery Tales of [1525]. Made into a dramatic personality of sorts in his own time, Skelton will become a dramatis persona in Elizabethan jest books and plays.

Within a year or two of Skelton's death in 1529 the basic elements of his reputation and the major modes of his influence were complete. To be sure not all his poems were available to the public. Bowge of Court had been twice printed (c. 1499 and c. 1510) by de Worde; the same printer had brought the Tunning of Elynour Rummyng to public eye in 1521 or thereabouts, as fragments of his edition discovered in the 1950's testify. Phyllyp Sparowe, in manuscript (or manuscripts) now lost, had stirred the indignation of Alexander Barclay by 1508. Skelton's ironic bio-bibliographical summary and defense of his calling, The Garlande of Laurell, in which PS is exonerated, had appeared in 1523. Just before his death two collections of his earlier and shorter poems, both lyric and sardonic, had issued from Rastell's press: Agaynste a Comely Coystrowne and Dyuers Balettys and Dyties Solacyous (c. 1527). As a sign of the times, his last piece, A Replycacion, a caustic rebuke of two graduates of Cambridge for having succumbed to the Lutheran heresy, had been printed by Richard Pynson, printer to the King's most noble grace, c. 1528.

In 1530 or thereabouts, a portion of his Collyn Clout was (hastily) copied in manuscript as the "Profecy of Skelton, 1529," as if he had literally predicted the fall of his chief satiric object, Cardinal Wolsey, who died in disgrace that autumn. By 1530 or 1532 the whole poem of CC had been printed; and at that approximate time Skelton's satirical morality play Magnyfycence came off the press. Both pieces were presumably freed now from censorship, by Wolsey's death.

Thus to the contemporary views of Skelton as learned and inventive, on the one hand, but unruly on the other, was added that of the inspired satirist, undaunted by the highest of the churchly or secular hierarchy. It is no wonder that by the 1530's we have scraps of evidence (see nos. 1531, 1531.1, 1534 and 1535 of the bibliography proper) that the association of Skelton with the witty, quick-minded scoffer in merry tales was coupled with the use of Skeltonics to represent lower-class characters and serving men, soon to harden almost into a convention that would flavor popular literature, including the drama, for a hundred years or more.

In the pages remaining, following the evidence of the bibliography as chronologically laid out, let us survey the larger periods of time that seem to mark the ebb and flow in Skelton's reputation and influence, or to contain within them shifting currents of interest. In each of these periods, I shall try to consider the views held on Skelton as poet and polemicist (and as perfecter of a particular verseform, the "Skeltonic," characterized by short 2-3 stress lines and shifting accents, often written in couplets and triplets but not infrequently in mono-rhyme leashes from 4 to 14 lines in length, connected within and between the lines by alliteration); as personality and persona; and as literary object (i.e., as an author about whom facts are to be collected, or whose works, printed or manuscript, are to be sought out, collected, described, compared and at last edited).

Major periods that mark the basic shifts in Skelton's reputation and influence fit into eight fairly definite blocks of time: 1530-1586 (Goodly Recognition yet Fading Laurels); 1589-1662 (Critical Division, Poetic and Dramatic Imitation, Installation as a Worthy); 1675-1737 (Notoriety Prevails); 1739-1821 (Antiquarian Recovery and Poetic Recrudescence); 1832-1882 (Editorial Restoration); 1883-1915 (Skelton Considered as Dramatist and Satirist); 1916-1933 (Skelton and the Modern Poets); and 1935-Present (Skelton and the Academic Critics).

None of these blocks is absolutely unrelated to another; all contain certain elements found earlier or later in greater or lesser prominence, not all of which are in harmony. Thus we set off 1832-1882 as "Editorial Restoration" because the former date marks the approximate time that Alexander Dyce began his labors on his splendid edition of Skelton (to appear in 1843) and the latter date marks the year that John Ashton published the latest recovered English text of Skelton's; yet seemingly the heading overlooks the fact that Thomas Hood and Elizabeth Barrett Browning continue and deepen the interest shown in Skelton by their fellow poets Wordsworth, Coleridge and

Southey. Or to designate 1675-1737 as a time in which "Notoriety
Prevails" because Edward Phillips at the beginning of that period had
noted that Skelton was now set aside because of his "miserable
loose...style, and galloping measure of verse" and Alexander Pope had
commented in his "First Epistle of the Second Book of Horace Imitated"
(1737) that "beastly Skelton heads of houses quote," is to overlook
Elizabeth Cooper's defense of the poet in 1737 and the issuance in
1718 of TER with a genial defense, the reprinting in 1736 of the 1568
Pithy, Plesaunt and Profitable Workes (which presumably prompted
Pope's remarks), and the additional reprinting of TER in the Harleian
Miscellany of 1744.

Nonetheless, the general feeling for what is happening to Skelton,
so to speak, seems to be borne out by the events as chronicled. Once
more, I must plead "reasonable arbitrariness," and allow the reader's
own perusal of these items to form a more sensitive arrangement of the
facts set down.

The period 1530 to 1586 may justly be termed that of "Goodly
Recognition yet Fading Laurels." As we have seen, at the very beginning of the period Skelton's memory as a poet was honored by the
initial publication of two of his major achievements, the satire
Collyn Clout and the morality play Magnyfycence. The first, in its
forcefulness, could now be safely printed with the fall and demise of
Cardinal Wolsey; the latter, more muted and diffuse in its comments on
Wolseyan policy, was likewise now considered beyond censorship. By
1568, with the publication of Pithy, Plesaunt and Profitable Workes
approximately halfway into the period, most of Skelton's poetry had
been printed, even though PPPW failed to include within its covers
the 1513 "Ballade of the Scottysshe Kynge," the lyrice printed in
Dyuers Balettys and Dyties Solacyous [c. 1527], and Magnyfycence.
John Stowe, if he were in fact the "editor" of PPPW for Thomas Marshe,
had before him the lesser collections of Certayne Bokes [c. 1545],
[1554] and [1560] (containing "A Treatise of the Scottes" (1513), an
augmentation of "BSK"; the two Latin "choruses" "Contra Gallos" and
"Contra Scottos," also of 1513; Ware the Hawke; the doubtful elegy on
Edward IV; and a reissue of TER) to draw upon as well as the three
printings of Why Come Ye Nat to Courte? of [c. 1545], [c. 1553] and
[1560], sturdy companions to the three mid-century editions of Collyn
Clout and Phyllyp Sparowe.

If imitation (as opposed to parody) be the greatest evidence of a
poet's high standing, then Skelton surely played a major role as the
developer of a verse form that delivered polemical poets of the full
burden of their choler in the 1530's and late 1540's. The Image of
Ypocrysy of 1533 or 1534 in 2544 lines of Skeltonics at times quite
outdoes the master in its tirading rhymes against the clergy and the
religious orders. In one passage in particular (11. 957 ff.) the
anonymous poet employs 54 lines of monorhyme, the first six of which
rhyme on three syllables, the last 48 of which rhyme on two syllables
and use but one polysyllabic word to a line! Needless to say the poem
abounds in echoes from CC, TER and WCY.

Similarly in the early years of the reign of Edward VI, the Skeltonic was a favored verse form of the writers of complaint of the day.
The anonymous author of Vox Populi [1547-48] and his almost equally
obscure contemporary, Luke Shepherd, the prolific pamphleteer of the
late 40's and presumed author of Doctour Doubble Ale, Phylogamus, The
Vpcheringe of the Marse, A Pore Helpe, Pathose, and John Bon and Master Parson, both resorted to Skeltonics to express social complaints
and religious polemic.

More subtle and less fully pervasive examples of Skelton "imitation" can be found between 1530 and 1586, as in Wyatt's application
of Jane Scrope's strange experience at her sampler to the form and
larger content of the strambotto "Who hath herd of suche crueltye before?" and in Spenser's reliance upon Skelton's Colin Clout as his
nom-de-plume in his Shepherdes Calendar of 1579, as well as his use
of CC for the tone of the pastorals of religious complaint within the
calendar.

The publication in 1567 of the collection entitled Merie Tales,
supposedly written by "Master Skelton Poet Laureat," is nearly coin-
cidental with the 1568 issuance of PPPW, the "collected poems," which
incidentally include pieces by Cornish and Watson, Skelton's contemporaries. The tales establish Skelton as a personality of popular
mythic quality whose sharpness and pungency will captivate alike the
writer of popular fiction, the presenter of popular aspects of drama,
and even the pedant. To be sure Skelton's reputation as a learned
poet and thus prophet persists in Richard Robinson's Rewarde of Wick-
ednesse [1574] and William Webbe's Discourse of English Poetrie, 1586,
but it is as a lively and mercurial personality in the "mad merry
veine" that Skelton mainly survives during the years of 1589-1662, a
period of "Critical Division, Poetic and Dramatic Imitation, and Installation as a Worthy."

By 1589 it becomes apparent that Skelton has become a bit old hat
among the cognoscenti, at least. Thus George Puttenham's dis-praise
of Skelton's "short distaunces and short measures" in 1589, and his
disbelief that Skelton, "I wat not for what great worthiness," be
"surnamed...poet laureate" is echoed by Francis Meres in 1598. Perhaps the fading of the laurels is best seen in Gabriel Harvey's varying use of, and views toward, Skelton. In his letter book of 1573-80,
begun when he was in his late twenties, Harvey makes use of the Skeltonic or alludes to Skelton in several places. He writes two pieces
of Skeltonic satire in 1573. He acknowledges in 1574 that his father,
as if clearing his throat in the morning, would "now & then merrily
kast out an owld Ryme, of sum Skeltons, or Skoggins making, as he
praetended." By 1577, however, he is more painfully aware of Skelton's reputation as a railing and scoffing satirist; by 1592 and 1594
he has definitely relegated Skelton to the ranks of the popular hacks
and drivellers of doggerel.

Brian Twyne, a giant among the Oxford antiquaries of his time,
continues the academic derogation of Skelton's powers begun by

Puttenham and repeated by Meres, when, in his <u>Antiquitatis Academie</u>
<u>Oxoniensis Apologia</u> of 1608 he terms the poet a <u>joculator</u> and a most
facile "bombologue." In 1622 Henry Peacham appropriates Puttenham's
phrasing to denigrate Skelton's reputation. By 1639, Skelton's
"<u>meere rime</u>" is described by the printer of <u>A Banquet of Jests</u> as
"once read, but now laid by." Skelton's general reputation as a poet
among the serious-minded commentators, not themselves poets, is perhaps most dramatically summarized by James Howell in 1655. He tells
of a "pitifully totter'd and torn" copy of Skelton that he found while
skulking in Duck Lane. He feared that it was not worth rebinding,
"for the Genius of the Age is quite another thing."

Yet critical opinion was not totally contemptuous of Skelton's
poetic worth. The picture of Skelton sketched by Francis Thynne,
Chaucer's late sixteenth-century editor (1598), is of the poet as undaunted, fearless and righteously angry in Wolsey's presence. The
author of <u>Pantagruel's Prognostication</u> [<u>c</u>. 1660] acknowledges Puttenham's criticism of the Skeltonic, as the instrument of a merry madcap
who can "run a poor rhyme out of breath until it pant or expire." At
the same time, however, he seems to have penetrated into the essence
of Skelton's manner, for he admits that Skelton's verse has "some
lucid intervalls of shrewd and poinant expressions."

If critical opinion about Skelton's poetic merit seems divided
during 1589-1662, the high esteem in which he is held by two prominent
poets of the first half of that period--Drayton and Jonson--is quite
otherwise. In 1619 Michael Drayton justified to his readers his experiment with the "short-breathed ode"--or if they would, "ballad"--
as a return to "the old English garb" as defensible as when "the
learned Colin Clout" (Spenser with more than a nod to Skelton) justified his "roundelay"--the use of older English forms in the <u>Shep-</u>
<u>heardes Calendar</u>: "'tis possible to clyme / to kindle or to slake /
All thoughe in Skeltons Rhyme." Ode 5 of the 1603 collection, 44
lines of Skeltonics, is Ode 7 of the 1619 collection and labelled "An
Amouret Anacreontick"! Ode 9 of 1603 becomes Ode 14 of the 1619 edition, where it is entitled "A Skeltoniad."

It is Ben Jonson, however, who most completely understands Skelton
as poet, personality, satirist, and as collector's object. As early
as 1600 Jonson turned to Skelton's morality play <u>Magnyfycence</u> to write
his comical dramatic satire of excess at court, <u>Cynthias Revels</u>. He
incorporates Skelton's careful balance of courtier-vices and fools;
and in the two masques performed in the long fifth act of the play he
reinforces Skelton's notion of the four cardinal virtues by presenting
qualities that complement them--the amenities of the courteous life--
and by demonstrating that courtly virtues without the restraint of
reason become courtly vices: undisciplined generosity becomes prodi-
gality, or variety of mind, voluptuousness.

Aware of the use of Skelton as a witty curmudgeon in the short
fiction of the time--as in the 1590 <u>Cobler of Caunterburie</u> or the <u>Life</u>

of Long Meg of Westminster (as entered in the Stationers' Register of
that year)--or as a playwright-in-cassock who liked to change costumes
and enter among the players (as in Anthony Munday's two plays of 1601
The Downfall and The Death of Robert Earl of Huntingdon), Jonson in-
troduces Skelton as a persona playing a major role in his masque The
Fortunate Isles and Their Vnion [1624]. In his masque Jonson also
shows his finely tuned sense of the popular, fitting, and contemporary, for he includes in the anti-masque the Elynour Rumming revived
in 1624 as "The Famous Ale-Wife of England, Written by Mr. Skelton."

The Masque of Owles, also written in [1624] for presentation at
Kenilworth, proves Jonson's historical awareness of Skelton as an
"object," since the masque's subtitle indicates the presence of the
ghost of Captain Cox, jibbering in Skeltonics. Almost fifty years
earlier in [1575] Robert Laneham had described the role played in the
royal entertainment at Kenilworth by the captain, a local antiquary
and book-collector. Among his holdings were proudly noted Skelton's
CC and TER.

This remarkable sense of the popular and fitting, flecked with a
historical propriety, had in fact already been demonstrated in Jonson's The Gypsies Metamorphosed of 1621, his most elaborate and most
popular masque. Although he may well have depended on Dekker's
Lanthorne and Candle-light (1608) for many of his gypsy canting terms,
Jonson seems to have known that Skelton's Tunning of Elynour Rummyng
made allusion (the earliest in English literature) to gypsies and
gypsy-dress (in the description of Elinor's headgear). At any rate,
the Patrico or gypsy chieftain expresses himself throughout the masque
in Skeltonics and at times in phrases directly reminiscent of TER.

There are other examples of Jonson's use of the Skeltonic in a
lesser degree in The King's Entertainment at Welbeck (1633), The Tale
of a Tub (1640), and The Devill is an Asse (1641). Perhaps recalling
the remark of his friend Richard James (1625) that the laurels of
Skelton and his Tudor contemporary Whittinton "Soone sprung" [were]
"soon fading," Jonson wrote a playful begging poem to "Master John
Burges" in the Skeltonic manner, personal evidence that with the
greatest of the Elizabethan-and-Jacobean poets, as would be true of
poets in the Romantic and Modern periods, Skelton was prized for his
verse, his satirical daring and the legend of his personality.

Jonson's use of TER in The Fortunate Isles and Gypsies Metamorphosed permits us a witting digression at this juncture. More than
any other poem in the Skelton canon, The Tunnyng of Elynour Rummyng
has captured the interest both of readers and also of book-illustra-
tors, for that matter, for over four-and-a-half centuries. It is in
that sense Skelton's most "representative" poem. Fragments of a first
edition of the poem dating from [c. 1521] were turned up in the 1950's
(see KINSMAN, no. 1955.3); the full poem appeared in Certayne Bokes
in [c. 1545], [c. 1554] and [c. 1560] and was included in PPPW, 1568.
In 1609 the play Pimlyco or Runne Red-Cap included a notice of Skelton

and directly incorporated into the play 240 lines of TER or almost
one-third of the poem. Jonson must have known the 1624 reprint of
Elynour Rvmmin, The Famous Ale-Wife of England with its clumsy, crude
wood-cut of Elynour and its pleasantly witty address by Skelton's
Ghost to the reader.

At the end of the seventeenth century a manuscript-copy of TER
was made with lettering that imitated the gothic textura letter-press
of a sixteenth-century edition of the poem. It was perhaps the 1718
edition of The Tunning, with its defense of Skelton's tavern-scenes
for the reader of "extensive Fancy and just relish," that prompted
the 1736 reprint of PPPW (a work which, as we have seen, occasioned
Alexander Pope's outburst in 1737 against "beastly Skelton"). At
least one other eighteenth-century publisher saw fit to reissue TER:
in 1744, reprinted from the edition of 1624, it appeared in the
Harleian Miscellany. The second, augmented version of this miscellany
introduced Elynour to nineteenth-century readers in 1808, two years
before Chalmers reprinted the 1736 version of Skelton's "complete"
works.

Not until 1928, however, was Elynour again to assert herself so
domineeringly. In that year, as illustrated by Pearl Binder for the
Fanfrolico Press of London, she made her blowsy re-entry, with her
ragged menage. In different guise she reappeared in 1930, this time
with decorations by Claire Jones under the auspices of Helen Gentry's
press in San Francisco. Once more, in 1953, Elynour was presented in
an edition splendidly furnished with wood-block cuts by Leonard Baskin
as printed by the Gehenna Press of Worcester, Massachusetts. Finally,
in 1968, scarcely recognizable under her foreign appellation, Elynour
was translated onto paper as "Noortje Neut" in K. Helsloot's Dutch
redaction of her poem as "De Kroeg van Noortje Neut" in Tirade, XII.

To return from our digression on TER to its seventeenth-century
starting point, we should note that in 1660, two years before Thomas
Fuller included Skelton in his Worthies of England, appeared the poem
"The Old Gill," a parodic imitation of the Tunning. Mistakenly assigned to the satirist John Cleveland, it has only recently been
relegated to anonymity by his modern editors. In a remarkable way
its anonymous character all the more demonstrates the extent to which
Skelton--in his most popular work at least--had penetrated the deeper
layers of seventeenth-century English literary consciousness.

Thirteen years lapse between Fuller's bestowal of the distinction
of a "worthy" upon Skelton in 1662 and Edward Phillips' 1674 account,
brief and divided, of the poet, whom he considers a "jolly English
rimer" as a personality but whose style he deplores as "miserable
loose" and "rambling" and whose verse he condemns as a "galloping
measure." Skelton's repute is once again that held of him by the
bookish Puttenham, Phillips' predecessor by a century; Phillips' remarks are, in their turn, repeated by William Winstanley in 1687. We
have begun a fifty year period (until 1737) in which Skelton will be

overlooked by the poets and essentially viewed by the literary historians as vulgar and forced: Notoriety Prevails.

Thus Miles Davies in 1716 will set Skelton down as one of the
"most notorious of all...Pamphlet writers, both in Prose and Verse,"
noticing TER as he does so, some two years in advance of its 1718
publication with its special defense of the poem for persons of "an
extensive Fancy." As we have noted in our digression on TER above,
Alexander Pope greeted the publication of PPPW in 1736 with distaste,
setting Skelton down as a poet "whose verses...lately reprinted" consisted almost wholly of "Ribaldry, Obscenity and Scurrilous language."
There are signs, to be sure, that not everyone shared Pope's views,
for in the same year of 1737, Elizabeth Cooper, editing selections of
English poetry from the time of the Saxons to Charles II, drew on the
Bowge of Courte, hailing Skelton as "The Restorer of Invention" to
English verse. Unconsciously she harkens back to Skelton's own contemporaries in her choice of epithet, even though she believes that
gift to have been "much debased by the Rust of [that] Age."

Despite an aura of notoriety that will cling to Skelton's yellow-
ing garland, during the next period 1739-1831, chroniclers of local
history and typographical antiquities will seek out Skelton in their
investigations and thus sufficiently pique the poets of the early
nineteenth century, chiefly Wordsworth and Southey, to refurbish
Skelton's poetic laurels.

In 1739 Francis Blomefield published the first two volumes of a
five volume history of Norfolk, presenting new findings on Skelton.
Ten years later Joseph Ames noticed certain Skeltonical works in his
Typographical Antiquities. Here again, admittedly, there is overlap
in my grouping of the years 1739-1831 as a period of "Antiquarian Recovery and Poetic Recrudescence." Actually Thomas Warton benefitted
from the edition of 1736 in preparing his History of English Poetry
(1778), for his dated signature in his copy of the edition, now at
the Huntington Library, indicates he owned PPPW in 1753. Moreover,
it was from his own reading of the 1736 edition that, in 1822, H.
Southern belatedly wrote a long appreciative essay on Skelton. Still,
the dates 1739-1831, from Blomefield's Norfolk to the year that a
third woodcut "portrait" of Skelton had been "recovered" and Robert
Southey had issued the call for a new edition of Skelton's Works,
accurately enough define the span of Skelton's "antiquarian recovery."
What can barely be adumbrated in this bibliography, of course, is the
activity in the book sales of the great collectors of the period--
Rawlinson, Steevens, Sykes to name but three--and Heber in especial,
without whose library Dyce might not have completed his edition of
Skelton in 1843.

Bishop Thomas Tanner in 1748 and Nasmith in 1777 give bibliographical indications that Skelton's dedicatory verses "I liber" and "Quamvis annosa est" had been located after two and a half centuries. John
Hawkins, a historian of music, in 1776 recovers Skelton's "Manerly

Margery" and its setting. Carrying on the study of "Typographical
Antiquities" begun by Ames in 1749, William Herbert properly locates
the first edition of <u>Collyn Clout</u> (1785-90), and Joseph Ritson in 1802
notes the manuscript version of <u>Speke Parrot</u> among his other Skeltonic
notations. T. F. Dibdin (1810-19) profits from the activity of the
older bibliophiles to correct them—he it is who first located the
<u>Replycacion</u> thought not "to be now extant" by Ritson a decade earlier,
and he it is who properly locates the unique copy of the <u>Garlande of</u>
<u>Laurel</u>.

The years 1739-1831, despite their marked recovery and identification of Skelton manuscripts and books as reported by such bibliographers of merit, were not all necessarily favorable to Skelton's
reputation, even though there was more of his work known to comment
on. Thus Thomas Warton, himself a lesser poet and essayist of some
distinction, perhaps the first great formal "historian" of English
literature, perpetuated Puttenham and Pope's views of Skelton as
coarse, obscene and scurrilous in the second volume of his <u>History of</u>
<u>English Poetry</u> (1778). He can little abide Skelton's choice of sub-
ject or of verse-form: "His subjects are often as ridiculous as his
metre: ...he sometimes debases his matter by his versification."
Skelton's "characteristic vein of humour" he calls "capricious and
grotesque. If his whimsical extravagancies ever move our laughter,
at the same time they shock our sensibility." Not only do the poet's
"festive levities" seem "vulgar and indelicate" but Warton finds them
also lacking in "truth and propriety." The famous description of the
tapestry depicting "The Triumph of Venus" in a Tudor bishop's manor
(presumably in Wolsey's seat at Hampton Court) is grudgingly conceded
to be "in the best manner of his petty measure: which is made still
more disgusting by the repetition of the rhymes." Less backhanded,
perhaps, is his praise, still divided, of <u>BC</u>. In it Skelton had
adopted the "grave and stately movement" of the Chaucerian stanza,
with the result that, for Warton, a great admirer of Spenser and his
stanza, Skelton had showed himself "not always incapable of exhibiting
allegorical imagery with spirit and dignity." He further acknowledges
that the poet, "not withstanding his scurrility," was a good writer of
the Latin elegiac couplet in his formal memorial verses for Henry VII
and Lady Margaret Beaufort. Warton would rather salute Skelton as a
promising writer of Latin poetry of an Ovidian elegance than acknowledge him as a proved poet in an English tradition, whatever the whimsical overtones "of Walter Mapes and Golias."

Warton is not without his own whimsies. Led by Bishop Tanner's
bibliography of 1747 to the "very splendid manuscript" in which was
preserved Skelton's earliest known poem, "The Death of the Earl of
Northumberland" (a Percy), he exclaims that Skelton "hardly deserved
such patronage." It may have been Warton's own excess in the "free
exertion of research" that led to his much bruited summary and description of <u>The Nigramansir</u>, a "lost" play printed by de Worde, he
claims, in 1504, and seen by him when it was in the possession of the
poet William Collins (d. 1759). Since we know that charges of

necromancy and also the moral abstractions of Simony and Philargyria,
allegedly characters in the interlude, can be found in Why Come Ye nat
to Courte?, Skelton's anti-Wolsey satire of 1522, and we know of the
existence of More's translation of the Necromantia of Lucian (STC
16895 [c. 1530]), we are inclined to share Ritson's doubt that the
play ever existed, or at least to fear that Warton was not always free
from confusion or bad memory. Rodney Baine, no. 1970, however, makes
a case for the Warton of 1778, in the light of recent discoveries, and
avers that "an incredulous rejection of [the actual existence of]
Skelton's Necromancer...is difficult to justify."

   The oscillations of Skelton's reputation, however, noted in the
previous "periods" into which we have divided his literary heritage,
insured that Warton's severe judgements were not long to prevail. In
1816 William Gifford, editor of Ben Jonson's works, attacked Warton's
pronouncements and defended his vein of poetry that shone through
"all the rubbish that ignorance has spread over it." Other men of
letters of the early nineteenth century, the scholarly poets Wordsworth and Southey, and a relatively young bibliographer-cum-biographer,
Philip Bliss, the reviser in 1813-20 of Anthony-à-Woods Athenae
Oxoniensis, provided positive incentive and encouragement for the
textual "restorer" of Skelton, Alexander Dyce and his two-volume
complete works of 1843.

   To begin with Bliss in order to make a nicer connection with Warton, one notes that he drew on the latter to augment Wood's original
notes--and for the attribution of the Nigramansir. He drew on Bishop
Tanner for some of his mid-eighteenth century discoveries and entries
(including two non-canonical works), on the catalogues of the great
Harleian manuscript collection (printed 1759) in which were itemized
for the first time Skelton's four flytings against Garnesche, and on
Hawkins' musicological treatise of 1776 for the restoration of the
unmannerly "Manerly Margery." Bliss thus continued in a more specialized way the syntheses effected by the older and broader bibliographic
compilers whose wider horizons were those of English books, manuscripts and collectors rather than just the vitae and accomplishments
of Oxford's graduates.

   Turning back to the year 1804 and to the poet Wordsworth, who had
assumed from Fuller--or his biobibliographical descendants--or from
local legend, that Skelton, too, was Cumberland-born, we find his
sonnet "With Ships the sea was sprinkled far and near," based on a
passage from Skelton's Bowge of Courte (11.36-39), presumably as ren-
dered in the 1736 edition. Two decades later, while writing to Allan
Cunningham on November 23, 1823, Wordsworth calls Skelton "a demon in
point of genius." Ten years later (in 1833), Wordsworth commends
Dyce for having progressed on his edition of Skelton, "A Writer deserving of far greater attention than his works have received." In
1844, the aging poet writes from Rydal Mount to thank Dyce for sending
him a present of the completed edition, "edited with your usual in-
dustry, judgment and discernment." Perhaps merely in politeness,

perhaps in genuine and "unavoidable" regret, Wordsworth confided that
he wished he could make "that profitable use of [Dyce's] labours,
which at an earlier period of life [he] might have done." He con-
cludes by noting that he is in much the same situation as Pope when
Hall's <u>Satires</u> were first--and belatedly--put into his hand.

In the long meantime, the almost ubiquitous <u>TER</u> had been reprinted (1808) and Alexander Chalmers (1810) had reprinted in its
turn the 1736 reprint of Skelton's poems, introducing the 1736 editor's preface with a summary of Skelton's life and some brief critical
remarks of his own. Before Robert Southey could get his review of
Chalmers' edition published in the <u>Quarterly Review</u> (1814), Dibdin in
1810 had properly located the unique copy of Skelton's <u>curriculum
vitae</u>, the <u>Garlande of Laurell</u>, and had reprinted excerpts from the
laureate's last poem <u>A Replycacion</u>, written, he commented, in "bastard
Hudibrastic verse." Bibliographically speaking, matters had now been
gathered to a head for Dyce's editorial generalship.

With candor and gratitude Dyce acknowledges in his preface to the
<u>Poetical Works of Skelton</u> that Southey's censure of Chalmers' reprint
in 1810 of the 1736 edition of <u>PPPW</u> had resolved him to undertake the
edition needed: "Prompted by this remark, I commenced the present
edition--perhaps with too much self-confidence, and certainly without
having duly estimated the difficulties which awaited me." In addition
to criticizing Chalmers' use of a "grossly corrupted text," Southey
had taken him savagely to task for his confused critical opinions,
"one sentence contradicting another." Chalmers, following Warton,
had opined that if Skelton's "vein of humour" had been directed to
subjects of legitimate satire, the poet would have been more worthy
of a place in his collection. "Did it ever occur to him," asked
Southey, "that Skelton's buffooneries, like the ribaldry of Rabelais,
were thrown out as a tub for the whale, and that unless he had thus
written for the coarsest prelates, he could not possibly have poured
forth such bitter and undaunted satire in such perilous times?"

Southey's own poetic practice, at least in the poem "The Cataract
of Lodore" (1821), intended, to be sure, as a rhyme for the nursery,
reflects his love of Skelton, written as it is under the direct influence of the "Skeltonic." Southey's "imitation" is followed the
next year by Walter Scott's harkening back to <u>Why Come Ye nat to
Courte</u>? which he briefly imitates in ten lines of verse introductory
to Chapter Five of <u>The Fortunes of Nigil</u>.

A chain reaction has begun. In 1822 H. Southern writes a retro-
active essay, a review of sorts, on the 1736 edition, whose feckless
reprinting by Chalmers had occasioned Southey's caustic review. He
uses Scott's verb "to Skeltonize" and seems to have been directed by
Scott to <u>WCY</u> in which he finds "most interesting matter." In 1840
and in 1842, as if impatiently heralding Dyce's long expected edition,
Isaac Disraeli and Elizabeth Barrett Browning each write enthusiastic
essays on Skelton, the one rhapsodizing on the "velocity" and

"corruscations" of Skelton's verse, the other on Skelton's dominion over the range of the vernacular--so suspect to Warton--and his claim almost to be the first English writer with a dramatic reputation, author of <u>Magnyfycence</u> and the <u>Nigramansir</u>. More remarkable still, a French literary historian, Philarète Chasles, in the <u>Revue des deux mondes</u>, as if in rebuke of Warton and in answer to Arthur Henry Hallam's remark in 1837 that Skelton's longer works were utterly contemptible, included Skelton with three other sixteenth century priests--Luther, Folengo and Rabelais--as a leader in the reaction against ecclesiastical corruption and the striving after an understanding of the senses.

With the publication in 1843, in two volumes, of Dyce's <u>Poetical Works</u> of John Skelton, a superb edition but one which Dyce confessed still contained "corruptions which defy my power of emendation, and passages which I am unable to illustrate," the long awaited and almost perfect Skelton was available to the reader. Long awaited it was, for Dyce in 1833 had editions of Collins and Greene behind him, and two of his three volumes of Peele in print before he could get down seriously to business on the Skelton, even then only one of several projects. Almost perfect, for it lacked the short strident "Ballade of the Scottysshe Kynge," not actually discovered until 1878 and brought out as an annotated facsimile by John Ashton in 1882. And almost perfect in that the conscientious and otherwise impeccable Dyce preserved as canonical some pieces of a very dubious nature as well as introducing into the canon some poems equally suspect. He preserved as canonical from the 1568 and 1736 editions the <u>Book of Three Fools</u>, actually three sections of Henry Watson's prose translation of Brant's <u>Narrenschiff</u>, made <u>c</u>. 1508, and the poems on Time, the Trinity, and the death of Edward IV, of no little dubiousness although of long attribution. Without sufficient evidence he introduced as canonical two poems that seemed to live up to Skelton's all-too-brief description of the "lost" titles in <u>GL</u>: "<u>Vexilla regis</u>" and "Wofully Araid."

By the end of 1856 Skelton's poetical works as edited by Dyce were published this side the water in two formats: in each instance connected with the series called "The British Poets," under the general editorship of F. J. Child. In [1855], surely by 1856, we find, significantly for moderns, the joint issuance, four volumes in two, of the <u>Poetical Works of Skelton and Donne</u>, the first pairing of two poets who were to affect, significantly, the literary sensibility of the twentieth century and who were each to be absorbed at his best by the witty, restless young Auden of the 1930's. In 1856 Skelton's poems appeared on their own in three volumes; from stereotypes of the 1856 edition his Poetical Works were reissued in 1864. Save for W. W. Skeat's inclusion of selected passages from Dyce (<u>WCY</u> and <u>PS</u>), the 1870's passed, however, without any further reissue of Dyce's edition, by now standard. Skelton's editorial restoration was finally completed in 1882, as noted the paragraph above, by John Ashton's facsimile edition of "BSK," limited to 500 copies. Ashton brought it out again in 1887, however, in the volume <u>A Century of Ballads</u>.

Although it is difficult to discern clear-cut patterns in popular
and learned reaction to the "restored Skelton" of Dyce's editorial
genius as finally complemented by Ashton, the most significant activities during the years 1883 through 1916 were devoted to popularizing
Skelton via anthology pieces, to examining his one known and surviving
play Magnyfycence, and to dating and explicating his long poems:
satirical (CC, SP, and WCY), "Goliardic" (PS), and allegorical (BC
and GL). Pieces despised and rejected by Warton and Hallam were now
deemed worthy of consideration; satirical pieces that had in places
vexed Dyce's learned mind were put under intense critical scrutiny;
and the play in hand, long neglected for the Nigramansir in the bush,
was brought to an editorial and critical focus.

As noted before, the phenomenon of "overlap" plagues the "periodi-
zer." As early as 1866 Skelton was labelled a "satirical laureate";
as late as 1877 Warton's ghost lived on in the Dublin University Magazine in whose columns Skelton was praised for his Latin, condemned for
his coarseness and vulgarity, and doomed to share a niche with the
"degraded but talented Charles Churchill." In 1916, the year that the
poet Robert Graves had published his earliest adaptation of the Skeltonic, the academe, A. S. Cook, also had published an article linking
Chaucer's House of Fame with Skelton's Garlande of Laurel.

The anthologists Ward (1880), Fitzgibbon (1887), Flügel (1895),
Arber (1900), and Williams (1902)--with some prominent exceptions,
noted on pp. xxiv-xxv above and in footnote six below--broadened their
offerings to include passages from the longer poems in addition to
selected lyrics from the Garland.

The scholarship of the period focusses most particularly on Skelton's political morality play Magnyfycence more as a transitional
piece bridging from religious to secular drama, from moral abstraction
to the political, from Christian time to historical chronology, than
as a work to be studied for itself and its own timely significance.
In 1881 a German Ph.D., Krumpholz, devoted his "inaugural dissertation" to the play. A. W. Pollard excerpted it in his anthology of
English miracle plays, moralities and interludes (1890). A. W. Ward
gave Magnyfycence space in his History of English Dramatic Literature
(new and revised edition, 1899) and, most important of all, Robert Lee
Ramsay brought great learning to bear on the play in his edition of it
for the Early English Text Society, 1908 (for 1906), a 1905 Johns Hop-
kins dissertation literally issued under new covers.

Ramsay had obviously profited from the rising tide of interest
that carried the early drama far beyond the highest high-tide line
previously recorded. Concentrating on the one work with all the intensity that Dyce had to diffuse over a corpus of poetry, Ramsay
divided his text between speakers more carefully than Dyce had done,
corrected some misreadings and prefaced it all with a long introduction on the various earlier editions of the poem, its date, its plot,
and such essential dramatic features as staging and characterization-
via-shifts in versification. In 1910 Farmer brought out a facsimile

text of the play (reissued in student's form in 1914) and in the same
year E. N. S. Thompson paid attention to Skelton's morality play in
his monograph on English moralities in general. G. R. Baskervill
studied the influence of Skelton among other early English poets upon
Ben Jonson, including Jonson's use of Magnyfycence in Cynthia's Revels,
to complete the significant work on Skelton's play during the pre-war
period, although Tucker Brooke and Madeleine H. Dodds briefly presented aspects of the play in 1911 and 1913.

An almost equally sustained interest in Skelton as a writer of
long satirical or allegorical poems can be found during the years
1883-1915. Although essentially presenting a bibliographical dis-
covery, the German scholar Zupitza printed in 1890 manuscript fragments of WCY, a poem of some brief interest in the 1820's. In 1896
Henry Bradley solved two cryptograms that had baffled Dyce: one in
the Garlande of Laurell, the other in Ware Hawk, a shorter and lesser
poem, to be sure. Three years later Albert Rey turned his attention
to Skelton's satirical poems as they related to Lydgate, Skelton's
predecessor; Barclay, Skelton's contemporary; and to Cock Lorell's
Bote. His interest in the relationship between Bowge of Courte and
other fools' literature seemed well-taken, although, following Dyce,
he mistakenly assumed that the Book of Three Fools was Skelton's and,
on his own, misdated both Bowge of Courte and Cock Lorell's Bote to
the impairment of his argument.

The very same year that the EETS actually published Ramsay's edition of Magnyfycence (1908), S. M. Tucker brought out a study of early
verse satire in England which discussed in some length Skelton's major
satires: BC, SP, CC, and WCY. Most important of all such discussions
were John Berdan's essays in 1914 and 1915 on the dating of Skelton's
satires and, in particular, on the gnomic and knotty Speke Parrot.

The third important strand in the period 1883-1915 is constituted
of biographical and bibliographical articles of some moment. James
Hooper (1897) re-examined the Norwich Diocesan Registers to ascertain
Skelton's successor at Diss; Sir Sidney Lee wrote a substantial piece
on Skelton, not without flaws, for the Dictionary of National Biography, also in 1897; and Gordon Goodwin, digging in the Comissary Court
records of Westminster, discovered the identity of the administrator
of Skelton's estate (1905). In terms of bibliography, we must note
that the German scholar, Friedrich Brie, made the first real attempt
systematically to determine the Skelton canon, in 1907; and in 1914,
of almost equal usefulness, the German woman scholar, Elise Bischoffberger, completed an eighty-page bibliography that traced Skelton's
influence on English literature.

By 1916, with the prolongation of a war that both sides had
thought should have soon ended, a young man about to make a name for
himself as poet, essayist, novelist and critic--Robert Graves--felt
that an era had collapsed to which he could say "Goodbye to All That,"
but soon realized "It All Goes On." From 1916 to 1933, and even

beyond, Skelton was to be embraced as a living writer in a vital metrical and satirical tradition by English poets, Robert Graves first and chief among them, and, a bit belatedly, by American poets. Save for his imitation by the polemicists of the late 1540's and his adoption by the Elizabethan-Jacobean poets who sensed the popular pulse--Churchyard, Drayton and Jonson--Skelton had never before been so warmly welcomed.

Precisely when Robert Graves turned to John Skelton's verse as a means of asserting poetic independence and direct and pithy expression is hard to determine. In his Oxford Addresses on Poetry (1962, p. 5), he declares that he discovered Skelton by accident in 1916, while on a brief leave from the Somme front. In Good-bye to All That (1929, p. 157), however, he quotes from a letter written in France on June 24, 1915, in which he cites a verse of Skelton's. Over the Brazier (1916), Graves' first published volume of verse, contains in its "Charterhouse" section (poems written at public school) his first poetry in short Skeltonics, "Free Verse," presumably set down in 1913-14 or perhaps among the poems sent from the Front in 1915 to a Cambridge friend, Edward Marsh. "Free Verse" did not indicate Graves' espousal of vers libre, but, rather, his advocacy of direct expression and his desire to avoid academically-uniform stanzas. The poem was included in his first collected volume, Fairies and Fusiliers (1917), a collection augmented by a lively poem warmly appreciating the Tudor poet, "John Skelton," in the master's mode and manner, and by the inclusion of the Skeltonic "David and Goliath," the title poem from his second volume of verse [late 1916].

With marvelous significance in a chapter entitled "'Control' by Spirits" in Poetic Unreason (1925), itself based on his B.Litt thesis at Oxford, Graves noted that "Skelton has had a stronger influence on my work than any other poet alive or dead: particularly have I admired in him his mixture of scholarship and extravaganza, his honest outspokenness and unconventionality in life and writings, his humour, his poetic craftsmanship, and, in spite of appearances, his deep religious sense."

Living as he then did in Islip, thus associating himself with Skelton's protector, the Abbot Islip of Westminster, who had started as a charity boy from the village, Graves felt under the control of the older poet: "Time and time again since I have caught myself playing at being Skelton, in literary affectations, in choice of metre and handling of words particularly...."

The links between Graves and Skelton in the early 1920s were many, their sometimes brief and petty utilitarian nature the more clearly showing a profound inter-relationship.[7] In Country Sentiment (1920), for example, Graves writes "Manticor in Arabia" with clear echoes of PS and "A Rhyme of Friends (In a Style Skeltonical)." In 1921 in Pier-Glass he begins a sustained habit of quoting brief passages from Skelton's poetry to help demonstrate the implications of a prose piece or suggest the ambience of a poem. His Poetic Unreason has a seven-line prologue from SP; My Head! My Head! (1925) likewise is keyed by a four-line quotation from Skelton. The volume of verse bearing the title Welchman's Hose (1925), itself a proverbial phrase used by Skelton in CC, is set off by a stanza from GL and contains two poems in the Skelton manner; so, too, Poems (1914-1926) includes a seven-line citation from Skelton in its preliminary matter.

Graves was to continue his interest in Skelton as a master of a single metric until the Marmosite's Miscellany of 1925, in which the title-poem, a satire on contemporary writers, was written in 59 stanzas, the majority of which were now in rhyme royal, Skelton-style, with eight stanzas of shorter-lined and less numerous rhymes quite in the manner of the stanza variations in Speke, Parrot. The marmosite, an elderly monkey, like Parrot, is caged and has a toy mirror in which to peer deeply. Like Parrot, the marmosite has the gift of tongues (he reads learned journals in Parrot's "Dowyche, with Spaynshe"). As in SP the poet takes down the words of the caged commentator; and as in SP the figure of Melpomene appears.

After 1927, however, Graves' interest in Skelton shifted from the man as versifier to be imitated, to the man as poet in the larger and deeper sense. To be sure, Graves was responsible in 1927 for writing the short prefatory note to the little collection of Skelton's verse in Humbert Wolfe's Augustan Books series, and for selecting and modernizing the poems that appeared therein. Moreover, he included most of his Skeltonic imitations in the two volume Poems, 1914-1926 and Poems, 1914-1927, both published in 1927. Nonetheless, Graves seems after 1927 to become more concerned with his own posture and role as a poet among Poets. True, he severely attacks Philip Henderson for his "Incomplete Complete Skelton"--a modernized edition (1931), based on Dyce, arranged by genre, with occasional substitution of words and without a sorely needed gloss. True, he is interested in Skelton's use of proverbs in GL (1934). Not until 1955, however, with his Clark Lectures at Cambridge and the decade and a half to follow, long after he had finished short stories, novels, works on profanity, mythology and the process of reading, plus reams of verse, do we have the opportunity to learn of Graves' exalted view of Skelton as the first "professional" English poet, devoted to Dame Occupation (GL) and Calliope. His Oxford Inaugural Lecture of 1961, entitled "The Dedicated Poet," deals at frequent intervals with Skelton and includes a skilled translation of the Latin part of Skelton's bi-lingual poem on Calliope, to him the true muse of poetry.

One would be perfectly happy to accept Graves' reception of Skelton as the model for other modern poets. To do so, however, would actually scant Skelton's standing on Parnassus. Richard Hughes, like Graves, had apparently cultivated a youthful familiarity with the Skeltonic, although he is less influenced by the older poet. His early poem "Poets, Painters, Puddings," after appearing in Gypsy-Night (1922), reappeared in Hughes' slender collected poems that bore the self-deprecatory title <u>Confessio Juvenis</u> (1926). Even before Graves, Hughes in 1924 edited a selection of Skelton's verse, much more substantial than Graves' collection that followed it three years later. Hardly surprisingly, Graves reviewed his friend's collection quite favorably.

Next to Graves, it was W. H. Auden who seemed most genuinely to incorporate Skelton (and Donne) into a sinewy and witty style. Perhaps Auden agreed with Graves, or at least unconsciously seems to have, in the latter's pronouncement that Skelton and Donne (memories of their prophetic coupling in the joint edition of 1881!) were the only (non-dramatic) geniuses of English poetry. Although the Sitwells (1923, 1927; 1930 and 1931) had made forays into Skeltonic meter and had chosen to preserve in later "Collected" pieces most of the booty they had gained, they seemed not quite so fully converted nor so subtly surrendered to Skelton as Auden.

Once more, as with Graves and Hughes, in a first collection of poems (1930), Auden shows in two of them that as a young man he had trained on the Skeltonic. We note Auden's name among the many reviewers of Philip Henderson's edition of <u>The Complete Poems of John Skelton Laureate</u> (1931), itself the work of a man of letters who had published his <u>First Poems</u> in 1930, dedicated to Laurence Housman and showing no sign of direct Skeltonic influence. In 1932, among the "Six Odes" of Book Three of <u>The Orators</u>, Auden wrote a birthday ode partly in Skeltonics to John Warner, to be reissued separately later that year in Sherard Vines' anthology, <u>Whips and Scorpions</u>.

In 1935 Auden showed his devotion to Skelton in three ways: he wrote a finely perceptive essay on Skelton's metrical dexterity and variety in <u>Magnyfycence</u>, he included some snippets from unfamiliar Skelton poems in an anthology he jointly compiled, and in the eminently successful verse drama that he wrote with Christopher Isherwood, <u>The Dog Beneath the Skin</u>, he adapted the Skeltonic to voices from the crowd. One must note, not without some reluctance, that after 1935 Auden went on to other modes and other verse forms. We see him nonetheless maintaining a respect of sorts for Skelton in the anthologies he edited or co-edited, such as his <u>Oxford Book of Light Verse</u> (1938) and <u>Poets of the English Language</u> (1950, with Norman Holmes Pearson).

Perhaps it is fair to say that 1935 marks the continental divide for Skelton's influence on poets practicing in the twentieth century. To be sure one can refer back to John Crowe Ransom's Skeltonical "Anne with her bird" of 1927, and look ahead to one of his last pieces, "Agitato ma non troppo" of 1969, in mono-rhyme. One can note that the Horace Gregory of 1933, not unlike the Graves of 1917, had offered "Praise" to John Skelton in Skelton's own verse form, and that Babette Deutsch in her own tour-de-force verse review of de Sola Pinto's selections from Skelton (1950), a review written for <u>Poetry</u> in 1953, had reflected the deeper preoccupation of academic commentators of the mid-thirties with <u>Speke, Parrot</u> as the critic of a

decadent age and a persistent voice for poetry. So the poet Richard
O'Connell in 1960 ended his poem on <u>Speke, Parrot</u> with the statement
that the proper habitat of the parrot is not here on earth, but, by
implication, in heaven, for "all men respect are the sparrow and
hawk." With even greater weariness, A. D. Hope, writing in June of
1972, urged parrot to speak, "flamboyant popinjay," for "although like
me you've nothing new to say," like the poet he is "Grubbing in the
dry springs of poetry" to transmit what a poet "scarcely apprehend[s]."

By 1935, nevertheless, the joyous and delightful adaptations have
left their mark behind; the pungent voice and daunting rhyme-leash
have hit their targets: verse forms are freer and more fluent, no
longer bound to fixed stanzas; diction is racy and sinewy with common
idiom. By 1935, Skelton will begin to be absorbed by academic critics
and the scholars of literary history. Much still needed to be done to
fit Skelton into Henrician times in the light of recent historical investigation (Pollard's <u>Wolsey</u> of 1929, for one example) and in the
light of lexical investigation (the <u>OED</u>, dedicated to Queen Victoria
in 1897, was completed in 1928 and presented to King George V) and in
renewed critical and editorial interest in the texts.

Academic commentators began to range freely over the expanses now
to be resurveyed as the domain in which Skelton ruled. By 1936 it is
quite clear that <u>Speke Parrot</u> is being examined in particular. That
year there appeared a flurry of notes and articles on the poem and on
particular passages in it. Among the inducements offered to parrot
were sweet cinnamon sticks and <u>"pleris cum musco."</u> The significance
of the latter as a sort of condiment had escaped Dryce but was to be
solved by Phyllis Abrams, one of almost a half dozen of writers on the
phrase in 1936. The most important single scholarly article on <u>Speke
Parrot</u> that year was that of William Nelson, an author whose investigations into Skelton were to stand scholarly scrutiny for forty years
and as of 1978 are still cited with respect and authority.

Nelson's book on <u>John Skelton, Laureate</u>, first published in 1939
and then reprinted in 1964, very firmly placed Skelton in the humanistic tradition of the late fifteenth century, a tradition that had been
imported into the English court by Henry VII. Nelson's work was firmly based on sound historical knowledge and intensive documentary research, as the various appendices to his book clearly show. He had
examined the petty legal quarrels of the day to find Skelton involved
as a kind of surety for the prior of St. Bartholomew in 1502 and as a
priest of academic integrity who could fittingly interrogate East
Anglian parishioners suspected of lacking health of soul. In his
scrutiny of Skelton's activities, Nelson sought to connect the origins
of the "Skeltonic" to the poet's <u>Speculum principis</u> written at the
court of Henry VII where Skelton tutored the young Henry (and possibly
his older brother Arthur), finding significant connections between the
rapid repetition of rhyme in the "Skeltonic" and the bunching of rhyming sounds in the Latin <u>reimprosa</u> in which Skelton wrote the treatise.
As a further example of Nelson's own wide range and deep-visioned

survey of the cultural scene, one notes with gratitude the intensive-
ness with which he investigated the quarrel among the grammarians in
1519 through 1521 as to the best method in which to teach Latin. He
also noted conservative resistance to the importation of Greek studies
then being sponsored by Cardinal Wolsey and related the grammarian's
war and conservative academic resistance to Skelton's major themes in
Speke Parrot.

At about the same time H. L. R. Edwards was beginning his studies
in Skelton. In 1935 he had looked at the genealogical background to
the Skelton family anew, a fresh investigation that lacked a certain
depth and breadth, nonetheless, as the French scholar Pollet was to
show in 1952. It was somehow fitting that Edwards should join with
Nelson in an exchange of opinions over the precise significance of
Speke Parrot and its position in Skelton's quarrel with Wolsey, a
quarrel in which it was the first and most obscure of three poems, the
other two being CC and WCY. As Nelson was to present Skelton as the
English-trained humanist, so Edwards in 1937 looked at the quarrel between the French humanist ambassador Robert Gaguin and the humanists
in Henry VII's employ during 1489-1490, when Gaguin had engaged in
sharp remarks over the negotiations at court. As Nelson had been
looking into the records in the PRO and the Norwich Consistorial
court, so Edwards had investigated some of the older records involving
Skelton. In examining the background to Skelton's mock-epitaph for
two parishioners in Diss, he came forward in 1937 with significant
emendations to text. Nelson and Edwards reached consensus on the matter of Skelton's "private calendar" which involved primarily the
numerals 33 and 34 found at the ends of the various envoys that pro-
longed Skelton's quarrel with Wolsey in SP. As a secondary means of
dating certain poems, the men agreed that the signature "Orator
regius" indicated Skelton's return to court in the spring of 1512 as
one of the king's recognized men of letters.

Not until 1949 was Edwards' own book on Skelton--The Life and
Times of an Early Tudor Poet--to appear. Although he relied heavily
on Nelson for the identification of essential records of Skelton's
life and ecclesiastical activity, Edwards attempted to make his biographical study far broader in nature than Nelson's more intensive
and thus necessarily narrower examination of Skelton as humanist and
poet. By the very nature of things Edwards' biography was inclined
to be conjectural, but in the best tradition of English books on the
life and works of a poet of distinction he worked into his presentation critical comments of value. For example, where Nelson had proposed that Reimprosa was an early and essential element in the "Skeltonic," Edwards derived it from Latin rhymed verse, as exemplified in
the medieval leonine hexameter. He showed how in Skelton's epitaphs
written at Diss against two quarrelsome parishioners, the poet had
begun them with rhyming Latin hexameters, and then had "tailed off"
into English Skeltonics.

Finally, it was entirely appropriate that Edwards, whose Cambridge
University D.Phil had dealt with Skelton as humanist and had presented

his classical background, should have joined forces with F. M. Salter
in editing and annotating Skelton's early translation of the Bibliotheca Historia of Diodorus Siculus in 1956 and 1959. The second
volume of the set contained a valuable introduction with notes and
appendices on Skelton's knowledge of Greek and his use of the Latin
classics, including a useful appendix on the poet's indebtedness to
the Cato Parvus, a schoolboy's text that suggested the aphoristic mode
followed by Skelton in the Speculum Principis. It had been Professor
Salter who had first published Skelton's "mirror for a prince" in 1934
in an issue of the journal Speculum. Prior to that by some dozen
years, Salter had written a master's thesis on Skelton's humanism, so
that he and Edwards, whatever the difference of age between them, had
ground in common upon which to join forces. Where Edwards seemed interested in the classical elements in Skelton's poetry, Salter was interested in the poet's contributions to the English language from
whatever source. Thus in 1945 in the Transactions of the Royal Society of Canada, by reviewing the novel terms naturalized from Poggio's
Latin translation of Diodorus, he lent formidable support to Skelton's
Tudor-reputation as "inventive Skelton," even though some of the words
introduced into evidence only appear to be "contributions" because of
the inaccuracies in the OED's recording and dating of the earliest use
of words.

We should not overlook two other scholars of the period who likewise brought forward books on our early Tudor poet: L. J. Lloyd and
Ian Gordon. Lloyd presented John Skelton: A Sketch of His Life and
Writings in 1938, a year before Nelson published his book. He had not
looked as deeply into Skelton's early years and into the ambience of
Henrician times as Nelson was to do, but as his title indicated he
sketched rapidly and in some instances vividly the progress of Skelton's career as a poet, presenting as he did so a heightened appreciation of Skelton's early poetry written in the Lydgatian manner. As
he was generously to admit in his note to the 1969 reprint of his
book, he was unaware that the cryptograms in WH and GL had been
solved, had oversimplified Skelton's "retirement" to Diss, and had
erred in stating that Skelton died unreconciled to Wolsey. Although
Ian Gordon had been working on Skelton at the same time that Nelson
and Edwards had been conducting their investigations, given the chair
in English Literature and Language at the University of New Zealand,
he was hindered by distance and the war in publishing his John Skelton, Poet Laureate. The book is chiefly important for its chapters
on Skelton as a "Goliard" poet, as seen in his skillful parody of the
Service for the Dead in PS, and as a "faithful son" of the church in
his religious lyrics, for whose continued attribution to Skelton
Gordon advances a spirited but perhaps mistaken argument.

As we have previously seen, Skelton's morality play, Magnyfycence,
seems to attract interests in widely scattered fits and starts. In
the late eighteenth and early nineteenth century, it was largely overlooked, to be sure, by an almost fantastic concern for a ghost play,
the Nigramansir. The interest of the 1950's and 60's in the play,

however, has had a firm historical basis thanks to Ramsay's edition of the play in 1908, reprinted in 1925, and has consisted to a large extent in a basic critical reorientation of notions about the play, its structure and meaning. In 1960 William O. Harris had argued that the play was not primarily an attack on Wolsey, as had been previously argued for almost half a century, thus bringing into high relief the more abstract argument of the play as it dealt with problems of the interrelationship between personal and public morality and the stress of acute financial adversity, rather than obscuring this larger theme in an elaborate network of local and personal references. David M. Bevington in 1962, in a chapter in his book From Mankind to Marlowe, examined Skelton's arrangement of his play, to shed new light on its dramaturgy, as reduced to the practicalities of a stage performance with limited cast.

As a result of this scholarly re-examination, it would seem, in the spring of 1963 the morality was staged for the first time ever by the Tower Theatre (Tavistock Repertory Company) of London, as adapted and directed by Michael Imison. The first production of Magnyfycence in the New World, incidentally, was not to come until February 1975, when the Poculi Iudique Societas of the University of Toronto staged the "goodly interlude and a mery" under the direction of Daniel De Matteis (reviewed by the Toronto Globe and Mail, February 13, 1975).

Professor W. O. Harris continued his analysis of the play in his book on Skelton's Magnyfycence and the Cardinal Virtue Tradition (1965), a book which took issue with Ramsay's Aristotelian interpretation of "magnificence" by relating the word to the Cardinal Virtue of "Fortitude" rather than to matters of liberality of dispense. In 1968, in his second book Tudor Drama and Politics, Bevington, although taking minor issue with Harris on the matter of the Wolsey's "presence" in the play, nonetheless agreed that Skelton's presentation established a model for the ideal king, who must be able to withstand prosperity as well as to endure adversity in a world that alternates between these two modes, a point underscored in an article by R. S. Kinsman (1966) on Skelton's deliberate use of proverb and sententia within the play to emphasize these themes. In addition, Bevington establishes the fact that the most daring topical meaning in the play is not in the selection of Wolsey as a primary target, but in the clearly implicit criticism of Henry VIII and his abuse of the old aristocracy, once his trusted advisors.

The early 60's (1961-1965) were also distinguished by a flurry of books that surveyed Skelton's achievements in wide spectrum. Two of them were general and eclectic, mingling documented biography, where useful, with literary history (not excluding fifteenth century traditions or early sixteenth century printing practices) and analogous developments in foreign literatures, written by the French scholar Pollet (1962) and the Italian scholar Schulte (1963). Two others presented more intensely theoretical and closely critical readings of Skelton's poetry—Heiserman (1961) and Fish (1965).

Pollet advanced the thesis that Skelton's name, elements of his
vocabulary, his earliest poem and connections show Yorkshire deriva-
tion or association. On the subject of <u>Magnyfycence</u> he clearly iden-
tified and dated the events alluded to in "Against Venomous Tongues,"
an immediate preliminary to the play, freshly analyzed the action of
the old morality play within its new framework of court life and its
range of characters from various classes and categories, and indicated its striking analogies with the mid-fourteenth <u>Chemin de Povreté
et de Richesse</u> adapted by Pierre Gringoire in 1499 under the title
<u>Chateau de Labour</u> and thence Englished in four editions between 1503
and 1510. With an ingenuity based on a detailed scrutiny of historical events he dated <u>TER</u>, and with an equal ingenuity founded in a
correspondingly detailed examination of Skelton's poems, distilled
the essence of Skelton's world, its physical, moral and mythological
topography.

Edvige Schulte's publication of <u>La Poesia di John Skelton</u> (Naples,
1963) brings a somewhat different "comparatist's" view to bear on
Skelton's accomplishment. While as concerned as Pollet with the
medieval background to Skelton's verse, Schulte made her most important contributions in examining Skelton's relationship, from quotation, paraphrase and chiefly analogue, with the Italian humanistic
tradition from Petrarch and Boccaccio to their successors Poggio,
Poliziano, Filelfo and Folengo. Three of them are directly mentioned
by Skelton: Petrarch is mentioned as one of the "clerks" and laure-
ates of the poetic "college" whose members honor Skelton in the <u>Gar-
lande of Laurell</u>, and is paraphrased in <u>WCY</u>; "John Bochas, with his
volumys grete" also attends Skelton in <u>GL</u> together with "Poggeus...
that famous Florentine" and his <u>Facetiae</u>. Thus in a chapter on <u>PS</u>,
Schulte nicely established connections between details of feature and
personality of Poliziano's heroine in his brief "De angeli puella"
and Jane Scrope; in a chapter on Skelton's flytings against Garnesche,
similarities in tone and epithet to the invectives of Filelfo and
Poggio; and in a chapter on <u>TER</u>, possible sources and significant
parallels between Folengo's mode of describing his characters Tognazzo
and Berta in his macaronic Latin poem <u>Baldus</u> (1517) and Skelton's
techniques in presenting Dame Elynour. Particularly in her eleventh
chapter on Skelton, Petrarch and the love of Glory or Fame in <u>GL</u>, did
she advance tantalizing evidence that Skelton may have known
Petrarch's Latin epic <u>Africa</u> and almost certainly knew his vernacular
poems <u>Il Trionfi</u> (especially "Triumphus fame" chap. iii) and the
<u>Canzoni</u>, however he was to expand and dramatize those passages he
"borrowed."

Thus well seated in the late medieval traditions of western
Europe by Pollet and Schulte, and hence with much more than a mere in-
sular curiosity, Skelton was to be systematically explored in a
generic and psycho-aesthetic way by two American scholars of the early
60's--Heiserman and Fish. Heiserman examined Skelton's satiric art in
terms of the conventions and traditions of medieval satire in general.
Dealing in separate chapters with <u>BC</u>, <u>Mag</u>, <u>SP</u>, <u>CC</u> and <u>WCY</u>, he began

each section with close analyses of the "objects" attacked and, having
finished his process of analysis, went on to examine earlier works
attacking similar objects and thus establish patterns and precedents.
More specifically, having discovered the real "objects" attacked in a
Skeltonic satire, Heiserman sought to describe its structural devices,
its personae, its diction and tone, and--all these matters combined--
its "manifest fiction," the means by which conventions have been made
vitally to refunction, or have been inadequately recombined into interesting failures, as in his judgment CC turns out to be.

Overlapping with Heiserman in some of the poems which he expli-
cated (BC, SP, CC, WCY), including the lyrics, WH and, briefly, GL
(all ignored by Heiserman), but excluding Mag, carefully scrutinized
by Heiserman, was Stanley Fish (1965). As he best put it himself,
whatever was new to his reading of Skelton was "the result of a single
assumption--that at the center of a Skelton poem is the psychological
(spiritual) history of its protagonist" (p. 240). The "informal signature" of Skelton's poetry, as Fish saw it, is a first-person narrator who loses his way, indulges for a time in questioning or complaint,
but who returns to, or calls for a return to, the ideals and restored
functions of an order "whose relevance has been reasserted rather than
weakened in the process of exploration and redefinition" (p. 242).
Heiserman, he would claim, tells us a good deal about the literary
possibilities available to Skelton, but very little about the poet who
manipulated those conventions to a purposeful end and the impact of
that poetry.

Since 1965 only one other full length book on Skelton has appeared,
that published by Nan Cooke Carpenter in 1967. She tried to maintain
that most difficult of balances, between the readable and the scholarly, between the general reader and the academic. In addition to sum-
marizing and using the scholarship of the 40's, 50's and 60's, Miss
Carpenter made genuine contributions of her own in emphasizing Skelton's "musical background and understanding," a facet of his writing
not previously explored with her depth and technical knowledge. She
noted their importance early and late in Skelton's work, in short
satirical lyrics, in the mock-elegiac PS and in the long satire CC.

The most recent decade, 1966-76, in terms of scholarly and critical publication has been chiefly characterized by a continuing interest in Magnyfycence, a renewed interest in Collyn Clout and Speke
Parrot, and a re-examination of The Garlande of Laurell, the one Skelton poem that has resisted detailed explication. At the same time
bibliographical and textual inquiries have been revived and extended,
and Skelton's general characteristics as a poet re-examined, including
a new identification of the "demotic" source of the Skeltonic (Norton-
Smith, 1973).

In addition to Kinsman's article on proverb and sententia in Magnyfycence (1966) and Bevington's chapter on the play in Tudor Drama
and Politics (1968), referred to earlier, one finds in 1969 F. P.

Introduction

Wilson and G. K. Hunter commenting on the play in the O.H.E.L. volume The English Drama (1485–1585), and Leigh Winser carefully examining it for its range of meanings, metaphors and methods of attack in a Columbia dissertation of that year. In an article derived from the dissertation, Winser in 1970 sought to place the play 10–12 years earlier (c. 1504–05) in Skelton's career than it had been placed before. Gordon Kipling in 1974, among other comments on the influence of Burgundian literature on Skelton, traced the concept of "Magnificence" to the Burgundian use of the term as designating an "architectonic virtue" on which both magnanimity and fortitude depend. Robert Potter, the next year, in his book on the English Morality Play, praised Magnyfycence as being dramatically even more revolutionary than previously thought in exemplifying the general problems of human nature through the specific problem of economic excess and deprivation and directing the attention of the audience to the problems of prince and state under such extremes rather than to the matter of individual salvation.

Collyn Clout has come in for renewed interest the last ten years as William Glassco's dissertation of 1966 shows and as Paul McLane's articles of 1972 and 1973 demonstrate, the first dating the poem as late as mid-1523 from its reference to "prestes" or Wolsey's forced "loans" of that year, and the second showing the pervasive influence of the poem on Spenser's Shepheardes Calendar. Also in 1973, K. J. Atchity brought a sharp focus to bear on the Latin epigraphs with which Skelton begins and ends the poem, for there he found reflected three levels of awareness: the individual, the body politic and the superhuman or divine.

Speke Parrot continued to command as much attention from scholars as it received from poets. In 1968, F. M. Brownlow examined the poem closely in terms of its strategic incorporation of materials from Psalm 82 of the Vulgate Bible. Three years later, he followed up certain implications that he had previously advanced to argue that the printed, short version of SP represents a completed state of the poem rather than merely an imperfect text, while the longer manuscript version, itself imperfect in lacking lines 59–265, represents "Version II" of Skelton's poem.

Perhaps the most interesting phenomenon during the decade was the attempt, finally, to explore the thickets from which Skelton's Garlande of Laurell was plucked and woven. In the first of his revisionist essays on the dating of the Garlande, M. J. Tucker argued in 1967 that lack of documentary evidence that Sheriff Hutton castle was occupied by Skelton's patrons, the Howards, in 1523, GL's traditional date, and the availability of evidence of Howard occupation of the castle in the 1490's led him to prefer the latter as a more likely time for Skelton's having at least begun GL. In 1969, with the distinguished American astronomer Gingerich, Tucker sought to date GL astrologically as having been completed in an early form by the late Spring of 1495, an interpretation by no means yet accepted. (See the

xlix

exchange of opinions between Tucker and Pollet in <u>Moreana</u>, nos.
1973.5 and 1973.7.) The <u>Garlande</u> has been interpreted by Colley
(1973) as an apologia for Skelton's ironic and satiric modes rather
than a comic denial of his claims to fame or a capitulation to Wolsey
(in the envoys); and by Lee (Wisconsin dissertation 1976) as a more
or less conscious demonstration of the validity that true Honour
(Fame) should accrue to the inspired moral poet, not the lesser types
of Honour discussed by Fame or defined by Aquinas. Lee's commentary
accompanies an edition of the poem based where possible on the defec-
tive manuscript-form as copy-text.

Finally the decade 1966–76 has shown that Skelton still delights
the bibliographer and still stimulates the poet-essayist. Kinsman
and Yonge in 1967 defined the canon more narrowly and presented it
more fully than Brie had done in 1907 and completed a census of sixteenth-century printed editions of Skelton's poetry. In 1965, two
years earlier, Robbins and Cutler had substantially supplemented the
<u>Index of Middle English Verse</u> to include alphabetically by first line
poetry written by, or claimed for, Skelton. <u>The New Cambridge Bibliography of English Literature</u> (1974) in its first volume brought
Skelton up-to-date in a selected way, as of 1970, actually by two
years more inclusive than Fishman's annotated "Recent Studies in
Skelton" in <u>ELR</u> (Winter 1971). With the issuance of the second
volume of the second edition of the <u>Short-Title Catalogue</u> in 1976,
Skelton in his various sixteenth and early seventeenth century guises
has been made clearly and succinctly accessible to the contemporary
Tudor scholar and reference librarian in a superbly printed volume.

Two poet-essayists, Robert Graves and Robin Skelton, completed
the consolidation of Skelton's reputation in our times. Graves' essays, admittedly, had appeared in the mid-50's and the first six years
of the 60's. The first of the Clark Lectures of 1954 at Cambridge
praised Skelton for a "stronger sense of poetic calling than almost
any of his successors"; the last, relying on Dame Occupacyon of the
<u>Garlande of Laurell</u>, praises him by implication for his poetic in-
tegrity and sturdiness. Graves' inaugural lecture at Oxford, par-
tially a defense of his being elected to the chair, was given over to
"The Dedicated Poet," John Skelton, "the first scholar to write popular English verse," and the "first muse-poet to appear in England,"
with verse written from the "back of the mind." Equally laudatory
but much less subjective and much more sustained and systematic is
the praise accorded John Skelton by the modern poet and scholar-
critic Robin Skelton in 1973.[8] Addressing himself to "The Master
Poet: John Skelton as Conscious Craftsman," Robin Skelton extols the
Tudor poet's "Apollonian" and conscious craftsmanship so notably
played down by Graves. As befits our earlier thematic analysis of
scholarly interests in the decade (1966–76), Robin Skelton notes that
old John had best displayed his "master poet <u>persona</u>" in <u>Garlande of
Laurell</u>, there establishing his lineage, his kinship with older poets,
his control of verse-forms and genres, his views on proper sources of
inspiration and proper models for his discipline.

It is all the more fitting to conclude this final ten year section on "Skelton and the Academic Critics (1935-Present)" with a quotation from Robin Skelton, one that restores John Skelton to the reputation he held among his own contemporaries--those who venerated him for his inventiveness, or those who disdained the academic qualities of his garland of laurel: "The Master-Poet, according to Skelton, must be omnicompetent, multi-lingual, and self-assertive." It was in this very mood that Skelton concluded his Latin admonition to trees of whatever kind to give place to the laurel, a poem that appropriately appears at the end of GL: "Arboris omne genus viridi concedite lauro!" These very words identify the poet on the title pages of two early Tudor collections of his minor verse: Agaynste a Comely Coystrowne and Dyvers Balettys and Dyties Solacyous. We have thus returned a master poet to the conditions of his own time.

NOTES

1. Botteghe Oscure, XXV (1960), 198.

2. See in the bibliography proper the following items: AUDEN 1930, 1932, 1933.1, 1935.2 (with Isherwood); RANSOM 1927.3, 1969.5; CARRUTH 1958; DEUTSCH 1953.1; GREGORY 1933.4; GRAVES 1916.1, 1916.2, 1917.1, 1920.1, 1921, 1923, 1925, 1925.1, 1927, 1927.1, 1928; HUGHES 1922, 1926; E. SITWELL 1923, 1930; and O. SITWELL 1927, 1931.
In addition to Auden and Graves as reviewers of Philip Henderson's 1931 edition of Skelton's Complete Poems, one finds two other practicing poets, William Rose Benét and Austen Clarke.

3. See Auden's essay on Skelton in The Great Tudors, ed. Katherine Garvan (1935); Edmund Blunden's long essay in the TLS (20 June, 1929) in praise of the living memory of Skelton whose death had occurred four centuries before; and Graves' Clark Lectures at Cambridge 1954-55 and his Oxford addresses 1961-66 as gathered in his collection On Poetry 1969. Note that Richard Hughes published a substantial selection of Skelton's poems in 1924 (reviewed by Graves in 1925), Graves a brief selection in 1927. Auden twice included excerpts from Skelton's poetry in more comprehensive anthologies in 1935 and 1938.

4. The CBEL of 1940 presented a carefully selected list of 74 Skelton items, almost a third of which dealt with editions and manuscripts; the NCBEL of 1974 offers 152 items, of which the number of critical pieces has more than trebled. Such an augmentation resulted not only from the increase in scholarly traffic over three decades but also from the reduction in enumerating sixteenth century bibliographical items made possible by including as a reference work Skelton: Canon and Census, compiled by R. S. Kinsman and T. Yonge in 1967.

5. English Literature in the Sixteenth Century (Oxford: Clarendon Press, 1954), p. 675.

6. This footnote, perhaps mistakenly, will be a single stone
   flung at three birds. First, there were distinguished anthologies of English verse that utterly ignored Skelton: Robert
   Anderson's The Works of the British Poets (London, 1795), in
   12 volumes, completely omits Skelton, as does Thomas Campbell's
   Specimens of the British Poets (1819), in 7 volumes. Similarly, Francis Palgrave's Golden Treasury of Songs and Lyrics
   (1861) fails to record even one of the Garland lyrics soon to
   become the "traditional" choice. Second, I have not included
   every nineteenth century anthologist, by any means: George
   Gilfillan is excluded, for example, since his Specimens...of
   the Less Known English Poets (Edinburgh, 1861) presents only
   one lyric from the Garland; similarly I have excluded William
   Cullen Bryant's A Library of Poetry and Song (New York, 1874)
   for its inclusion of only a single lyric from GL, "Mistress
   Margaret Hussey" (p. 38). As a final item let me list some of
   the twentieth century anthologies omitted on the basis of their
   failure to include five full pages of poetry from the Skelton
   canon, even though they have included two or three of his
   shorter pieces together, in some instances, with such doubtful
   poems as "Wofully Araid" or "Petually Constrained": John Bet-
   jeman and Geoffrey Taylor, English Love Poems (1964), pp. 16-
   18; Sir E. K. Chambers and F. Sidgewick, Early English Lyrics
   (1917), [3 from GL]; A. N. Jeffares, Seven Centuries of Poetry
   (1960), pp. 15-18; J. M. Manly, English Poetry (1170-1892)
   (1907), pp. 61-62; W. Peacock, English Verse (1928), I, 106-109;
   Herbert Read and Bonamy Dobrée, The London Book of English
   Verse (1949) [3 GL lyrics and "Wofully Araid"]; James Reeve,
   The Cassell Book of English Poetry (1965), Nos. 64-69 [but two
   longer poems "Wofully" and "Petuelly" are dubious]; and A. J. M.
   Smith, Seven Centuries of Verse, English and American (1947),
   pp. 71-72.

7. I make no claim to utter completeness in my remarks concerning
   Graves' indebtedness to Skelton. I have not included, for example, his comments on Skelton in the Woman's Leader, XII
   (1920), 462-463 or his incidental comments on the poet in his
   essay "The Future of Poetry," Fortnightly Review, DCCXI--(1926),
   pp. 205-206. Nor have I incorporated anything save "major"
   remarks by Graves on Skelton in the 40's and 50's, omitting,
   perhaps to my disadvantage, his passing comments in the White
   Goddess of 1948 and The Common Asphodel of 1949. For his help-
   ful comments on, and encyclopedic knowledge of, Graves' use of
   Skelton, I am particularly indebted to A. S. G. Edwards, who
   has most generously dug into his own "cunning bag" to provide
   some of the examples I have adduced.

8. It would be both provincial and misleading to suppose that historians of whatever kind are wholly in accord with the notion
   that John Skelton has been restored to high claims of true
   merit. G. R. Elton in his England under the Tudors (2nd edn.,
   London: Methuen and Co., 1974), p. 443, grumps: "When

historians of literature have to fall back on the tedious
Alexander Barclay...English poetry was in a parlous state.
Nor can much more be said for John Skelton...not the last poet
laureate hardly to deserve the first part of his title, though
his idiosyncratic doggerel breathed vigour, a crude humour,
and--especially in his attacks on Wolsey (Speke Parrot and Why
Come Ye Nat to Courte, c. 1522-23) a genuine savagery." Elton
also delivers himself of two somewhat contradictory but equally
dyspeptic views in his Reform and Reformation, England 1509-
1558 (Cambridge, Massachusetts: Harvard University Press,
1977), pp. 38, 65-66.

John Skelton, Early Tudor Laureate:
An Annotated Bibliography *c.* 1488-1977

1488   SKELTON, JOHN. The Bibliotheca Historia of Diodorus
        Siculus.
              Translation by Skelton [c. 1488] of five books with-
        out title, from Poggio's Latin version of the Greek
        original translated before 1449; mentioned by Caxton
        (see 1490 below), "For [Skelton] hath late translated
        the boke of dyodorus syculus," and by Skelton himself in
        the Garlande of Laurell (see 1523.3), vv. 1498-1502.
        The work is found in a contemporary manuscript, Corpus
        Christi College, Cambridge MS. 357, copied by three
        scribes for Robert Pen (d. 1538), a Gentleman of the
        Chapel under Henry VII and Henry VIII; it is defective,
        with loss of material, and breaks at Bk. IV, chap. 19 of
        the original, Bk. V in Poggio's and Skelton's reckoning.
        For a photographic reproduction of Skelton's manuscript,
        see no. 1925.4; for an annotated edition of the work, in
        2 volumes, see no. 1956.2+.

1489   SKELTON, JOHN. "The Doulourous Dethe and Muche Lamentable
        Chaunce of the Most Honorable Erle of Northumberlande."
              Skelton's earliest undoubted poem, it was written
        after 25 April 1489, the occasion of the Earl's death,
        in 217 lines of rhyme royal, preceded and followed by
        short Latin poems. It is found in a manuscript version,
        B.L. MS. Royal 18. D. II, fols. 165-6^v; it was first
        printed in PPPW, sigs Y6-Z2^v, no. 1568 below.

1490   CAXTON, WILLIAM. The Boke of Eneydos.
              In his preface to his translation of the Eneydos, STC
        24796, sigs 42^{r-v}, printed after 22 June 1490, Caxton
        makes a laudatory reference to the power of translation
        displayed by "mayster Iohn Skelton, late created poete
        laureate in the vnyuersite of Oxenforde" for his versions
        of Cicero's letters and of Diodorus Siculus. For an
        available modern print of Caxton's statement, see
        W. J. B. Crotch (ed.), The Prologues and Epilogues of
        William Caxton, EETS, CLXXVI (1928), p. 109.

1

1492-3   GRACE BOOK B (Pt. I)...of the University of Cambridge.
          Edited by Mary Bateson. Cambridge: Cambridge Univer-
          sity Press, 1903, p. 54.
               Reproduces a Cambridge University record of the year
          1492-93, certifying that Skelton was there awarded the
          laureate degree in rhetoric, as previously granted him
          at Oxford and "overseas," presumably at Louvain: "Con-
          ceditur Johanni Skelton poete in partibus transmarinis
          atque oxonie laurea ornato ut apud nos eadem decorare-
          tur." The record is reprinted in Nelson, p. 43, no.
          1939.8 below, and Edwards, p. 287, no. 1949 below.

1495   SKELTON, JOHN. Garlande of Laurell.
               The poet, in the Spring of 1495, had perhaps begun
          and conceivably finished a first version of the poem.
          See no. 1969.1 for argument for early dating of the
          poem; see also no. 1523.3 for first printed version.

1495.1   SKELTON, JOHN. "Manerly Margery, Mylk and Ale."
               30 untitled lines beginning "Ay beshrewe yow, be my
          fay," in B.L. MS. Additional 5465, ff. 96^v-99; written
          sometime c. 1495-1500. For first printed version, see
          no. 1776.1; the poem is included in Dyce, no. 1843.1 and
          has been freshly edited by Stevens, pp. 378-79, no.
          1961.5 below. For other short poems written in this
          period, presumably chiefly c. 1495-1500, see ACC and
          DBDS, nos. 1527 and 1527.1.

1496   GRACE BOOK B (Pt. I)...of the University of Cambridge.
          Edited by Mary Bateson. Cambridge: Cambridge Univer-
          sity Press, 1903, p. 92.
               Two items for meals eaten by Skelton in London with
          John Suckling (Syclyng) of Godshouse, after Pentecost,
          1496 are recorded: the first with the Bishop of Salis-
          bury, the second at Symson's Inn. The records are re-
          printed in Edwards, p. 287, no. 1949 below.

1498   ORDINATION RECORDS for 31 March, 14 April, and 9 June 1498
          on which days Skelton was ordained sub-deacon, deacon,
          and priest, respectively, as recorded in Register 'Hill'
          (1489-1505) of the diocese of London, Guildhall Library
          MS. 9531/8, fol. 5^v, col. 1, are printed by Dyce, I, xx-
          xxi, no. 1843.1 below and Edwards, p. 288, no. 1949
          below.

1498.1   OFFERING RECORD of 20 shillings by Henry VII "at master
          Skelton masse," 11 November 1498 is found in P.R.O. MS.
          E101, 414/16, the account book of John Heron, Treasurer
          of the Chamber, 13-15 Henry VII. Printed by Nelson, p.
          71 n. 37, no. 1939.8 below and Edwards, p. 288, no. 1949
          below.

1499   ERASMUS, DESIDERIUS. "Carmen Extemporale."
                 Specifically mentions Skelton three times: the first
            time as "Aeterna vates Skelton dignissime lauro," found
            in B.L. MS. Egerton 1651, f. 6ᵛ, printed by Edwards,
            p. 289, no. 1949 below. In an attempted revision of the
            poem, Erasmus varies the line as "...Skelton dignissime
            lauro ut habetur," on fol. 10, printed by Edwards, p.
            290, no. 1949 below. See also no. 1934-13 for note lo-
            cating poem in Preserved Smith's life of Erasmus.

1499.1   ERASMUS, DESIDERIUS.
                 Calls Skelton "vnum britannicarum litterarum lumen ac
            decus" in his dedication of B.L. MS. Egerton 1651 during
            the autumn of [?1499] to young Prince Henry, f. 1,
            printed in part by Edwards, p. 290, no. 1949 below and
            in whole from the Adagia (1500) by P. S. Allen, Opus
            Epistolarum Des. Erasmi Roterodami (Oxford: Clarendon
            Press, 1906), I, No. 104, pp. 239-241. For a modern
            translation of the letter, see The Correspondence of
            Erasmus, trans. R. A. B. Mynors and D. F. S. Thomson
            (Toronto: University of Toronto Press, 1974), I, 197.

1499.2   SKELTON, JOHN. The Bowge of Courte. First edition: "En-
            prynted at Westmynster by me Wynkyn the worde" [c. 1499],
            sigs. A-B⁶ [539 lines of rhyme royal]; STC 22597.
                 Reproduced by University Microfilms, Reel No. 1188;
            described in K&Y, pp. 46-47; for dating see no. 1937.1.
            See also second edition, no. 1510.3 below.

1501   COURT OF REQUESTS.
                 Skelton is mentioned as the defendant in the case of
            Peter Ottey, one of the royal chaplains, "contra Iohannem
            skelton"; found in P.R.O. Court of Requests Misc. Bks.
            II, f. 133, and printed by Nelson, p. 242, no. 1939.8
            below and by Edwards, p. 290, no. 1949 below.

1501.1   GRACE BOOK B (Pt. I)...of the University of Cambridge.
                 Edited by Mary Bateson. Cambridge: Cambridge Univer-
            sity Press, 1903, pp. 148-149.
                 "Mayster Skelton" mentioned four times by John Suck-
            ling as his guest for supper in a Westminster inn, during
            Hilary term, January-March 1501. The records are re-
            printed by Edwards, p. 287, no. 1949 below.

1501.2   SKELTON, JOHN. Speculum Principis.
                 Skelton finished this rhyming Latin prose pamphlet
            proper (B.L. MS. Addit. 26,787) by 28 August 1501, with
            an "Epigram," a Palinode, and a Complaint to be added
            c. 1510-11; first printed by F. M. Salter, no. 1934.16
            below. See also 1925.5 for photographic reproduction.

1502   COURT OF REQUESTS.
                 On 10 June 1502, Skelton, as surety for an obligation
            incurred by the prior of St. Bartholomew's, to Sir
            Reginald Bray and others, was committed "carceribus
            genitoris domini regis" (? to the prison of the king's
            mother [the Lady Margaret Beaufort]) on failure of the
            prior to pay; found in P.R.O. (Court of Requests Misc.
            Bks. II, fol. 3). The record is printed by Nelson, with
            reading "ianitoris" for "genitoris," pp. 242-43, no.
            1939.8, and by Edwards, p. 290, no. 1949 below.

1504   BLOMEFIELD, FRANCIS. Topographical History of the County
            of Norfolk. Fersfield, 1739, I, 11 and 18.
                 First noticed that Skelton succeeded Peter Greves as
            Rector of Diss, Norfolk before 10 April 1504, as shown
            by fact that the will of Margery Cowper of Diss, Norfolk
            was witnessed by "Master Iohn Skelton laureat parson of
            disse" and John Clark, Soul Priest, as recorded in Nor-
            wich Consistory Court Register R. ix. 212b (1504-07).
            The record is noted by Nelson, p. 81, n. 47, no. 1939.8
            below and reprinted in Edwards, p. 291, no. 1949 below.

1504-05   GRACE BOOK Γ. Edited by William George Searle. Cambridge:
            Cambridge University Press, 1908, p. 37.
                 Skelton granted grace at Cambridge for incorporation
            from Oxford, with the privilege of wearing a special
            habit "sibi concesso a principe," during Spring of aca-
            demic year 1504-05. Record reprinted by Nelson, p. 102,
            n. 9, no. 1939.8 below, and by Edwards, p. 287, no. 1949
            below.

1505   SKELTON, JOHN. Ware the Hauke.
                 Skelton may have finished this heavily Latinate poem
            of 329 lines of Skeltonics, an attack on a hawking priest,
            before 15 August 1505. See CB, no. 1545 below, for
            earliest surviving print.

1505.1   SKELTON, JOHN. Phyllyp Sparowe.
                 Skelton may have finished the "Dirge" and "Commenda-
            tions" sections, 11. 1-1267 of the poem, in late 1505,
            before the death of Jane Scrope's mother in December
            1505. The "Addition," vv. 1268-1382, was probably
            written c. 1509.

1507   SKELTON, JOHN. "A Devout Trentale" and "Epitaph for Adam
            Uddersale."
                 Mock epitaphs on two of Skelton's parishioners at
            Diss, John Clarke and Adam Uddersall, copied down by the
            Vicar of Trumpington, the scribe to Cambridge university
            on 5 January 1507; first printed in PPPW, no. 1568, sigs.
            X8V-Y3V.

1507.1   SKELTON, JOHN. "Diligo rusticulum" and "Lamentatio urbis Norvvicen."
        The first an elegiac couplet, the second 10 lines of elegiacs, occasioned by a fire that severely damaged the city of Norwich in 1507; first printed in PPPW, no. 1568, sig. Y3^v.

1509   BARCLAY, ALEXANDER. The Shyp of Folys. STC 3545 (1509), fol. cclxxii.
        Skelton is apparently referred to in the penultimate section "Of the syngularyte of some newe Folys" as a jesting or wanton poet for having written Phyllyp Sparowe (c. 1505): "It longeth nat to my scyence nor cunnynge / For Phylyp the Sparowe the (Dirige) to synge," stanza 1962. For a more readily available text of Barclay's work, see that edited by T. H. Jamieson (Edinburgh: W. Paterson; London: H. Sotheran, 1874), II, p. 331. See also BARCLAY, nos. 1514 and 1515 for further hostile remarks.

1509.1   CONSISTORY COURT, NORWICH.
        Records show that Skelton was involved in an interrogation concerning the "health of the soul" of one of his parishioners, Thomas Pykerell of Diss, in the Consistory Court at Norwich on 3 December 1509; from Consistory Court Act Book, Norwich Cathedral; excerpt printed in Nelson, p. 243, no. 1939.8, and Edwards, p. 291, no. 1949.

1509.2   SKELTON, JOHN. "A Lawde and Prayse Made for Our Sovereign Lord the Kyng."
        A poem written for Henry VIII's coronation in 56 lines, found in Skelton's own hand in P.R.O. MS (TR) E. 36/289, fols. 67-70; printed by Dyce, I, pp. ix-xi, no. 1843.1; see also no. 1914.5 for reprint from manuscript and no. 1973.2 for full photographic reproduction with transcription.

1509.3   SUPPLEMENTARY PATENT ROLLS.
        A routine royal pardon for all persons imprisoned for petty matters in Henry VII's time was extended among others to "Iohannes Skelton...clericus, poeta laureatus ac Rector ecclesie parochialis de Dysse" on 21 October 1509; excerpted from P.R.O. Supp. Patent Rolls C. 67/57/2 m. 31, as printed by Edwards, p. 298, no. 1949.

1510   CONSISTORY COURT, NORWICH.
        Records show a second summons to defendant, 14 January 1510, "In Skelton contra pykerell...," Consistory Court Act Book, Norwich Cathedral; excerpt printed by Nelson, p. 243, no. 1939.8, and Edwards, p. 291, no. 1949.

1510.1   CONSISTORY COURT, NORWICH.
          Records show Pykerell suspended "In Skelton contra
          pykerell" 4 February 1510; excerpt from Consistory Court
          Act Book, printed by Nelson, p. 243, no. 1939.8, and
          Edwards, p. 291, no. 1949.

1510.2   THE GREAT CHRONICLE OF LONDON. Edited by A. H. Thomas and
          I. D. Thornley. London: Privately printed, 1938, p.
          361.
          Refers to Skelton along with Cornysh and More as a
          satiric poet, reference dating c. 1510, in Guildhall
          Library MS. 3313; see also no. 1960.7 for note calling
          attention to this reference.

1510.3   SKELTON, JOHN. Bowge of Courte. The second edition, "En-
          prynted at London by Wynkyn de Worde in Flete strete /
          in the sygne of the sonne" [c. 1510], sigs. A⁶-B⁴; STC².²
          22597.5. For full description, see K&Y, p. 47.

1511   INSTITUTION BOOK, NORWICH CATHEDRAL. Book XIV, fols. 60k-
          kᵛ, 1ᵛ and o.
          Records show that on 11 November 1511 Master John
          Skelton, Rector of Diss, was appointed one of the Ar-
          bitrators in an ecclesiastical court case involving the
          Rector of Redgrave. Excerpts printed in Edwards, pp.
          291-292, no. 1949.

1511.1   SKELTON, JOHN. "Palinode" and "Soliloquy."
          The poet added 12 hexameters and a brief prose so-
          liloquy of complaint to the manuscript of Speculum Prin-
          cipis which then, evidently, was sent to Henry VIII as a
          birthday gift from "Skeltonis Laureatus, didasculus
          quondam Regius" on, or about, 28 June 1511.

1511.2   WESTMINSTER ABBEY MUNIMENTS.
          Records show that on 5 July, 1511, with Prior of
          Westminster Abbey, there dined "Skelton the poet wᵗ
          othere"; excerpt from Westminster Abbey Muniments 33,325
          fol. 17ᵛ printed in Nelson, p. 118, no. 1939.8, and Ed-
          wards, p. 298, no. 1949.

1512   DU RESNEL [DU BELLAY], ABBÉ [JEAN FRANCOIS]. Recherches sur
          les Poëtes Couronnez in Mémoires de l'Académie des In-
          scriptions. 1736, X, p. 522.
          According to a record (now long lost), du Resnel as-
          serts that Skelton was recognized by letters patent as
          poet laureate to Henry VIII in the fifth year of his
          reign (1512-13). The claim is cited by Dyce, I, p. xv,
          no. 1843.1.

1512.1   SKELTON, JOHN. "Quamvis annosa est" and "I, liber et
          propera, regem tu pronus adora."

Two brief Latin poems in holograph, dedicating Skelton's New Year's gift in 1512 to Henry VIII of a 13th
century chronicle of the wars against the Saracens; the
manuscript is now Corpus Christi College, Cambridge, MS.
432, the poems on fols. 1^v-3^v. For printings of the
verse, see nos. 1748, 1777 and 1913.1.

1512.2   SKELTON, JOHN. "Why Were Ye, Calliope, Embrawdered with
            Letters of Golde?"
                 In English and Latin, this is the first of Skelton's
            poems to be signed "Orator regius," possibly because of
            the royal grant of late April or May above; it was first
            printed in PPPW, sig. 2A3^v, no. 1568 below.

1512.3   SKELTON, JOHN. "Henrici septimi epitaphium."
                 This Latin poem, commissioned by John Islip Abbot of
            Westminster to hang over Henry VII's tomb, was written
            by 29 November 1512. To its 24 lines of elegiac couplets
            were added four additional lines of Latin verse cele-
            brating the victory of Flodden (1513) over Henry's old
            opponent. The poem was first printed in PPPW, sigs.
            Z4^{r-v}, no. 1568.

1513   BRADSHAW, HENRY. The Holy Lyfe and History of Saynt Wer-
            burge. STC 3506 [1521], sig. S2. Modern edition by
            Carl Horstmann, EETS, LXXXVIII (1887), p. 199.
                 Bradshaw, who died in 1513, mentions "inventive Skel-
            ton and poete laureate" in the 2nd stanza of the envoy
            to his poem, in company with "Maister Chaucer," "Ludgate
            sentencious" and "preignaunt Barkley."

1513.1   BRADSHAW, HENRY. The Lyfe of Saynt Radegunde. STC 3507
            [1521], sig. D1^v.
                 The "Lyfe" was perhaps written c. 1500, before no.
            1513 above. As edited in a modern edition by F. Brit-
            tain, Cambridge University Press, 1926, p. 37, Bradshaw
            mentions Lydgate, Chaucer and Skelton as "fathers of
            eloquens" together with "religious Barkley."

1513.2   SKELTON, JOHN. "Eulogium pro suorum temporum conditione."
                 This Latin poem of 36 elegiacs, followed by a 4 line
            "Tetrasticon Veritatis," was written on parchment and
            hung over the tomb of Henry VII as a companion piece to
            no. 1512.2; from its content it may have been completed
            in the early Spring of 1513. It was first printed in
            PPPW, sigs. Z5-Z5^v, no. 1568.

1513.3   SKELTON, JOHN. "Chorus de Dys contra Gallos."
                 Written after 22 August 1513, when the English took
            Thérouanne; 16 lines of elegiacs, celebrating surrender
            of the city; first printed in CB, sig. B4, no. 1545
            below.

7

1513.4   SKELTON, JOHN. "A Ballade of the Scottysshe Kynge."
          The poem in 73 lines was written after 9 September,
          1513, the English victory over the Scots at Flodden, but
          before 22 September when the full details of battle became
          known; printed by [R. Faques], [ ]^2, unsigned; STC 22593
          [1513]; University Microfilms, Reel no. 19, K&Y, p. 37;
          for reprints, see nos. 1881.2, 1882, 1887, and 1969.

1513.5   SKELTON, JOHN. "Chorus de Dys Contra Scottos."
          This Latin poem, in 20 lines of elegiacs was written
          after 9 September but before 22 September, probably
          after "BSK," for it seems a bit more accurate; first
          printed in CB, sig. B3^v, no. 1545 below.

1513.6   SKELTON, JOHN. "Agaynst the Scottes."
          This is a revised and augmented version of "BSK" in
          180 lines, with 4 lines of Latin and a defense of his
          strident tone called "Unto Dyuers People that Remord
          this Rymyng," of 38 lines; first printed in CB, sigs.
          A8-B3, no. 1545 below.

1514   BARCLAY, ALEXANDER. The fourth Egloge of Alexander Barclay,
          entituled Codrus and Minalcas, treating of the behauiour
          of Riche men agaynst Poetes. STC 1384b [?1521], sig.
          ciii.
          The poem, written c. 1514, states, "Then is he decked
          as poete laureate, / When stinkyng Thays made him her
          graduate." For a modern edition consult Beatrice White
          (ed.), The Eclogues of Alexander Barclay, EETS, CLXXV
          (1928), p. 165; her note to Ecl. iv, 685-686 shows that
          Barclay has expanded the Latin of his original into a
          gratuitous and covert reference to Skelton.

1514.1   SKELTON, JOHN. "Agenst Garnesch."
          Skelton's half of the flyting of "Skelton Lauriate
          Defender agenst Master [Christopher] Garnesch, Chalen-
          ger" by "the kynges most noble commandement," 4 poems
          totalling 469 lines, written c. 1514. First printed by
          Dyce, I, pp. 116-131, no. 1843.1 below, from B.L. MS.
          Harley 367 [c. 1550], a manuscript at one time owned by
          John Stowe, the Elizabethan antiquary, fols. 101-109^v.
          The manuscript is severely damaged by damp and mold and
          some lines thus are rendered imperfect. For dating of
          flyting, see 1928.3; for Manuscript copy of original,
          consult Folger MS. N.b. 49, fols. 23-28, a late copy of
          the damaged ms. made by Joseph Haslewood (1769-1833).

1515   BARCLAY, ALEXANDER. The Life of St. George.
          There is a possible reference to Skelton in this manu-
          script poem, written c. 1515, in vv. 113-119: "Let

raylynge poetes for helpe on V́enus call; / ...he which
is lawreat / Ought not his name with vyce to vyolate."
For a modern edition see William Nelson's edition, EETS
(1955 for 1948), CCXXX, p. 14.

1516   SKELTON, JOHN. "Against Venemous Tongues."
                Written perhaps after early May 1516, it consists of
82 lines of 4-beat Skeltonics attacking carping critics,
possibly a prolegomenon to Magnyfycence, no. 1516.2 below. It was first printed in PPPW, sigs. 2A1-2A3, no.
1568.

1516.1   SKELTON, JOHN. "Elegia in serenissime principis et domine,
          domine Margarete."
                The elegy in 26 lines of elegiacs was completed 16
August 1516, to be hung over tomb of the Lady Margaret
Beaufort, mother to Henry VII and Skelton's erstwhile
patroness. It was first printed in PPPW, sigs. Z3-Z3^V,
no. 1568. See also nos. 1600 and 1752 for another version and a translation.

1516.2   SKELTON, JOHN. Magnyfycence.
                "A goodly interlude" of 2567 lines, it was written in
1516 or 1517 but not printed until c. 1530; see no.
1530.3 for that edition.

1516.3   SKELTON, JOHN. "Vilitissimus Scotus Dundas allegat caudas
          contra Angligenas."
                This is Skelton's reply to some accusatory Latin hexa-
meters by the Scottish humanist George Dundas, in 63
lines of macaronic Latin and English Skeltonics, written
c. 1516; it was first printed in PPPW, sigs. Y3^V-Y5, no.
1568.

1517   SKELTON, JOHN. The Tunnyng of Elynour Rummyng.
                An "ale-wife poem," written in seven passus of 623
lines of Skeltonics plus two lines of Latin elegiacs and
four of Latin hexameters at end; probably written in late
Spring, 1517. See no. 1521 below for fragments of first
printed edition.

1518   SKELTON, JOHN. "In Bedel quondam Belial incarnatum,
          devotum epitaphium."
                This mock-epitaph of 20 lines against William Bedell,
the Treasurer of Lady Margaret's Household, whose will
was proved prior to 11 July 1518, seems to have been
written in early July of that year. It was first printed
in PPPW, sigs. Y5^V-Y6, no. 1568. For Bedell's will, see
Edwards, pp. 299-301, no. 1949.

1518.1   WESTMINSTER ABBEY MUNIMENTS.
           According to an indenture of 8 August 1518, "Iohannes
Skelton laureatus" dwelled in a tenement located within
the sanctuary of Westminster Abbey on the south side of
the Great Belfry; record taken from the Westminster
Abbey Muniments, Register II, fols. 146-147; printed by
Edwards, pp. 298-299, no. 1949. See also 1921.1.

1519   WHITTINTON, ROBERT. "In clarissimi Scheltonis Louaniensis"
and "Schelton Anglorum vatum gloria" in his Opusculum,
STC$^{2.2}$ 25540.5, sigs. C4^v- C7^v.
           The first is an "epigram" in 138 lines of elegiacs,
the second a distich; both are reprinted by Dyce, I,
pp. xvi-xix, no. 1843.1. See also no. 1520.1.

1520   LILY, WILLIAM. "Quid me, Scheltone, fronte sic aperta."
           These are the first of 7 lines of Latin hendecasylla-
bics written by William Lily against Skelton for the
latter's attack on his verses; it was either in response
to, or in provocation of, no. 1520.1 below; found in
B.L. MS. Harley 540, fol. 57^v; printed by Dyce, I, p.
xxxviii, with Fuller's translation of 1662, no. 1843.1
below.

1520.1   SKELTON, JOHN. "Vrgeor impulsus tibi Lille retundere
dentes."
           This is the only line remaining of Skelton's verse
attack on the grammarian William Lily, himself involved
in a grammarian's war with the conservative Robert Whittinton, friend to Skelton (see no. 1519 above). It was
first recorded in print by Bale, Catalogus [1557-59].

1521   SKELTON, JOHN. The Tunnyng of Elynour Rummyng. STC$^{2.2}$
22611.5 [1521?]. First edition.
           Surviving only in fragments, the poem was probably
printed by de Worde sometime in 1521; for a description
of the fragments see K&Y, pp. 72-73. For dating and
Pepwell as possible printer, see no. 1955.3; for de Worde
as printer see no. 1961.5 below. See also nos. 1545,
1554 and 1560.4 for editions of CB in which TER was printed; see also nos. 1624, 1660, 1693, 1718, 1744, 1808,
1928.1, 1930.1, 1953.5 and 1968 for later individual
editions, versions, imitations or translations of this
poem.

1521.1   SKELTON, JOHN. Speke Parrot.
           Written, perhaps, in two stages: the first repre-
sented by its earliest printed form in CB, no. 1545,
sigs. A2-A6, presenting the first 237 lines of the poem,
completed by mid-August 1521; and the second stage represented in B.L. MS. Harley 2252, fols. 133-140 (MS. dating

$\underline{c}$. 1525-35, a collection which included $\underline{CC}$). The second or "extended version," offering the epigraph, lines 1-57 and 238-513, including the Galathea addition, 4 envoys, and Parrot's complaint, was finished before mid-December, 1521. <u>See</u> nos. 1554 and 1560.4 for later prints of $\underline{CB}$.

1522   SKELTON, JOHN. <u>Why Come Ye Nat to Courte?</u>
        The poem, 1248 lines of English Skeltonics plus 27 lines of Latin Skeltonics, 10 leonine hexameters and 4 hexameters, like $\underline{SP}$ and $\underline{CC}$ was written in several journalistic sections and was probably finished shortly after 28 October 1922, the Lord Mayor's Day. <u>See</u> no. 1545.3 for the first printed version and for the MS. fragment ($\underline{c}$. 1525-50) preserved; <u>see</u> $\underline{CB}$, no. 1545, for its inclusion of "All Noble" (the prologue) as a separate piece.

1522.1 SKELTON, JOHN. <u>Collyn Clout.</u>
        The major portion of this poem was completed before 3 October 1522, then perhaps added to in the Spring of 1523. It survives in two major forms: a MS version of the poem, B.L. MS. Harley 2252, fols. 147-153^V (MS. dating $\underline{c}$. 1525-35, a collection which included $\underline{SP}$, as above), lacking 162 lines of the printed text but providing the epilogue; and a printed version which first appears in [$\underline{c}$. 1531], for which <u>see</u> no. 1531.2 below. For a dating of the poem <u>see</u> no. 1972.3 below. For the "Profecy of Skelton, 1529" ($\underline{CC}$ 462-80), <u>see</u> B.L. MS. Lansdowne 762, fol. 75 (71).

1523   HEYWOOD, JOHN. <u>A Dialogue Concerning Witty and Witless</u> (fr. ms., not in <u>STC</u>). Edited in a modern edition by John S. Farmer in <u>The Dramatic Writings of John Heywood</u>. London: for the Early English Drama Society, 1905, p. 194.
        In the interlude, written $\underline{c}$. 1523, "John" berates the "witless wretch" in a series of Skeltonic rhyming couplets, both masculine and feminine, 11.32-43.

1523.1 ?HEYWOOD, JOHN. <u>The Playe Called the Foure PP.</u> <u>STC</u> 13300 [?1544].
        This play, attributed to Heywood, written between 1521 and 1525, may variously echo poems of Skelton's; thus line 33 of the play may echo <u>PS</u>, v. 247, while 11. 302-303 may reflect <u>TER</u> (vv. 370-371); one commentator (<u>see</u> no. 1938.4) believes that the action taken by the pardoner to release Dame Margery's soul from Hell (11. 916-970) shows an expansion of the reference in $\underline{CC}$ (vv. 874-878) of the release of "Dam Margeries soule out of hell." For a modern edition of the play, <u>see</u> that edited by John S. Farmer in <u>The Dramatic Writings of John Heywood</u> for the Early English Drama Society (London, 1905), pp. 27-64. <u>See also</u> no. 1534 below.

11

1523.2   SKELTON, JOHN. "Gentle Paule, laie down thy sweard."
           This couplet criticizing Wolsey's dissolution of Con-
           vocation was written in late April 1523; it was attribu-
           ted to Skelton by Hall, Vnion of the Two Noble and
           Illustre Families of Lancastre & Yorke, STC 12722 (1548),
           sig. TTt2^V. It is also found in a late eighteenth cen-
           tury manuscript copy, Folger Library MS. N. b. 49 (olim
           Phillips MS 10112), fol. 3.

1523.3   SKELTON, JOHN. A Ryght Delectable Tratyse Vpon a Goodly
           Garlande or Chapelet of Laurell by Mayster Skelton Poete
           Laureat Studyously Dyuysed at Sheryfhotton Castell, sigs.
           A6, B-F^4. STC 22610 (1523). First edition, printed by
           Richard Fakes (Faques) on 3 October 1523.
           This "biobibliographical" dream allegory in 1572 lines
           of rhyme royal, with 7 lyrics in various meters inter-
           spersed, includes at its end a 13 line Latin poem
           "Fraxinus in silvis" and the trilingual "En Parlament à
           Paris" (8 lines in French, 6 lines as translated in
           Latin, 15 lines as translated into English, plus a 2 line
           motto in French. It is also printed in PPPW, on sigs.
           A2-F3, no. 1568, a version which adds 2 stanzas (vv. 337-
           343, 407-413) and the concluding "L'autre envoy" (vv.
           1587-1602); "Fraxinus in silvis" is there printed as a
           separate poem on sig. Y5; "En Parlament" without the
           motto on sigs. X8^{r-v}. For a description of this 1523
           edition, see K&Y, pp. 70-71; the edition is reproduced
           on University Microfilm Reel no. 19.
           A manuscript version of GL, B.L. MS. Cotton Vitellius
           E.x., fols. 208-225^V exists, fire-damaged and imperfect,
           yielding 658 lines of the total of 1602 verses (ll. 1-
           245 and 721-1140) and has been printed as a conflated
           text by E. P. Hammond, no. 1927.5 below; see also LEE,
           no. 1976.

1523.4   SKELTON, JOHN. The Douty Duke of Albany.
           This invective poem, composed in 507 lines of Skel-
           tonics, followed by two envoys of 16 and 19 lines respec-
           tively, was written after 3 November 1923 when the
           invading Duke of Albany was forced to abandon the siege
           of Wark. It was first printed in PPPW, sigs. F2-G3,
           no. 1568.

1525   ALSOPPE, THOMAS. "The Breuyate and Shorte Tragycall
           Hystorie of the Fayre Custance." STC$^{2-1}$ 538.5 [1525],
           sig. [F3^V].
           A 62 line envoy in Skeltonics from 2 to 10 lines in
           length concludes Alsoppe's metrical condensation in
           rhyme royal of Chaucer's Man of Law's Tale. The entire
           poem is reprinted with commentary by Franklin B. Williams,
           Jr. in ELR, VI (1976), 351-367 ["Lenuoy" on p. 367]; see
           no. 1976.4 below.

1525.1   GODLY QUEEN HESTER. STC 13241 [1561].
          This play against a tyrannical chief minister is
          sometimes erroneously attributed to Skelton, as of the
          latter days of his career, and was probably written
          sometime between 1525 and 1529. See no. 1561 for the
          full entry for this play.

1525.2   A C [HUNDRED] MERY TALES. STC 23633 [1525].
          This collection contains as Tale No. 41 the story "Of
          mayster Skelton that broughte the byssop of Norwiche ii
          fesauntys." Called "daw" and "fool" by the Bishop,
          Skelton names the pheasants "Alpha" and "Omega," his
          first and last gifts. The tale is reprinted by Dyce, I,
          pp. lxxiv-lxxv, no. 1843.1 below, and by P. M. Zall,
          pp. 102-103, no. 1963.10 below.

1527   SKELTON, JOHN. Skelton Laureate Agaynste a Comely
          Coystrowne, fols. [ ]⁴; unsigned; STC 22611. Printed by
          John Rastell [c. 1527].
          For a description of this edition, see K&Y, pp. 71-72;
          the volume is microfilmed on University Microfilms, Reel
          no. 860.
          Contents: "ACC"; "Contra asinum"; "UDH"; "WW". For
          the printer and date of printing, see no. 1953.3; for
          dating of UDH (?late 1490's), see 1953.4.

1527.1   SKELTON, JOHN. Here Foloweth Dyuers Balettys and Dyties
          Solacyous, fols. [ ]⁴; unsigned; STC 22604. Printed by
          John Rastell [c. 1527].
          Contents: "Lullay"; "Aunc Acq"; "Knolege"; "Cuncta-
          licet" (Lat. & Engl.); "Go."
          For a description of this edition, see K&Y, pp. 60-61;
          it is microfilmed on University Microfilm Reel no. 860;
          for printer and date of printing, see no. 1953.3 below.

1528   ABJURATION OF THOMAS BOWGAS.
          The abjuration of Bowgas, a fuller of St. Leonard's
          Parish, Colchester, before Cuthbert Tunstall, Bishop of
          London, on 4 May 1528 in the chapel of the Norwich Inn
          near Charing Cross, was witnessed by "Magister Skelton,"
          among others. The record is excerpted from Strype's
          Ecclesiastical Memorials (1822), by Edwards, p. 303,
          no. 1949 below.

1528.1   ? BARLOWE, WILLIAM. The Burial of the Mass. STC².¹ 1462.7
          [1528].
          Listed wrongly in bibliographies under "Roy, William,"
          and as commonly mistitled Rede Me and be Not Wrothe.
          Edited under that title by E. Arber (London, 1871), this
          Reforming, anti-Wolsey satire, commissioned by William
          Roy, takes over words and phrases from Skelton's satires

of the 1520's; cf. <u>WCY</u> 217ff. and 294ff., for example,
with <u>Burial</u>, sig. D2 (Arber, pp. 55-56); <u>CC</u> 626-632 with
<u>Burial</u> sig. D3 (Arber, p. 56). <u>See</u> E. G. Rupp, <u>Studies</u>
<u>in the Making of the English Protestant Tradition</u> (1947),
p. 53 ff. for the correct author and title.

1528.2   SKELTON, JOHN. <u>A Replycacion Agaynst Certayne Yong Scolers</u>
<u>Abjured of Late, &c.</u>, sigs. A⁶-B⁴; <u>STC</u> 22609. Printed
by Richard Pynson [<u>c</u>. 1528].
  This, Skelton's last poem, was probably written in
June or July 1528, after the release of Thomas Bilney
from the Tower (<u>see</u> <u>Rep.</u>, vv. 176-196, and Nelson, pp.
213-214, no. 1939.8, Edwards, p. 248, no. 1949.
  <u>Contents</u>: Latin prose dedication to Wolsey; "Argument"; "Protestacion"; "<u>Eulogium Consolationis</u>"; 408
lines chiefly in Skeltonics; "<u>Epitoma</u>."

1529   CHURCHWARDEN'S RECORDS FOR ST. MARGARET'S, WESTMINSTER.
  Under "accompte for buryallis, obittes and lyghtis,"
we find "Item of Master Skelton for iiij taper ij s
viijd" and "for iiij torches iiijs." Also included are
items for his knell and peals (6s 8d) and a payment to
Our Lady Brotherhood of 20d, plus a second payment of
12d for the ringing of his knell and peals. The records
are printed by Edwards, p. 304, no. 1949, from vol. E2
[unpaginated] at Caxton Hall, <u>sub fin</u>. acct for 27 May
1528-2 June 1530.

1529.1   COMMISSARY COURT, WESTMINSTER.
  On 16 November 1529, permission to administer Skelton's estate was granted to William Mott (or Mote),
curate of St. Margaret's, Westminster (6 Bracy); <u>see</u> no.
1905 below, record reprinted by Edwards, p. 304, no.
1949.

1529.2   NORWICH INSTITUTION BOOK XVIII.
  According to an entry in this book for 17 July 1529,
Thomas Clerk was instituted Rector of Diss "<u>per mortem</u>
<u>naturalem magistri Johannis Skeltoune</u>" at the presenta-
tion of Robert, Lord-Fitz-Walter. The record was first
noticed by Blomefield, <u>Topographical History</u> (1739), I,
p. 11 from the entry in the Norwich Institution Book,
xviii, f. 9; it is extracted by Nelson, p. 220, n. 22,
no. 1939.8. <u>See</u> WESTLAKE, no. 1923.3, for record in
W.A.M. no. 33325.

1529.3   SKELTON'S BURIAL INSCRIPTION.
  On 21 June 1529, Skelton died; he was buried in St.
Margaret's, Westminster, before the high altar, with an
inscription on alabaster "<u>Ioannes Skeltonus vates Pierius</u>
<u>hic situs est</u>." The inscription is reprinted from Bale's

Index and his Catalogus by Edwards, pp. 254, 305 and
306, no. 1949.

1530 THE FANTASY OF THE PASSYON OF THE FOX LATELY OF THE TOWN OF
   MERE. STC 10685 [c. 1530].
     This mock-eulogy and testament for a pet fox, "Curri-
   bus," is similar in places to Skelton's PS; cf. in particular the "Exclamatio inuidorum" (Arber, pp. 275-278)
   with Jane Scrope's "Exclamatio" in PS. It can be found
   in Henry Huth (ed.), Fugitive Tracts, First Series, No. 4
   (1875) [unpaged]; and in Edward Arber (ed.), Selections
   from the English Poets, the Surrey and Wyatt Anthology
   (London: H. Frowde, 1901), pp. 268-283.

1530.1 THE PRODIGAL SON.
     Fragment of an interlude printed c. 1530, in Malone
   Society Collections, I.1, 1970. On pp. 29-30, the speech
   of "Servus" (Robyn Ren-Awaye), vv. 70-80 is in Skeltonics:
   "Iynckyn iumbler / Rafe rumbler / Philyp slumber /
   Thomkyn tumbler," &c. [names of his fellow stable-lads.]

1530.2 "THE PROFECY OF SKELTON, 1529."
     A corrupted version of CC vv. 462-480, B.L. MS. Lans-
   downe 762, fol. 75 (71); see nos. 1531 and 1531.2 below.

1530.3 SKELTON, JOHN. Magnyfycence, A Goodly Interlude and a Mery,
   sigs. A-G⁴, A²; STC 22607. First edition, printed c.
   1530 by Treveris and John Rastell.
     For a description of the edition, see K&Y, pp. 61-63;
   the edition is microfilmed on University Microfilms,
   Reel no. 483. For later reprints or editions, see nos.
   1821, 1908.2, 1910.1, and 1925.3. For title-page compartment, see no. 1976.6.

1530.4 TREASURER'S ACCOUNTS.
     A couplet referring to "Dame Elynour Rummyng / by her
   hummyng sunnynge [? summynge]" is found scribbled on
   dorse of the account book of the keeper of the manors at
   Westminster c. 1530-33; see no. 1952.1; Nelson, p. 120,
   no. 1939.8, gives text as "Dame Elyner of Rumyng by her
   mumyng dumeryng."

1531 "THE JESTES OF SKELTON." (?)
     A manuscript collection, allegedly in the possession
   of Thomas Cromwell [c. 1530-32], since lost. For the
   mention of the title see L&P Hen. VIII, vol. VII, p. 341,
   no. 923 (vii).

1531.1 REDFORD, JOHN. Wit and Science.
     Preserved in B.L. MS. Addit. 15233, defective at the
   beginning, it has been edited by Arthur Brown in Malone

Society Reprints, LXXXVII (1951). With the entrance of
the vice "Tedyousness," we find a use of hemistich qua-
trains after the manner of Skelton, vv. 144-174, and
"true Skeltonics" (the dimeter couplets of PS and TER)
in vv. 175-196 of this morality written c. 1531, or sometime between 1531 and 1547 when Redford was Master of the
Choristers of St. Paul's.

1531.2   SKELTON, JOHN. Collyn Clout, sigs. A-D^8; STC$^{2.2}$ 22600.5.
First edition, printed c. 1531 by Thomas Godfray, lacking
the Latin verse epilogue.
    A manuscript version of the poem, roughly contempora-
neous, 162 lines shorter than the "full text" but providing the 11 lines of Latin hexameters at the poem's
end, is found in a commonplace book belonging to John
Colyns, a London mercer (fl. 1518-30), B.L. MS. Harley
2252, fols. 147-153. In addition, a badly transcribed
"Profecy of Skelton" (CC vv. 462-480) can be found in
B.L. MS. Lansdowne 762, fol. 75 (71), no. 1530.2 above.
For a description of this edition, see K&Y, pp. 54-55;
for later editions of the poem see nos. 1545.1, 1553.1,
1560.5, 1831.1, and 1966.2 below.

1534   HEYWOOD, JOHN. A Play of Love. STC 13303 [c. 1534].
    This play has been edited by John S. Farmer in The
Dramatic Writings of John Heywood (London: for the
Early English Drama Society, 1905). For songs sung by
the Vice, in Skeltonic manner, see pp. 150 and 153 of
that text.

1534.1   IMAGE OF YPOCRYSY.
    2544 lines of Skeltonics preserved in B.L. MS. Lans-
downe 794, printed in Ballads from Manuscripts, edited
by F. J. Furnivall (London: Ballad Society, 1868), I,
pp. 167-274. The poem constitutes a broadside attack on
the clergy, religious orders, and those connected with
them from bell-ringer to Pope.

1535   TALES AND QUICK ANSWERES, VERY MERY, AND PLEASANT TO REDE.
STC 23665 [c. 1535], sigs. A3^v-A4.
    Tale no. 13 of this collection presents "The beggers
answere to M. Skelton the poete"; it is reprinted by
Dyce, I, pp. lxxv-lxxvi, no. 1843.1, and by P. M. Zall,
pp. 252-253, no. 1963.10 below.

1536   WYATT, SIR THOMAS. "Who hath herd of such crueltye before?,"
in Collected Poems of Sir Thomas Wyatt. Edited by Kenneth
Muir and Patricia Thomson. Liverpool: Liverpool University Press, p. 32.
    No. 68 in Tottel's Miscellany (1557-1587) as edited
by Hyder E. Rollins (Revised edn., Cambridge, Massachusetts: Harvard University Press, 1965), I, p. 51; and

No. 125 in the <u>Arundel Harington Manuscript of Tudor Poetry</u>, edited by Ruth Hughey (Columbus, Ohio: Ohio University Press, 1960), I, p. 157. This <u>ottava rime</u> "epigram" seems based on <u>PS</u> vv. 210-226 in which Jane Scrope, sewing a "representacyon" of her dead sparrow on her sampler, believes she has pricked him on the head; Rollins believes that A. K. Foxwell's suggestion of Wyatt's indebtedness here to Skelton (1913, II, pp. 58-59) "lacks weight," <u>op. cit.</u>, II, p. 182; Hughey opines that it is "quite reasonable," <u>op. cit.</u>, II, p. 157.

1537   A NEW INTERLUDE CALLED THERSYTES. <u>STC</u> 23949 [<u>c</u>. 1560], but written by October 1537.
        We find dialogue between Mulciber and Thersites in Skeltonics, on sig. A2^v; Thersites resorts to Skeltonics in his battle against the snail (<u>see</u> especially sig. C1^v) and his response to his mother on D3^v-E1; cf. the conclusion of Telemachus' letter from Ulysses on C3 with the ending of Skelton's "ACC."

1540   "MASTER SKELTONS DOCTERS OF COWNSELL."
        Three lines of doggerel, in an early Tudor hand (? 1540), found on the margin of a flyleaf to <u>Stephanus Langton super XII Prophetas</u>, printed by M. R. James in <u>A Descriptive Catalogue of the Manuscripts in the Library of Corpus Christi College, Cambridge</u> (Cambridge University Press, 1909), Pt. 1, p. 63.

1542   [HUNTINGDON, JOHN.] <u>A Genealogye of Heresye</u>.
        Brief passages showing Skeltonic influence from this now lost piece of Huntingdon's are cited <u>seriatim</u> by JOHN BALE, in his <u>A mysterye of inyquyte contayned within the heretycall Genealogye of Ponce Pontolabus</u>, <u>STC</u> 1303 [written <u>c</u>. 1542 but printed 1545], sig. B1^v, pp. 4, 6, 8, 11^v, 15^{r-v}, 22^v, 24^v, 26, 28, 30^v, 32^v, 35 &c. An excerpt from the <u>Genealogye</u> is printed in Dyce, I, pp. cvii-cix, no. 1843.1 below.

1545   SKELTON, JOHN. <u>Here after foloweth Certayne Bokes</u>, sigs. A-D^8, <u>STC</u> 22598. First edition, printed by Richard Lant for Henry Tab, <u>c</u>. 1545; the volume contains <u>SP</u>, "Edw. IV" [doubtful], "Ag Scottes"; "<u>Chorus contra Scottos</u>"; "Chorus contra Gallos"; <u>WH</u>; "All Noble"; "Tyme"; "Prayers"; <u>TER</u>.
        For descriptions of the volume <u>see</u> <u>K&Y</u>, pp. 47-50, and nos. 1939.9, 1940.1, and 1947 below. The edition is available on University Microfilms, Reel no. 10; for later sixteenth century editions of <u>CB</u>, <u>see</u> nos. 1554 and 1560.4 below.

1545.1   SKELTON, JOHN. Colyn Cloute, sigs. A-D⁸, STC 22601. Second
          edition, printed by [William Copland for] Rycharde Kele
          [c. 1545].
              A microfilm reproduction is available in University
          Microfilms, Reel no. 19. For a description of this edi-
          tion, see K&Y, pp. 55-56 and no. 1940 below. For later
          sixteenth century editions of CC see nos. 1553.1 and
          1560.5.

1545.2   SKELTON, JOHN. Phyllyp Sparowe, sigs. A-D⁸, STC 22594.
          First edition, printed by [William Copland for] Rychard
          Kele [c. 1545].
              A microfilm reproduction is available in University
          Microfilms, Reel no. 19. For a description of this edi-
          tion, see K&Y, pp. 38-40. For later editions, see nos.
          1553.2, 1560.6, and 1831.1 below.

1545.3   SKELTON, JOHN. Why Come Ye Nat to Courte? sigs. A-D⁸, STC
          22615. First edition, printed by [William Copland for]
          Richard Kele [c. 1545].
              A microfilm reproduction of the edition is available
          in University Microfilms, Reel no. 19. For a description
          of the edition, see K&Y, pp. 73-76, and nos. 1940.1 and
          1947 below.
              Contents: "All Noble" as prologue, WCY, Latin epi-
          logues. A manuscript version, written c. 1525-1540 has
          survived: Bodleian MS. Rawlinson 813, fols. 36-43ᵛ, pre-
          senting "All Noble" plus 11. 838-1246. It was printed
          by Zupitza, Archiv, LXXXV, 429-436, no. 1890.1 below.
          For other editions of WCY, see nos. 1553.3, 1560.7 and
          1966.2 below.

1547   [SHEPHERD, LUKE.] Doctour Doubble Ale. STC 7071 [listed
          1548?, but ? Fall 1547].
              The poem presents a satirical portrait of a parson
          "endurate / and earnest in the cause / of piuish popish
          lawes" in 438 lines of Skeltonics. It is available in a
          nineteenth century edition as edited by W. Carew Hazlitt,
          in Remains of the Early Popular Poetry of England (Lon-
          don, 1866), III, 297-321.

1547.1   [SHEPHERD, LUKE.] Phylogamus. STC 19882 [c. 1548].
              This is a satire preserved in two fragments, totalling
          139 lines of Skeltonics, against an unnamed poet "hyghly
          professyng Romery," perhaps a certain "Mason." It is the
          Englishing of a tract by Bartholomaeus Latomus (1485-
          1566), and probably written c. 1547. It has been re-
          printed by Friedrich Germann, Luke Shepherd ein
          Satirendichter der Englischen Reformationszeit (Augs-
          burg, 1911), pp. 101-104.

1547.2   [SHEPHERD, LUKE.]   The Vpcheringe of the Messe.   STC 17630
          [c. 1548].
               The prologue and conclusion of this anti-Catholic
          satire is in Skeltonic couplets, arranged in octaves;
          the rest of poem imitates Skeltonic rhyme leashes and
          comic rhyme, Latin and macaronic lines.

1547.3   VOX POPULI, VOX DEI.   Edited by F. J. Furnivall from B. L.
          Harley MS. 367 in Ballads from Manuscripts.   London:
          reprinted by the Ballad Society, 1876 from the first
          issue of 1868, I, pp. 108-151.
               The poem was written [c. 1547] in 815 lines of Skel-
          tonic meter and rhyme-leash expressing wide-ranging
          social complaint against raised rents and prices, de-
          basement of currency, and the covetousness of merchants
          and upstart gentlemen.

1548   BALE, JOHN.   Illustrium Maioris Britanniae Scriptorum...
          Summarium.   STC 1296 [1548], fol. 254^v.
               "Skeltonus poeta laureatus" is given a two line entry
          in the Additio.   See also nos. 1549, 1556, and 1559.

1548.1   BARNES, -----.   The Treatyse Answeringe the Boke of Berdes,
          Complyed by Collyn Clowte, Dedycatyd to Bernarde Barber
          Dwellynge in Banbery.   STC 1465 [1548], sig. Bl ff.
          Edited by F. J. Furnivall, EETS (1870), E.S., X, pp. 305-
          316.
               The treatise is a retort purportedly by "Collyn Clowte"
          to Andrew Borde's lost attack on beards; in octaves aaaa/
          bbbb with refrain "C."   Cf. WH, no. 1505 above, in tone.

1548.2   MARDELAY, JOHN.   Here is a short Resytal of certayne holy
          Doctours.   STC 17318 [1548].
               The poem opens with couplets in the Skeltonic metrical
          pattern.

1548.3   [SHEPHERD, LUKE.]   Pathose, or an Inward Passion of the
          Pope for the Losse of hys Daughter the Masse.   STC 19463
          [1548].
               This polemical poem, apparently written after 31 July
          1548, when Bp. Stephen Gardiner was committed to the
          Tower, consists of 749 lines of Skeltonics as preserved,
          with three leaves containing approximately 156 lines miss-
          ing; a mock-sympathetic satire on the Mass.   It is re-
          printed in Germann, Luke Shepherd (see no. 1547.1), pp.
          104-111.

1548.4   [SHEPHERD, LUKE.]   A Pore Helpe, the Buklar & Defence of
          Mother Holy Kyrke.   STC$^{2.1}$ 13051.7 [1548].
               397 lines of Skeltonics that only pretend to favor
          Bp. Stephen Gardiner's party.   It is reprinted in W.

Carew Hazlitt (ed.), Remains of the Early Popular Poetry of England. London, 1866, III, pp. 253-266. For the dating of A Pore Helpe, see M. Channing Lenthicum, "A Pore Helpe and its Printers," Library, n.s. IX (1928-29), 169-183.

1548.5   [SHEPHERD, LUKE.] [The Interlude of] John Bon and Mast[er] Parson. STC$^{2.2}$ 3258.2 [1548].
          The poem is a satire on Corpus Christi (feast day and Sacrament), written in lines reflecting the influence of the Skeltonic. It is printed in Tudor Tracts 1532-1588 with an introduction by A[lbert] F. Pollard. New York [1906], pp. 159-169.

1549   BALE, JOHN. The Laboryouse Journey & Serche of Johan Ley- lande...enlarged...by Iohan Bale. STC 15445 [1549], sig. H1.
          Here Bale lists "Joannes Skelton" in "A Regystre of the names of English Wryters" to be included in his Catalogus, as corrected and augmented; see also BALE, nos. 1556 and 1559 below.

1550   JACKE OF THE NORTHE, BEYOND THE STYLE, in Ancient Metrical Tales. Edited by Charles Henry Hartshorne. London, 1829, pp. 288-292.
          Transcribed from a folio ms., Corpus Christi College, Cambridge MS. 106, the poem is written (c. 1550) in Skeltonic couplets: "It is but a whyle / Sins, that I Jacke of the Style / Came forthe of ye Northe &c." Jack defends himself from charges of murder, and refers to the greater crimes of the enclosures of commons.

1553   BALDWIN, WILLIAM. A Marvellous Hystory Intitulede Beware the Cat. STC 1245 (1584), sigs. D1^{r-v}.
          This prose piece written c. 1553, and first printed 1570, survives in 4 leaves; we take our information from the 1584 edition, as edited by William P. Holden (New London, Connecticut, 1963), p. 46; in the piece one finds 18 lines of rhyming prose in the tradition of Skelton's Replycacion, reproducing the "poeticall furie" overcoming the narrator, who has trained and sensitivized his ears to understand cats: for example, he could not hear be- cause of "barking of dogges, grunting of hoggs, wauling of cats, rumbling of ratts, gagling of geese, humming of bees" &c.

1553.1   SKELTON, JOHN. Colyn Cloute, sigs. A-D^8, STC 22602 [c. 1553]. Third edition, printed by [William Copland for] John Wyghte.
          A printing with a variant colophon [William Copland for] Thomas Marshe is found, STC$^{2.2}$ 22602.5. A microfilm

of STC 22602 is found in University Microfilms, Reel no. 353; the edition is described in K&Y, pp. 57-58.

1553.2   SKELTON, JOHN. Phillyp Sparowe, sigs. A-D^8, STC 22595 [c. 1553]. Second edition, printed by [William Copland for] John Wyght.
    With variant colophon, [William Copland for] Robert Toy, STC$^{2.2}$ 22595.5. Microfilm reproduction in University Microfilms, Reel no. 153; and description in K&Y, pp. 41-43; additional description in no. 1940 below.

1553.3   SKELTON, JOHN. Whi Come Ye Nat to Courte? sigs. A-D^8, STC 22616 [c. 1553]. Second edition, printed by [William Copland for] Robert Toy.
    Found with variant colophon, [William Copland for] John Wyght, STC$^{2.2}$ 22615.5; contents as in no. 1545.3 above. The edition is described in K&Y, pp. 76-77.

1554   SKELTON, JOHN. Certaine Bokes, sigs. A-D^8, STC 22599 [c. 1554]. Second edition, printed by John Kynge and Thomas Marshe.
    Contents as in no. 1545 above. Microfilm reproduction in University Microfilms, Reel no. 353; edition described by K&Y, pp. 50-52.

1555   BRADFORD, JOHN. The Copye of a letter sent...to the erles of Arundel, Darbie, &c. STC 3480 [c. 1555].
    Written in prose with frequent internal rhyme, it is analogous in form to Skelton's Replycacion. It is excerpted in Dyce, I, pp. cxvii-viii, no. 1843.1 below.

1556   BALE, JOHN. "Ioannes Skelton," in Index Britanniae Scriptorum [from Bale's autograph notebook Bodl. Cod Seld supra 64, written down before 1557]. Edited by Reginald Lane Poole, with the help of Mary Bateson. Oxford: Clarendon Press, 1902, pp. 252-255.
    Presents a biographical sketch of Skelton in Latin, apparently based on notes, since lost, of the Tudor antiquarian Edward Braynewood; offers a Latinized list of Skelton's works based on (a) William Horman's memoranda, including the opening line of Skelton's "Carmen inuectiuum" against Lily (the only line preserved of the 64 constituting the attack); (b) Edward Braynewood's holdings (GL, PS, WCY, and "AVT"); (c) lost poem "Anglie tubam" from the shop of Richard Grafton; (d) Skelton's own list in GL, vv. 1170-1504, itemizing 47 pieces. The biographical portion of the entry is reprinted in Edwards, p. 305, no. 1949 below. See also Bale, no. 1559 below.

1557   CHARNOCK, THOMAS. The Breviary of Natural Philosophy.
        First printed by Elias Ashmole, in Theatrum Chemicum
        Britannicum. London, 1652, Wing 3987, pp. 303-304.
            The anonymous original compiler of the Breviary,
        writing in verse [c. 1557], describes the young "un-
        lettered" Charnock's alchemical writings in prose and
        meter as acts that exceeded Chaucer "at his yeares" and
        "Skelton at his yeares" who was "even further to seeke,"
        wherefore Charnock, because of his "knowledge, gravity
        and witt" might well "be crowned Poet Laureat."

1559   BALE, JOHN. Scriptorum illustrium maioris Brytannie, quam
        nunc Angliam & Scotiam vocant: Catalogus. Basel, 1557-
        1559, cent. viii, no. 66, pp. 651-652.
            The biographical sketch of Skelton is an expansion
        and rearrangement of the material written down in the
        ms. Index (see no. 1556 above), e.g., the opening sen-
        tence is expanded by addition of "clarus & facundus in
        utroque scribendi genere, prosa atque metro" and the
        penultimate sentence concerning Skelton's death by "cap-
        tiuitatis suae tempore"; but lacks the statement of the
        Index that Skelton was buried before the high altar of
        St. Margaret's Church, Westminster. In listing Skelton's
        works, does not mention sources of information; presents
        essentially the same list as in Index, although in a
        somewhat different order, adding two new entries: the
        prophecy of Wolsey's death (see under CC, no. 1531.2
        above) and De bono ordine, comoediam, a play still lost
        (but see nos. 1944.1 and 1956 below). The biographical
        sketch only is reprinted by Edwards, p. 306, no. 1949
        below.
            Note: the Catalogus (derived from the unpublished
        Index) is the source of later writings about Skelton's
        life through PITSEUS (Pits), no. 1619, FULLER, no. 1662,
        Anthony à WOOD, no. 1691, to Bishop Thomas TANNER, no.
        1748. It perpetuates (and perhaps perpetrates) three
        legends: 1) that Skelton warred constantly with the
        friars, principally the Dominicans; 2) that Skelton had
        confessed on his deathbed that he had pretended that the
        woman he had secretly wed was his concubine, lest she be
        taken for his wife (and thus run counter to Bishop Nix's
        views against priestly "marriage"); 3) that Skelton was
        forced into sanctuary in Westminster because of his
        writings against Wolsey.

1560   COPLAND, ROBERT. Jyl of Braintfords Testament. STC 5730
        [c. 1560]. Edited by F. J. Furnivall. For private cir-
        culation, 1871.
            The poem, perhaps written c. 1545, has some points of
        similarity with TER in that Jyll, like Elynour, keeps an
        inn and provides a social center for her low-life

community; further, the tricked priest is dispatched by
Jyl in lines reminiscent of WH: "Syr John whypdok, Syr
Jak whypstoke, / Syr John smelsmok, as wyse as a woodcok"
(vv. 329-330).

1560.1   GRYFFYDD, ELIS. MS. Mostyn 158 (National Library of Wales),
fols. 471-472.
A version in Welsh, c. 1560, of Skelton's witty re-
fusal to write an inscription for Wolsey's tomb (cf.
Merie Tales of Skelton, Tale X, no. 1567). The version
is printed by Edwards, pp. 306-307, no. 1949 below.

1560.2   "A LIBELL WRITTEN AGAINST [EDWARD] BASHE." Edited by Ruth
Hughey, in The Arundel Harington Manuscript of Tudor
Poetry. Columbus, Ohio: Ohio State University Press,
1960, I, pp. 225-233.
Cited here from the Arundel Harington MS. but found
also in CUL MS. Dd 5.75, it is a ms. poem of 295 lines
starting in the Skeltonic manner and imitating CC (221-7),
TER (190-3) and WCY in various places.

1560.3   A NEWE INTERLUDE OF IMPACYENTE POUERTIE. STC 14114 [1560].
Edited by R. B. McKerrow, in Materialen zur Kunde des
älteren Englischen Dramas. Louvain, 1911.
The argument between Envy, the Vice, and Peace in the
play, despite occasional unrhyming lines, is in the Skeltonic manner, 11. 23-94: e.g., (Envy) "A, constable,
quod ha, nay, that wyll I not abyde / For I am lothe to
go shorter tyde / Yet long horson for al thy pryde" &c.

1560.4   SKELTON, JOHN. Certain Bokes, sigs. A-D⁸, STC 22600 [c.
1560]. Third edition, printed by Jhon Day.
Contents the same as in nos. 1545 and 1554 above. A
microfilm reproduction of the edition is available in
University Microfilms, Reel no. 153; the edition is
described in K&Y, pp. 52-54; and also in nos. 1939.9 and
1940.1 below.

1560.5   SKELTON, JOHN. Colyn Cloute, sigs. A-D⁸, STC 22603 [c.
1560]. Fourth edition, printed by [John Day for] Anthony
Kytson.
Found with variant colophons: [for] Abraham Veale,
STC 22603a, [for] Jhon Wallye [sic], STC 22603b. The
edition is on microfilm, University Microfilm, Reel no.
353; it is described in K&Y, pp. 58-60.

1560.6   SKELTON, JOHN. Phillip Sparow, sigs. A-D⁸, STC 22596 [c.
1560]. Third edition, printed by [John Day for] Anthony
Kitson.
Found with variant colophons: [for] Abraham Veale,
STC 22596a; [for] John Walley, STC 22596b. Available on

microfilm in University Microfilm, Reel no. 939; described by K&Y, pp. 43-46, and in no. 1940.1 below.

1560.7   SKELTON, JOHN. Whye Come Ye Nat to Courte?, sigs. A-D⁸,
STC 22617 [c. 1560]. Third edition, printed by [John
Day for] Anthony Kytson.
Found with variant colophons: [for] Abraham Veale,
STC 22617a; [for] John Wallye STC².² 22617a.5. Contents
as in nos. 1545.3 and 1553.3 above. The edition is de-
scribed in K&Y, pp. 77-79, and also in no. 1940.1 below.

1561   A NEWE INTERLUDE DRAWEN OUTE OF THE HOLY SCRIPTURE OF GODLY
QUEENE HESTER. STC 13251 (1561). Edited by W. W. Greg,
in Materialien zur Kunde des älteren Englischen Dramas.
1904, V.
The play is sometimes attributed to Skelton; it was
perhaps written 1525-29 if the character Aman is to be
associated with Wolsey and his policy by which Henry's
mood was directed against Hester (Catherine); it contains
some reminders of Skelton's vice-characters in Mag. and
some verbal echoes in 11. 402-416 from WCY 297-322; in
417-425 from WCY 1051-1065; and in 430-434 from CC 78-86
and 560.564. See no. 1525.1 above.

1564   BULLEIN, WILLIAM. A Dialogue bothe pleasaunt and pietifull
against the Feuer Pestilence. STC 4036 [published by 12
March 1564]. Edited by Mark W. and A. H. Bullen, EETS
(1888), E.S., LII, p. 16.
In the dialogue, Bullein incidentally represents Skelton as choleric poet, "kindled" against Wolsey, and presents a pastiche of 14 lines from CC (798-800, 585-594).

1566   "MY FRIEND, THE LYFE I LEAD AT ALL." Edited by Ruth Hughey,
in the Arundel Harington Manuscript of Tudor Poetry (see
no. 1560.2 above), I, pp. 314-315.
The poem, entered as a broadside by Thomas Colwell in
the Stationer's Register, 1565-66, mentions "A phillip
Sparrow to be fedd At her owne handes with Crommes of
bread" (vv. 41-42).

1567   MERIE TALES, NEWLY IMPRINTED & MADE BY MASTER SKELTON POET
LAUREAT. STC 22618 [1567], sigs. A-C⁸, D6.
15 tales in number: 1) How Skelton came home late
to Oxford from Abington; 2) How Skelton drest the Ken-
dallman in the sweat time; 3) Howe Skelton tolde the man
that Chryst was very busye in the woodes with them that
made fagots; 4) Howe the Welshman dyd desyre Skelton to
ayde hym...; 5) Of Swanborne the knave [based on Skelton's "Devout Trental"]; 6) How Skelton was complayned
on to the bishop of Norwich; 7) Howe Skelton, when hee
came from the bishop, made a sermon; 8) Howe the fryer

asked leave of Skelton to preach at Dis; 9) How Skelton
handled the fryer that woulde needes lye with him in his
inne; 10) How the cardynall desyred Skelton to make an
epitaphe upon his grave; 11) Howe the hostler dyd byte
Skelton's mare under the tale...; 12) Howe the cobler
tolde maister Skelton it is good sleeping in a whole
skinne; 13) Howe Master Skelton's miller decevyed hym
manye tymes...; 14) How Skelton was in prison at the com-
mandement of the cardinal; 15) Howe the vinteners wife
put water into Skelton's wine.

Reprinted by Dyce, I, pp. lvii-lxxiii, no. 1543.1; by
W. C. Hazlitt in his Shakespeare's Jestbooks (London:
Willis & Sotheran, 1864), II, pp. 2-36; and by P. M.
Zall, pp. 326-348, no. 1963.10 below. See also PARK-
HURST, no. 1573.1, for Latin epigram based on Tale Seven
above.

1568   JOHN SKELTON. PITHY, PLESAUNT AND PROFITABLE WORKES OF
MAISTER SKELTON, POETE LAUREATE, NOWE COLLECTED AND NEWLY
PUBLISHED. ANNO. 1568, STC 22608.

Contents: 1) "Salve" [doubtful]; 2) [124 lines of
commendatory verse by Thomas Churchyarde, praising Skelton for his learning, art, judgement, "great practies of
the pen," and noting that "His terms to taunts did lean,
His talke was as he wraet"]; 3) Table of contents; 4) GL;
5) BC; 6) DDA; 7) SP [version "A"]; 8) "Edw. IV" [doubt-
ful]; 9) "Ag Scottes"; 10) "Chorus contra Scottos";
11) "Chorus contra Gallos"; 12) WH; 13) "All Noble";
14) "Tyme" [doubtful]; 15) "Prayers" [doubtful]; 16) TER;
17) WCY; 18) CC; 19) PS; 20) "ACC"; 21) "Contra asinum";
22) "UDH"; 23) "WW"; 24) BTF [non-canonical]; 25) "En
Parl"; 26) "Dev Tr"; 27) "Ep. Adam"; 28) "Diligo"; 29)
"Lamentatio" [bis]; 30) "VSD"; 31) "Frax. in silvis";
32) "In Bedel"; 33) "DEN"; 34) "En Marg"; 35) "H VII";
36) "Eulogium"; 37) Trouth and Information [by Cornishe,
non-canonical]; 38) "AVT"; 39) "Calliope" (Engl. & Lat.).

Compiler: for the identification of the "Collector"
of the pieces, one "I.S." ([ ]4v) as John Stowe, see
no. 1956.1 below; for Stowe's conception of his role as
editor--an uncertain one--see A. S. G. Edwards and J. I.
Miller, N&Q, ccxviii, 365-369 and A. S. G. Edwards and
J. Hedley, SB, xxviii, 265-268. As "editor" Stowe seems
to have based his text of what he prefers to call "The
Crowne of Laurel" (4) upon a manuscript, since lost,
which supplies two stanzas (vv. 337-343, 407-413) and the
concluding envoy (vv. 1587-1602) missing from Faukes'
edition of the poem (1523), but which lacked Skelton's
initial 4 lines of self-laudatory Latin verse and the
elaborate marginalia which accompanied Dame Occupacyoun's
presentation of "Skeltons bokes and baladis with ditis
of plesure" (vv. 1170-1260 and 1376-1511). For BC (5),

he seems to have depended chiefly on de Worde's second
edition of the poem [c. 1510], although upon occasion
checking it against the first edition of [1499]. He is
presumably uniquely responsible for the text of DDA (6),
not previously printed, nor now known to exist in ms.
form. Items 7-16, however, he had set directly from CB
[c. 1560], for the order of items is the same, and lines
dropped in TER, peculiar to that third edition of CB, are
likewise missing in the PPPW version (lines 87, 134, 178)
together with certain shared misreadings or variants
(e.g., "dogges" for "hogges," TER 169; "it dothe" for
"doth it" in TER 50). In accepting the printed contents
of CB uncritically, Stowe incorporated into PPPW three
poems that at the best are doubtful (nos. 8, 14 and 15).
For his text of WCY (17), he turns to the most recently
published edition, the third, of c. 1560, as shown for
example by the corrupted reading "heons" for "urcheons"
in line 165 which the two prints share; similar petty
blunders indicate that Stowe went to the most recent
editions of CC (18) and PS (19) for his collection.

For items 20-23, he relied on the ACC printed by
Rastell [c. 1527], but overlooked his edition of DBDS of
about the same time and the five lyrics that it contained. Stowe also overlooked other available Skelton
pieces in print, Mag [1530], Rep [1528], and "BSK" (1513),
and was unaware of the existence of the contemporary manuscript versions of GL, SP and CC. On the other hand,
Stowe went to manuscript material to print "DEN" (from a
manuscript that still survives, BL MS. Royal 18, D. 11)
and for "Dev. Tr." & "Ep. Adam," "AVT," "Diligo," "Lamentatio," the mock-epitaph on Bedel, and the epitaphs
for Henry VII and Lady Margaret--all from manuscripts
that have long since disappeared. In fine, considering
what he did preserve, we should not unduly tax him for
also including the non-canonical BTF and Cornishe's
satirical Trouth and Informacion. See also nos. 1736.1,
1810, and 1970.5 below for reprints of this edition; see
further nos. 1843.1, 1855, 1856, 1864, 1881.1, 1931, 1948,
1959.2, 1964 for later complete editions of Skelton. The
edition is microfilmed, University Microfilms, Reel no.
471 and is described by K&Y, pp. 63-69, by no. 1940.1 below, and in the Grolier Club Catalogue, "Langland to
Wither" (1893), pp. 192-193.

1569   AVALE, LEMEKE [a pseudonym: John Avale was a servant to
        Bp. Bonner]. A Commemoration or Dirige of Bastarde
        Edmonde Boner, alias Sauage.... STC 977 [1569].
            Presents verses in the Skeltonic manner, e.g., "Fifth
        Lesson," sigs. B3ᵛ-B6 (167 lines); "Response to Sixth
        Lesson," B7ᵛ-B8 (21 lines); "Response to Seventh Lesson,"
        B8ᵛ-C1 (10 lines); "Response to Eighth Lesson," C1ᵛ-C1

(10 lines); excerpts of the poem are printed in Dyce, I,
p. cxxiii, no. 1843.1.

1570   W., R. <u>A Recantation of Famous Pasquin of Rome</u>. <u>STC</u>$^{2.2}$
        24913a.5 (1570).
             This is a mock Requiem Mass for Bishop Bonner, with
        frequent comic rhymes in the Skeltonic manner (e.g.,
        "Maria, lia [lie], fria tria [try]" on A4), and extended
        Rhymes (e.g., in the <u>Oremus</u> "O most ungracious Pope, /
        Which was old Boners <u>hope</u>, / Now send helpe with a
        rope, / Your old frendes wanteth scope" on A4^v, or the
        <u>Lavabo</u> on B$_2$ with its details of what Bonner had washed
        from his hands, including, as rhymes, "equitie," "pitie,"
        "humilitie," "veritie," "fidelitie," "gracility," "chari-
        tie" &c.).

1573   HARVEY, GABRIEL. <u>The Letter-Book of Gabriel Harvey, A.D.
        1573-1580</u>. Edited by E. L. J. Scott from B.L. MS. Sloane
        93, in Camden Society, N.S. XXXIII (1884).
             "The Schollers Loove," and "A Milk Maid's Letter,"
        pp. 102-129 and 90-92, respectively, are satiric poems
        "scribbled at the first in a hurlewind of conceit," and
        in the Skeltonic manner. See also HARVEY, nos. 1574,
        1577.1, 1578.1, 1592 and 1593.1 for further references
        to Skelton.

1573.1 PARKHURST, JOHN. "De Skeltono vate & sacerdote," in <u>Ludicra
        siue Epigrammata Juuenilia</u>. <u>STC</u> 19299 (1573), p. 103.
             Fourteen lines of elegiacs based on the Seventh Tale
        of <u>The Merie Tales of Skelton</u>, no. 1567 above. The poem
        is reprinted in Dyce, I, pp. lxxix-lxxx, no. 1843.1
        below.

1574   HARVEY, GABRIEL. <u>Gabriel Harvey's Marginalia</u>. Edited by
        G. C. Moore-Smith. Stratford-upon-Avon, 1913.
             Among his marginalia for 1574 we find on p. 154: "My
        father would now & then merrily kast out an owld Ryme, of
        sum Skeltons, or Skoggins making, as he praetended"
        [followed by 10 line example in Skeltonics beginning
        "Ego, et Ille / Ar not so sille"]; and in the marginal
        note to p. 146 of Oικογομια seu Dispositio Regularum...
        (1570) and on p. 200 we find other brief marginal remarks
        by Harvey himself, in Skeltonics, as he comments on
        <u>Joannis Foorth Synopsis Politica</u>. See also HARVEY, nos.
        1577.1, 1578.1, 1592 and 1593.1 below for further refer-
        ences to Skelton by Harvey.

1574.1 ROBINSON, RICHARD. <u>The Rewarde of Wickednesse</u>. <u>STC</u>$^{2.2}$
        21121.7 [1574].
             The author claims to have written his poem to avoid
        "Idlenesse," one of charges brought against Skelton in

GL (v. 120); he is hailed by "Richard Smith" for having
scaled the House of Fame, where he now occupies the stage
alone, "Aboue [his] head a Garland gaye, of liuelye Laurel Tree" (sig. A4ᵛ); upon returning from Pluto's King-
dom, where he had seen Bishop Bonner, bloody as a butcher,
he is greeted by Melpomene, laurelled; he is there shown
the House of Fame of Helicon, and sees the Laurel tree
from which the names and pictures of famous poets hang,
among whom, as English poets, he sees Chaucer, Skelton,
and Lydgate (sig. Q2ᵛ.).

1575   GASCOIGNE, GEORGE. "The Praise of Phillip Sparrowe," in
The Posies. STC 11636 (1575). Edited by John W. Cun-
liffe. Cambridge: Cambridge University Press, 1907, I,
pp. 455-456.
    This poem of 54 lines actually owes little to PS save
for possible analogues in phrasing (e.g., cf. v. 23, w.
PS 119) and the general laudatory tone.

1575.1   LANEHAM, ROBERT. A Letter Whearin Part of the Entertainment
untoo the Queen at Killingwoorth Castl. is Signified.
STC 15191 [1575]. Edited by F. J. Furnivall under the
title Captain Cox, His Ballads and Books: or Robert
Laneham's Letter. London: Ballad Society, 1871.
    On p. 30 of Furnivall's edition, we find that CC and
TER are listed among the Captain's holdings. See also
Jonson, The Masque of Owles...Presented by the Ghost of
Captain Coxe, no. 1624.2 below.

1577   GRANGE, JOHN. The Golden Aphroditis. STC 12174 (1577).
Edited by Hyder E. Rollins, in Scholars' Facsimiles and
Reprints. New York, 1939, sig. N4.
    Grange mentions WH, TER, WCY, PS; compares Skelton
with Erasmus in that both "vttered their mindes...at
large..." by cloaking their thoughts in "mery conceytes,"
and "writing of toyes and foolish theames. Or who would
haue hearde his fault so playnely tolde him if not in
suche gibyng sorte?"

1577.1   HARVEY, GABRIEL. The Letter-Book of Gabriel Harvey [1577].
Edited by E. L. J. Scott, Camden Society, N.S. XXXIII
(1884).
    On page 57 Harvey, in a "delicate poeticall" device
on the death of George Gascoigne, presents Skelton "that
same malbraynd knave, / Looke how he knaws a dead horse
bone." See also HARVEY, nos. 1578.1, 1592, and 1593.1.

1577.2   HOLINSHED, RAPHAEL. The Laste Volume of the Chronicles of
England, Scotlande and Irelande..., STC 13568 (1577), p.
1612, col. 1.
    In the summary of "lerned men that lived in the dayes
of this moste famous prince [H VIII]," along with Colet,

Lillie, Linacre and Pace, we find listed "John Skelton, a pleasant Poet."

1578 BUTTES, THOMAS. [Notebook entry, Huntington Library MS. HM 9, sig. L6].
    Written down <u>c</u>. 1578 by Buttes, son of Sir William Buttes, physician to Henry VIII, we find: "Skelton wryteth on the wall / what is it y^t Moony [money] may not? <u>do all thinges</u>. / One other wryteth vnder y^t / All the monye is this place / Cannot make Skelton a good face."

1578.1 HARVEY, GABRIEL. <u>Gabriel Harvey's Marginalia</u>. Edited by G. C. Moore-Smith. Stratford-upon-Avon, 1913.
    Harvey notes the loan of the [<u>Merie</u>] <u>Tales of Skelton</u> (no. 1567 above), given him at London by "Mr. [?Edmund] Spensar, xx Dec. 1578," together with the jests of Scogan and tales of Howleglasse and Lazarillo; he compares all four unfavorably for "false and crafty feates" with Joe Miller, "whose witty shiftes and practices are reported among Skelton's Tales" (a reference, presumably, to "John Miller" of Tale xiii).

1579 <u>I</u>. <u>C</u>., Gent. <u>A Poore Knight his Pallace of Priuate Pleasures, Written by a Student in Cambridge</u>. STC 4283 (1579), sig. C3^v. The poem is reprinted in <u>Three Collections of English Poetry of the Latter Part of the Sixteenth Century</u>. Roxburghe Club, 1844, 1td. edn.
    In the chapter "Of Cupid his Campe," the student lists Homer, Hesiod, Virgil and Ovid among classical poets, and includes Skelton with Chaucer and Gower among the English poets.

1579.1 SPENSER, EDMUND. <u>The Shepheardes Calendar</u>, <u>STC</u> 23089 (1579). Edited by Ernest de Selincourt in <u>Spenser's Minor Poems</u>. Oxford: Clarendon Press, 1910.
    In the first line of the "January" eclogue, "Colin Cloute, a Shepeheardes boye" appears; the name is glossed as "not greatly vsed, and yet I have sene a poesie of M. Skelton's vnder that title." In E. K.'s Epistle to Gabriel Harvey, it is explained that under Colin's name, "the Author selfe is shadowed." <u>See</u> no. 1973.4, McLANE, for a detailed discussion of Spenser's use of Skelton in <u>The Shepheardes Calendar</u>.

1581 RICHE, BARNABY. <u>His Farewell to the Militarie Profession</u>. <u>STC</u> 20966 (1581).
    As edited by Thomas M. Cranfill (Austin: University of Texas Press, 1959), on p. 150, 1.38 we find a reference to "an olde mother Elenour, a disciple of the Spanishe Celestina," a possible reference to Elynour Rummynge as she is seen in no. 1590 below.

1583   SIDNEY, SIR PHILIP. "Good brother <u>Philip</u>, I have borne you
            long" in <u>Astrophel and Stella</u>, <u>STC</u> 22536 (1591), pp. 34-
            34^v; and as revised in <u>The New Arcadia</u>, <u>STC</u> 22541 (1598),
            p. 548, Sonnet no. 83.
                As edited by William A. Ringler, Jr., in <u>The Poems of</u>
            <u>Sir Philip Sidney</u> (Oxford: Clarendon Press, 1962), the
            poem, written 1581-83, appears on p. 208, with notes on
            pp. 482-483. While it is in no large part indebted to
            <u>PS</u>, it echoes phrases from <u>PS</u> 119, 125-126 and 140 in
            vv. 3, 8, and 12 respectively.

1583.1   SIDNEY, SIR PHILIP. "A Shepheard's tale no height of stile
            desires," in <u>The Old Arcadia</u>, <u>STC</u> 22540 (1593), pp. 44^v-
            45.
                Verses 84-104 of the poem as edited by Ringler, in
            Poems of <u>Sir Philip Sidney</u> (1962), pp. 244-245, present
            a description of a pet sparrow and his activity reminis-
            cent of those presented in <u>PS</u>, vv. 120-140.

1586   DAY, ANGEL. <u>The English Secretorie</u>. <u>STC</u> 6401 (1586), sig.
            B2.
                A cancellandum, unique to the Folger copy prints a
            non-canonical, bawdy poem of 5 lines, ascribing it to
            Skelton: "Humbly complayneth to your high estate, / The
            Lady Prioresse of Margate: / For that the Abbot of S.
            Albones did stoppe, / With two stones and a stake her
            water gappe / Helpe Lord for God sake." <u>See also</u> nos.
            1605 and 1951.2 below for a variant and for note calling
            attention to the cancellandum, respectively.

1586.1   WEBBE, WILLIAM. <u>A Discourse of English Poetrie</u>. <u>STC</u> 25172
            (1586), sig. C3^v.
                As printed in G. Gregory Smith, <u>Elizabethan Critical</u>
            <u>Essays</u> (1904), I, p. 242, after discussion of Chaucer,
            Lydgate and <u>Pierce Ploughman</u> [sic], Webbe mentions Skel-
            ton as one who had "obtayned the Lawrell Garland" and as
            "doubtless a pleasant, conceyted fellowe, and of a very
            sharpe wytte."

1589   PUTTENHAM, GEORGE. <u>The Arte of English Poesie</u>. <u>STC</u> 20519
            (1589). Edited by Gladys Doidge Willcock and Alice
            Walker. Cambridge: Cambridge University Press, 1936.
                Puttenham, who may have begun his book in 1569 and
            augmented it in 1584, after mentioning Chaucer, Gower,
            Lydgate, the author of Piers Plowman, and Hardyng the
            chronicler, lists Skelton, "I wot not for what great
            worthiness surnamed the poet laureate" on p. 60; then
            calls him a "sharpe Satirist, but with more rayling and
            scoffing then became a Poet Laureate" on p. 62, and
            recommends that Skelton's use of "short distaunces [be-
            tween rhymes] and short measures, as pleasing only the

popular ear," be banished from the repertory of "courtly makers."

1589.1　A SKELTONICAL SALUTATION, Or Condigne Gratulation, / And Iust Vexation, Of the Spanish Nation, / That in a Brava-do, / Spent Many a Crusado, / in Setting Forth an Arma-do, / England to Invado. STC 22619 (Oxford, 1589), sigs. A6-B6.
　　The poem is entirely in Skeltonics, English and Latin; excerpts from it are printed in Dyce, I, pp. cxxvi-cxxviii, no. 1843.1 below and the whole poem in no. 1880 below. A second edition of the poem, STC 22620, was printed in 1589.

1590　THE COBLER OF CAUNTERBURIE. STC 4579 [1590].
　　The Cobler presents six tales, in a unifying frame: that of a barge trip between Billingsgate and Gravesend, in a bourgeois burlesque of a Canterbury Tales presided over by the Cobbler. It has clear echoes of Skelton's description of Elynor Rumming in the verse presentation of the Old Woman of the fifth tale (pp. 59-60), her ker-chief "tied with a whim-wham, knit up againe with a trim-tram, much like an Egiptian." The tale of old lady is dropped, however, in the 1630 revision of the piece as The Tincker of Turvey, no. 1630.1 below.

1590.1　THE LIFE OF LONG MEG OF WESTMINSTER, entered in the SR in 1590. [Our comments are from the edition of 1635, STC 17783.]
　　Doctor Skelton, in his "mad merry veine," addresses Meg at the Eagle Inn of Westminster (2nd tale), couching his remarks in Skeltonics that are reminiscent in diction of WH and providing a "portraiture" reminiscent of his description of Elynour Rummynge in TER; Skelton also ap-pears as a character in chap. 4. The work is excerpted in Dyce, I, pp. lxxxi-lxxxv, no. 1843.1 below and re-printed in Charles C. Mish, Short Fiction of the Seven-teenth Century (New York: Norton Library, 1968), pp. 79-113.

1591　THE TROUBLESOME RAIGNE OF KING JOHN. STC 14644 (1591), sigs. E4v and F1. Edited by John S. Farmer, in Old Eng-lish Drama, CVI (1913).
　　The Friar's plea to Philip is in 10 lines of Skel-tonics, printed as 5 lines of monorhyme with internal rhyme: "Benedicamus Domine, was euer such an iniurie, / Sweete S., Withold of thy levitie, defend vs from ex-tremitie" / &c.

1592　HARVEY, GABRIEL. Fovre Letters and Certaine Sonnets. STC 12900.

The second letter as edited by Alexander B. Grosart (Huth Library, 1884), I, p. 165, concerns "father Elderton, and his sonne Greene, in the vaine of Skelton, or Scoggin, [who] will counterfeit an hundred dogged Fables [&]..."; and speaks sardonically of the garland of bays bestowed on Greene, at his death, by his mistress: "I know not whether Skelton, Elderton, or some like flourishing Poet were so enterred...." See also 1593.1.

1593   FOULFACE, PHILIP, of Ale-ford [pseudonym]. Bacchus Bountie, STC 11208 [1593].
         The poem, finished by 9 December 1592, contains 30 lines of Skeltonics to "Bonny Bachus" despite two examples of cross-rhyme on sig. B1^v and lists Skelton with Chaucer and Lydgate among the English poets, themselves in the company of the great Greek and Latin poets, on sig. C1.

1593.1   HARVEY, GABRIEL. Pierces Supererogation. STC 12903 (1593).
         As edited by Alexander B. Grosart (Huth Library, 1884), II, pp. 109 and 132, we find references to Skelton and Scogan, with Skelton being called "the Malancholy foole" on p. 132.

1593.2   PEELE, GEORGE. King Edward the First. STC 19535 (1593).
         As edited by W. W. Greg, in Malone Society Reprints, XXIII (Oxford, 1911), sig. F2, in scene viii, 11. 1490-1502 we find dialogue in the Skeltonic manner; the Friar's speech is at times characterized by mild Skeltonics as in 11. 1467-1470, 1531-1533.

1594   GREENE, ROBERT. The Honorable Historie of Frier Bacon and Frier Bongay [sic]. STC 12267 (1594).
         In the play, performed in 1592, as edited by Brooke and Paradise, in English Drama 1580-1642 (Boston: D. C. Heath & Co., 1933), pp. 69-96, we find traces of Skeltonic verse in the Dr. Dawcock fashion of WH on the lips of Miles, the servant of Bacon, in Scene vii, 41-46; 73-84; 102-113; 124-131.

1594.1   THE LIFE AND DEATH OF JACK STRAW. STC 23356 [1594].
         As edited by Kenneth Muir and F. P. Wilson, in Malone Society Reprints, XCVIII (Oxford, 1957), in Act II, sc. 1, 11. 518-522, we find Skeltonics in the mouth of Hob Carter.

1594.2   LODGE, THOMAS. The Wounds of Civil War. STC 16678 (1594).
         As edited by J. Dover Wilson, in Malone Society Reprints, XIX (1910), on sigs. G3^v and G4, in Act IV, sc. ii, 11. 1781-1786; 1800-1805 we find Skeltonics in the mouth of the Clown, printed as prose.

1595   DANDO, JOHN [pseudonym]. <u>Maroccus Extaticus or Bankes Bay</u>
            <u>Horse in a Trance</u>. STC 6225 (1595).
                 On sigs. B4 we find 5 lines of Skeltonics; on B4ᵛ a
            total of 14 lines of Skeltonics against economic profit-
            eering, spoken by Bank's horse to crown his brilliant
            performance.

1597   BRETON, NICHOLAS. <u>The Will of Wit, Wits Wil, or Wils Wit</u>.
            STC 3705 (1597). As found in <u>The Works of Verse and</u>
            <u>Prose of Nicholas Breton</u>. Edited by Alexander B. Grosart.
            [Edinburgh]: for private circulation [1875-79].
                 In II, pp. 7 and 8 there are 54 lines in Skeltonic
            tradition and in II, p. 31, there are 28 lines in the
            Skeltonic manner at the end of a long moralistic dia-
            logue entitled "The Schollar & The Soldiour."

1598   HALL, JOSEPH. <u>Virgidemiarum</u>. STC 12716 (1598), p. 83.
                 As edited by Arnold Davenport, in <u>The Collected Poems</u>
            <u>of Joseph Hall</u> (Liverpool: University of Liverpool
            Press, 1947), in Satire VI, i, 76 there is a reference
            to "angry <u>Skeltons</u> breath-less rimes"; further borrowings
            or adaptations from <u>CC</u> can also be found in <u>Virgidemiarum</u>
            I, vii, 23; II, ii, 64; and V, i, 117ff.

1598.1   MERES, FRANCIS. <u>Palladis Tamia, Wit's Treasury</u>. STC 17834
            (1598), sig. 279ᵛ.
                 As edited by Don Cameron Allen, in <u>Francis Mere's</u>
            <u>Treatise "Poetrie," A Critical Edition</u> (Urbana, 1933),
            p. 72 and reprinted by Don Cameron Allen in <u>Scholars'</u>
            <u>Facsimiles and Reprints</u> (New York, 1938), p. 279ᵛ, we
            find Meres comparing "<u>Skelton</u> (I know not for what great
            worthines, surnamed the Poet Laureat)" with "<u>Sotades</u>
            <u>Maronites</u> the Iambicke Poet" who gave himself over to
            "impure and lascivious things" as Skelton has "applied
            his wit to scurrilities and ridiculous matters...."

1598.2   <u>THE RIDDLES OF HERACLITVS AND DEMOCRITUS</u>. STC 13174 (1598).
                 On Alᵛ, we find 16 lines dedicatory in Skeltonic
            couplets: "Prophesies, predictions, / Stories and fic-
            tions, / Allegories, rimes / and serious pastimes / For
            all manner men, / Without regarde when" &c.

1598.3   THYNNE, FRANCIS. <u>Animaduersions uppon the Annotacions and</u>
            <u>Corrections of Some Imperfections of Impressiones of</u>
            <u>Chaucer's Workes</u>.
                 As edited from manuscript by G. H. Kingsley, for EETS,
            IX (1865), p. 7, in his criticism of Speght's edition of
            Chaucer (1598), Thynne mentions that his father, William,
            an earlier editor of Chaucer (1532), was "called in ques-
            tion by the Bysshopes, and heaved at by cardinall Wolsey,"
            chiefly because he had encouraged Skelton to publish <u>CC</u>
            against Wolsey, while the poet was sheltered at the elder

Thynne's home in Erith, Kent (a lease which, one notes, was not obtained until 1531, 2 years after Skelton's death).

1600   CAMDEN, WILLIAM. Reges, reginae, nobiles & alii.... STC 4518 (1600).
           Camden prints "El Marg" on sigs. Z3-Z3ᵛ, "Eulogium," with "Tetr." on sigs. D1-D1ᵛ, and "HVII" (lacking vv. 25-28), on sigs. D2-D2ᵛ.

1600.1 [DRAYTON, MICHAEL.] The First Part of the True and Honor-able Historie of the Life of Sir John Oldcastle. STC 18795 (1600).
           As edited by T. William Hebel, in The Works of Michael Drayton (Oxford: Shakespeare Head Press, 1931), I, p. 448, we find "Ellen of Rumming" anachronistically men-tioned in 1. 1994 along with Owleglasse, the "Friar and the Boy," and Robin Hood, by Harpool, Oldcastle's ser-vant, in his defense of "English books." See also DRAYTON, no. 1606+ below for other uses of Skelton by Drayton.

1600.2 HATHWAY, R[ICHARD] and W[ILLIAM] RANKINS. Scogan and Skelton.
           The play of this title is a "lost" play; see Harbage and Schoenbaum, Annals of English Drama, 975-1700 (1964), pp. 80-81, where it is listed as of 1601-02; references to the playbook in Henslowe's Diary (edited by Foakes and Rickert), however, show that payments made to the playwrights ranged from late January to early March 1600.

1600.3 JONSON, BEN. Cynthias Revels or the Fountaine of Selfe-Love. A Comicall Satyre. Written c. 1600, first appear-ing in print in the folio of 1640, vol. 1, STC 14753, pp. [153]-235; edited by C[harles] H[arold] Herford and Percy Simpson (Oxford: Clarendon Press, 1925-52), IV, 1-183.
           Despite the difference between late medieval and neo-classical type names, Jonson seems indebted to Skelton's Magnyfycence in the construction of this play: his Crites resembles Skelton's Measure; his four courtier-vices, Amorphus, Hedon, Anaides and Asotus, resemble Skelton's four courtier-vices, Counterfeit Countenance, Cloaked Collusion, Crafty Conveyance and Courtly Abusion; two of his female vices, Moria and Phantaste, resemble Skelton's two fools, Folly and Fancy. In addition, Jon-son follows Skelton in disguising the follies as virtues and in grouping qualities of character in one class and qualities of conduct in another. See no. 1911 below; see also JONSON, nos. 1621, 1624.1, 1624.2, 1633, 1640, 1640.1 and 1641 below; note that vols. VI-XI of the Her-ford and Simpson are edited by C. H. Herford, Percy and Evelyn Simpson, as used in these later references.

34

1600.4 LOOKE ABOUT YOU. STC 16800 (1600).
     As edited by W. W. Greg, in the Malone Society Re-
     prints, XXXIV (1913), fol. G2, scene xi, 11. 1831-1832,
     we find Block's announcement of the arrival of Prince
     Richard made in Skeltonics to "Lady Faulconbridge"
     (Robin Hood disguised).

1600.5 NASHE, THOMAS. Summers Last Will and Testament. STC 18376
     (1600).
     In the play, written c. 1592, as edited by R. B. Mc-
     Kerrow in The Works of Thomas Nashe (rev. edn; Oxford:
     Clarendon Press, 1958), III, p. 252, line 588, we find a
     punning reference to "the riffe raffe of the rumming of
     Elanor" (TER).

1600.6 R[OBERTS], H[ENRY]. Haigh for Deuonshire. A Pleasant Dis-
     course or Sixe Gallant Marchants of Deuonshire. STC
     21081 (1600), sigs. B1-B2.
     "To the friendly Readers," beginning "In Storie olde, /
     It hath ben tolde / That many a Franion / And boone com-
     panion...&c." continues with over 158 lines of Skeltonic
     verse.

1600.7 THE WISDOME OF DR. DODYPOLL. STC 6991 (1600). sig. C4.
     As edited by M. N. Matson, in the Malone Society Re-
     prints, CVIII (1965 for 1964), we find Skeltonics marking
     the speech of Haunce, "our man": "Farewell Dr. Doddy, /
     [I]n minde & in body, / An excellent Noddy: / A Cockscomb
     in Cony, / [B]ut that he wonts mony, / To give legem
     pone."

1601 CHAMBER, JOHN. A Treatise against Iudicial Astrologie. STC
     4941 (1601), sigs. P1 and Q4.
     Here are found three references to the "merrie Skel-
     ton" of the jest-book tradition. The examples are re-
     printed in Samuel Egerton Brydges (ed.), Censura
     Literaria (1805), IX, pp. 385-386.

1601.1 MUNDAY, ANTHONY. The Downfall of Robert Earl of Huntingdon.
     STC 18271 (1601).
     As edited by John C. Meagher, in the Malone Society
     Reprints, CVII (1965 for 1964), we find Skelton playing
     an active part in this play as a playwright, the "Pro-
     logue" to explain the preliminary dumb-shows, and then
     as a player (Friar Tuck) who frequently resorts to Skel-
     tonics, e.g., when he assumes his habit as Friar Tuck
     (sigs. A3v-A4), or when as the Friar he inveighs against
     the corruptions of a barbarous age (sigs. D2-D3).

1601.2 MUNDAY, ANTHONY. The Death of Robert Earl of Huntingdon.
     STC 18269 (1601).

The play is a sequel to <u>Downfall</u> above; as edited by
John C. Meagher, in the Malone Society Reprints, CXII
(1967 for 1965), we find Skelton, a bit addle-pated,
continuing the plot of <u>Downfall</u> in his opening speech as
Friar Tuck in Skeltonics printed as prose lines; and when
his play, in which Skeltonics are <u>not</u> prominent, ends
with the death of Robin Hood, Skelton is asked to continue by the "Earl of Chester" with "Matilda's Tragedy."
<u>See also</u> MUNDAY, no. 1615 below.

1602   A PLEASANT CONCEITED COMEDIE, WHEREIN IS SHEWED HOW A MAN
       MAY CHUSE A GOOD WIFE FROM A BAD. <u>STC</u> 5594 (1602).
          As edited by A. E. H. Swaen, in <u>Materialien zur Kunde</u>
       <u>des älteren Englischen Dramas</u>, XXXV (Louvain, 1911), we
       find that the schoolmaster, Sir Aminadab, is given to
       short couplets, frequently macaronic or with Latin ele-
       ments in them, of the school of Skelton, as in 11. 743-
       751, 1347-1350, 1397-1408, for examples.

1602.1 SHAKESPEARE, WILLIAM. <u>The Merry Wives of Windsor</u>.
          In the play, perhaps written as early as 1597, but
       first published in 1602, in II, i, 10-15 Falstaff signs
       off his letter to Mistress Page in 5 lines of Skeltonics.

1603   DENT, ARTHUR. <u>The Plaine Mans Path-way to Heauen</u>. <u>STC</u>
       6627 (2nd edn. 1603), pp. 162-167.
          (On Drunkenness): Dent resorts to Skeltonical-like
       catalogues of nouns and gerunds in which rhyme occasion-
       ally occurs, as in the passage on the fruits of drunken-
       ness, p. 164: "babbling, brabbling, fighting, quarreling,
       surfetting..."; or p. 166 (how drunkards misspent their
       money): "in gaming, rioting, swearing, staring, swilling,
       bezzeling, bibbing, brawling, and brabbling." The charac-
       ter "Antile" does mention "Ellen of Rummin" as pleasant
       and merry while the character Asunetus, on the other hand,
       includes <u>TER</u> among "Vaine and friulous bookes of Tales,
       Iestes and lies" (p. 371).

1604   "SKELTONICALL OBSERVATIONS OF BISHOPS VISITATIONS, PRETEND-
       ING REFORMATIONS, INTENDING PROCURATIONS."
          This is a MS. poem, CUL MS. Mm. iii.12, from the col-
       lection of Anthony Harrison (b. 13 November 1563, d.
       1638), a diligent collector of all things concerning the
       Bishop of Norwich, whom he served as secretary and col-
       lector of tithes, 1603-08; is written in 17 lines of
       Skeltonics. It is printed by F. J. Furnivall in <u>Ballads</u>
       <u>from Manuscripts</u> (London: for the Ballad Society, 1876),
       I, footnote 4 to pp. 210-211.

1605   MAURITIUS, JOHANNES (John Morris).
          In his commonplace book, BL MS. Royal 12. B. v., fol..
       14^V, Mauritius records a variant of the <u>jeu d'esprit</u> also

attributed to Skelton in a cancellandum in Angel Day's
1586 English Secretorie, no. 1586 above. Here it is the
Lady Prioresse of "St. Margarate" (not "Margat") who com-
plains, and a "water gate" rather than "water gappe" that
has been stopped up by the Abbot of St. Albans "w<u>th</u> two
stones and a stike."

1605.1   ROWLEY, SAMUEL. When You See Me, You Know Me. STC 21417
(1605).
     As edited by F. P. Wilson and John Crow, in the Malone
Society Reprints (1952), on sig. A4, Henry VIII bids
Queen Jane to call Will Sommers to make her merry, but
is told: "He was met my liege, they say, at London /
Earely this morning by Doctor Skelton," to which the King
replies, "Hes neuer from him, goe let a grome be sent, /
And fetch him home...."

1606+   DRAYTON, MICHAEL. Poemes, Lyrick and Pastorall (Odes,
Eglogs, The Man in the Moone. STC 7217 (?1606).
     Ode 1, sig. B2ᵛ ends with a defense of the short
"measure" used in the odes: "'tis possible to clyme /
to kindle or to slake / All thoughe in Skeltons Ryme";
Ode 5, sig. B6ᵛ-B7, 44 lines of Skeltonics, becomes no.
7 in the 1619 edition (STC 7222) and is there labelled
"An Amouret Anacreontick"; Ode 9, 36 lines of trimeter
couplets with irregular stress, sigs. C2-C2ᵛ, becomes
no. 14 in the 1619 edition and is there entitled "A
Skeltoniad."

1606.1   WEST, RICHARD. News from Bartholomew Fayre. STC 25264
(1606).
     This work borrows at times the Skeltonic mode in
rhyme and meter as in lines at the bottom of A2ᵛ-A3; in
the assignment of duties to mourners for "Maximus" (cf.
PS), sigs. A3-A3ᵛ; and in the incorporation of vv. 56-65
of "Dev Tr" in the Dirge.

1608   TWYNE, BRIAN. Antiquitatis Academie Oxoniensis Apologia.
STC 24405 (1608), p. 14.
     Twyne mentions CC and Skelton slightingly: "& Coleni
Clouti fabula, quae a Ioanne Skeltono postea multo auc-
tior extitit, ioculatore quidem illo & bombologo
facetissimo."

1609   PIMLYCO OR RUNNE RED-CAP. STC 19936 (1609).
     We find here a notice of Skelton plus the inclusion
of part of TER, on sigs. B2-B2ᵛ; in addition there are
three long quotations from TER (ll. 1-100; 101-234; 243-
250) on sigs. B3-B4ᵛ and C2ᵛ-C5. See also no. 1624 for
notes on this piece.

1611   FLORIO, JOHN. <u>Queen Anna's New World of Words, or Diction-arie of the Italian and English Tongues</u>. <u>STC</u> 11099, p. 198.

          Florio defines <u>Fróttola</u> as "a countrie song or rounde-lay, a wanton tale, or skeltonicall riming" (this last phrase newly added, to fill out his earlier definition of the word in <u>A Worlde of Wordes</u> (1598), <u>STC</u> 11098, p. 140).

1612   ROWLANDS, SAMUEL. [Actually written by Nicholas Breton?], <u>Cornu-copiae, Pasquines Night-cap: or Antidot for the Head-ache</u>. <u>STC</u> 3639 (1612), sig. O2.

          In two stanzas ironically celebrating the Cuckoo and the Cuckold, ?Rowlands or ?Breton mentions Skelton "with his Lawrel Crowne" and "ruffling rimes...empty quite of marrow" as the creator of Philip Sparrow [<u>PS</u>], whose accomplishments are still short of the Cuckoo's; Skelton is also mentioned on sig. Q3.

1613   KING, HUMPHREY. <u>An Halfe-penny-worth of Wit, or The Her-mites Tale</u>. <u>STC</u> 14973 (1613) [3rd impression].

          After a discussion between the writer and a hermit over various evils of the world, the author promises a tale "in Skelton's rime" on sig. D2^v; Skelton is mentioned later, on E1.

1613.1   MARKHAM, GERVASE. <u>Hobsons Horse-load of Letters or A Presi-dent for Epistles, The First Booke</u>. <u>STC</u> 17360 (1613).

          In Letter LIIII, "A merry-mad-Letter to a merry mad wench, chaste and ingenious" on sig. H2^v, and Letter LV, "An answere to the former Letter in the same Kinde" on sig. H3; we find letters in Skeltonic monorhyming stanzas of 8, 8, and 4 lines respectively, the first beginning "Lady of beauty possitiue, / Peerelesse beyond compara-tiue, / Shew your sweet selfe superlatiue" &c., the second commencing, "The true forme desideratiue, / Of your fayre speech affirmatiue, / Maketh me all medita-tiue, / How to propound a negatiue."

1614   [BROWNE, WILLIAM, of Tavistock.] <u>The Shepheardes Pipe</u>. <u>STC</u> 3917 (1614), sig. C7.

          At the end of Eclogue i we find praise of Thomas Occleve as Chaucer's "Scholler" with disparagement of those who "haue garlands for their meed, / That but iarre as <u>Skeltons</u> reed"; in modern edition as edited by Gordon Goodwin, <u>Poems of William Browne of Tavistock</u> (London: Routledge, 1893), II, 119.

1615   M[UNDAY], A[NTHONY]. <u>Metropolis Coronata, The Triumphes of Ancient Drapery...In Honour of the aduancement of Sir Iohn Iolles, Knight, to the high Office of Lord Maior of London....</u> <u>STC</u> 18275 (1615), sig. C2^v.

Friar Tuck replies to Robin Hood, who has granted his request that the band of merry men be of pleasureable service to the Lord Mayor, in six lines of Skeltonics preparatory to a Hunting Song: "Thankes my deare Domine, / And to you noble Homine, / For this indenter, / Friar Tuck subscribes <u>Libenter</u>, / How lest we offer wrong / Fall to your Sing Song."

1616   FARLEY, HENRY. <u>The Complaint of Paules, to All Christian</u>
        <u>Soules</u>. <u>STC</u> 10688 (1616).
            The subtitle of the work is in Skeltonic rhythm and rhyme: "Or an humble Supplication, / To our good King and Nation, / For Her newe Reparation."

1618   BOLTON, EDMUND. <u>Hypercritica</u>.
            Written 1618 but taken from an Oxford collection of 1722, <u>Nicolai Triveti Annalium Continuatio</u>, edited by Anthony Hall, to which Bolton's <u>Hypercritica</u> was added as the last item, p. 235. Bolton states that Edmund Spenser is no more to be praised (other than in his Hymns) "for practic <u>English</u>" than Chaucer, Lydgate, Pierce <u>Ploughman</u> or "Laureat Skelton."

1619   PITSEUS, IOANNIS [John Pits]. "De Ioanne Sceltono," in <u>Relationum historicarum de rebus angliciis</u>. Paris, p. 701.
            While essentially this work is a rewriting of Bale's <u>Catalogus</u>, no. 1559 above, Pitseus adds the "<u>Epitaphia</u> <u>Regum, principium, magnatum, nobilium</u>," "incised" at Westminster Abbey (<u>see</u> no. 1600 above), and locates Skelton's translation of Diodorus Siculus, "MS Cantabrigiae in Collegio S. Benedicti" (Corpus Christi College, Cambridge MS. 275), the first notice of this ms.

1620   <u>WESTWARD FOR SMELTS. OR THE WATERMANS FARE OF MAD-MERRY</u>
        <u>WESTERN WENCHES...WRITTEN BY KINDE KIT OF KINGSTONE</u>.
        <u>STC</u> 25292 (1620).
            As edited by James O. Halliwell, in Percy Society, XXII (1848), pp. 10, 19-20, 36-37, 47, 51-52, 57-58 show the use of Skeltonics by Kit the boatman to describe each of his fishwife passengers on the trip up the Thames to Kingston.

1621   JONSON, BEN. <u>The Gypsies Metamorphosed</u>. <u>STC</u> 13798 (1640).
            The work was written in 1621 as shown in the Huntington Library ms. version (HM 741) but published with Jonson's translation of Horace and given the title <u>The</u> <u>Masque of the Gypsies</u> and a printing date of 1640. As edited by Herford and Simpson, VII, pp. 539-622, we find throughout the masque the Patrico expressing himself in Skeltonics with words and phrases particularly reminiscent of <u>TER</u>, which had made one of the earliest

references to gypsies in English literature (vv. 74-79).
For particular examples we note Part I, Dance 1, Song,
ll. 132ff; the gypsy in Dance 2, strain 3, with a Jon-
sonian rendering of the Skeltonic at beginning (410-413)
and end (449-457); and 1180-1182 where the rhyme is taken
from TER 15-17 (lines to be used in Fortunate Isles 374-
376). See also JONSON, nos. 1624.1, 1624.2, 1633, 1640,
1640.1 and 1641 below for other examples of his use of
Skelton.

1621.1   PEACHAM, HENRY. The Compleat Gentleman. STC 19502 (1621),
          pp. 91 and 95. Modern edition from 1634 edition by
          G. S. Gordon. Oxford: Clarendon Press, 1906.
              Peacham compares Skelton's rhymes adversely to
          Petrarch's stanze, and alludes to Skelton as a poet
          laureate "for what desert I could never heare" and men-
          tions Skelton's epitaph on H VII; cf. his remarks with
          those of Puttenham and Meres nos. 1589 and 1598.1 above.

1624   ELYNOVR RVMMIN, THE FAMOUS ALE-WIFE OF ENGLAND, WRITTEN BY
          MR. SKELTON, POET LAUREAT TO KING HENRY THE EGIHTH [sic].
          London, for Samuel Rand, sigs. A⁴, B⁴, C²; STC 22614.
              Contents: In the Huntington Library copy, only, ap-
          pears the woodcut of Elynour Rummyng known as "The Lin-
          coln Nosegay" on recto and verso, both, of title page;
          then an address to the reader by "Skelton's Ghost" (in
          Skeltonic couplets); the text of TER; "Skelton's Ghost
          to the Reader," and the woodcut portrait of E.R. a
          second time.
              Two copies of this edition are located in the Bodleian,
          each without title page: 8° T. 27 Art. Seld. [lacking
          C2] and 8° R. 17 Jour. Seld. Both have been erroneously
          reported in the STC as copies of STC 22613 [TER], actu-
          ally a "ghost." Similarly STC 22612 [TER] is a "ghost,"
          arising from the fact that part of TER is incorporated
          into Pimlyco, or Runne Red-cap, STC 19936, no. 1609
          above. For the 1814 purchase for 500 guineas by T. F.
          Dibdin of the "Lincoln Nosegay Books," see William A.
          Jackson, Records of a Bibliographer (Cambridge, Massachu-
          setts: Harvard University Press, 1969), pp. 149-155;
          see no. 1794 for copy of the "Lincoln Nosegay" portrait
          of E. R.
              See nos. 1744 and 1808 for reprintings of TER from
          this edition.

1624.1   JONSON, BEN. The Fortunate Isles and Their Vnion. STC
          14772 (1624).
              As edited by Herford and Simpson, VII, pp. 707-729,
          Skelton, "The Worshipfull Poet Laureat to K. Harry"
          (1. 317), is mentioned in a preliminary way in ll. 279,
          306, 309 &c., before coming on stage in a major role with

Scogan, Edward IV's jester (John Scogan, fl. 1480, of a
Norfolk family, was often confused with the poet Scogan,
Chaucer's friend); Skelton speaks in Skeltonics in 11.
339-341, 350-361 (with echoes of Mag ?), 368-380 borrowings from TER 1-6, 15-21), and 400-414 (with borrowings
from TER 49, 50, 80-84); Iohphiel also has a few lines
in Skeltonics, while Elynour Rumming is one of the
figures in the anti-masque.

1624.2   JONSON, BEN. The Masque of Owles...at Kenilworth, Presented
          by the Ghost of Captain Coxe.
              The masque was the first printed in Folio Workes of
          1640, vol. 2, pp. 125-143, STC 14754, but wrongly dated
          1626 on the t.p. As edited by Herford and Simpson, VII,
          pp. 781-786, it consists of 179 lines of Skeltonics. See
          no. 1575.1 above for the appropriateness of linking Skel-
          tonics with Captain Cox; see also JONSON, nos. 1633, 1640,
          1640.1 and 1641 below.

1626   JAMES, RICHARD. "To Mr. Benj. Jhonson on his Staple of News
          first presented," 11. 9-14, in The Poems, etc. of R.
          James, B.D. Edited by A. B. Grosart (London: for private
          circulation, 1880), p. 221; play entered SR 14 April 1626.
              Skelton and his younger contemporary Whittinton are
          mentioned as laureates whose laurels were "Soone sprung,
          soon fading."

1626.1   VAUGHAN, SIR WILLIAM [under the pseudonym of "Orpheus
          Junior"]. The Golden Fleece Divided into Three Parts.
          STC 24609 (1626).
              Skelton is mentioned p. 83; Skelton interrupts, in
          quatrains with alternating rhymes, however, p. 88; is a
          mischievous character in a play, p. 93.

1630   TAYLOR, JOHN, The Water-Poet. "A Skeltonicall salutation
          to those that know how to reade, and not marre the sense
          with hacking or misconstruction," in All the Workes of...,
          being 63 in Number, STC 23725 (1630), p. 245.
              The poem is printed as 15 lines of prose but with in-
          ternal rhyme so regularly prominent that it seems in-
          tended to have been printed as verse, as the last two
          lines of the passage show: "...my wits I could bristle,
          for a better Epistle, but yet at this time, this Skel-
          tonicall Rime, I send to thy view, because it is new.
          So reader, adue."

1630.1   THE TINCKER OF TVRVEY, HIS MERRY PASTYME IN HIS PASSING FROM
          BILLINGSGATE TO GRAVES-END. STC 4581 (1630).
              As reprinted by Charles C. Mish, in Short Fiction of
          the Seventeenth Century (New York: Norton Library,
          1968), pp. 115-191, the work is a revision of THE COBLER

OF CAUNTERBURIE, no. 1590 above. Before each of the six traveler's tales, two of which are new, a description of the teller is given in octosyllabic couplets with rhythmic variations in the Skeltonic manner, on sig. A3, in the Tinker's epistle praising the ale of Mother Twattlebum, we find mention of the fact that her Grandma was "old Mother Elianor Rumming..., and Skelton her Cozen, who wrote fine Rimes in praise of her High and Mighty Ale."

1631   WEEVER, JOHN. Ancient Fvnerall Monvments Within the Vnited Monarchie of Great Britain, Ireland and the Islands Adiacent. STC 25223 (1631).
          On p. 476, Weever unwarrantedly ascribes to Skelton the shortest of the several Latin poems that hung over the tomb of Henry VII: "Septimus hic situs est Henricus gloria regum"; on p. 477, he quotes Skelton's "terrible curse" (4 lines) upon the potential desecrators of Lady Margaret's tomb (see "El Marg," no. 1516 above); on pp. 497-498 he gives a thumbnail sketch of Skelton, including the statement "This John Skelton was that pleasant merry Poet (as his rimes yet extant doe testifie)," the first part of which will be quoted by Blomefield, no. 1739 below; cites Lilly's lines on Skelton, no. 1520, from "the collections of Master Camden.

1632   BROME, RICHARD. The Northern Lasse, STC 3819 (1632), in The Dramatic Works of Richard Brome. London: J. Pearson, 1873, III, p. 52.
          In Act III, Sc. ii, in dialogue playing on "Sir Philip" as a lover, Constance sings a song "A bonny bonny Bird I had, / A Bird that was my Marrow: / A Bird whose pastime made me glad / And Philip 'twas my Sparrow," with references to its ability to "keep cut" (cf. PS 118).

1633   JONSON, BEN. The King's Entertainment at Welback. Written in 1633 but printed for first time in 1640 Folio, vol. II, STC 14754, pp. 272-283 of The Under-wood.
          As edited by Herford and Simpson, VII, pp. 791-803, we find Accidence and Father Fitz-ale using Skeltonics and Jonson's own longer-lined Skeltonic rhyme in dialogue, lines 113-148, 158-200, 255-272. See also JONSON, nos. 1640, 1640.1 and 1641.

1633.1   NASHE, THOMAS, of the Inner Temple. Quaternio or a Fourefold Way to a Happie Life, STC 18382 (1633).
          Parts of "Edw. IV" are printed, described as "made by Skelton, which I find inserted amongst the reprinted Workes of Lydgate," pp. 239-240; brief comments on Skelton's reputation and the date of death given in marginalia on p. 240. (Since no collected Works of Lydgate

are known to be in print in 1633, it is remotely possible
that Nashe had seen a copy of the suppressed printing of
Lydgate's most compendious work in print, his translation
of Boccaccio's <u>Fall of Princes</u>...Whereunto is added the
<u>Fall of Al such as since that time were noteable in Eng-</u>
<u>land</u> (1555?), now known only through a t.p. and a single
leaf of text. It seems more likely, however, that Nashe
is confusing Lydgate's "Workes" with William Baldwin's
"continuation" of the <u>Fall of Princes</u> in the <u>Mirror for</u>
<u>Magistrates</u>, Pt. I (1557), which ended with "Mayster"
Skelton's "oracion" for Edward IV, doubtfully ascribed to
the poet.)

1633.2   PRYNNE, WILLIAM. <u>Histrio-Mastix, The Players Scourge, or</u>
          <u>Actors Tragaedie</u>. <u>STC</u> 20464 (1633), p. 834.
              Approves "Skeltons Comedies <u>de Virtute</u> [lost], <u>de</u>
          <u>Magnificentia</u>, & <u>de bono Ordine</u> [lost]" together with
          such works as "<u>Geffrey Chaucers</u> & <u>Pierce</u> the Plowmans
          tales and Dialogues," and pieces of Nicholas Grimald as
          "penned only to be read, not acted," their subjects being
          "al serious, sacred, divine, not scurrilous, wanton or
          prophan, as al modern Play poems." As his marginalia
          indicates, Prynne derived his information vis-à-vis
          Skelton from Bale's <u>Catalogus</u>, no. 1559 above.

1638   HEYWOOD, THOMAS. <u>The Wise-woman of Hogsdon, A Comedie</u>.
          <u>STC</u> 13370 (1638), sigs. C4^V, D3^V, F2 and F2^V. In
          <u>Dramatic Works of Thomas Heywood</u>. London: J. Pearson,
          1874, V, pp. 303, 307, 320, 321.
              We find Sir Boniface, the "pedanticall" schoolmaster,
          resorting to short, macaronic couplets, in the Skeltonic
          manner, as in his entrance, Act II, Sc. 1 (C4^V), and
          triplets in the Skeltonic vein, as in Act III, Sc. i
          (D3^V), "Curro, Curris, Cucurris: / My cheeks are all
          Murry, / And I am gone in a hurry." The language of
          Spenser, "a conceited gentleman" is also in comic Skel-
          tonic rhyme, as in his comic dispute with Sir Boniface
          in Act IV, Sc. i, (F2 and F2^V): "<u>vos estis, vt, egosum</u>
          <u>testis</u>, / that what he confest is / as true as the
          pestis."

1639   <u>A BANQUET OF JESTS OR CHANGE OF CHEARE</u>. <u>STC</u> 1372 (1639),
          sig. A5^V.
              This is actually the "fifth impression" of BANQUET
          (1630), <u>STC</u> 1370, reprinted as Archie Armstrong, <u>A Ban-</u>
          <u>quet of Jests and Merry Tales</u> (1889). "Skelton's <u>meere</u>
          rime" is mentioned, in "The Printer to the Reader," 1. 6,
          as "once read, but now laid by," an item lacking in first
          edition of 1630.

1640   JONSON, BEN. <u>A Tale of the Tub</u>.
        The play was originally written 1596 or 1597, and in
        1633 issued with satire on Inigo Jones; then printed in
        1640.
        As edited by Herford and Simpson, III, p. 85, in Act
        V, vii, 23-25, Skelton is mentioned in an argument be-
        tween Squire Tub and In-and-in Medlay over the true au-
        thorship of the Tale. To Medlay's claim that he was the
        author, the Squire retorts: "The Workeman Sir! the Arti-
        ficer! I grant you. / So <u>Skelton</u>-Laureat; was of <u>Elinour
        Rumming</u>: / But she the subject of the Rout, and Tunning."

1640.1 JONSON, BEN. "To Master John Burges," in <u>The Underwood</u>.
        Edited among Jonson's other poetry by Herford and Simp-
        son, VIII, pp. 231-232.
        The poem consists of 28 lines of short, irregularly
        cadenced couplets in the Skeltonic manner: "Father <u>John
        Burges</u>, / Necessitie urges / My wofull crie, / To Sir
        <u>Robert Pie</u>: / And that he will venter / To send my De-
        bentur," &c.

1640.2 ROUS, JOHN. <u>The Diary of John Rous</u>. Edited by Mary Anne
        Everett Green, Camden Society, LXVI (1856) [diary begun
        in 1625, ended in 1642], pp. 118-119.
        Resorts to 6 lines of Skeltonics on "The strange al-
        teration begun in this nation."

1641   JONSON, BEN. <u>The Divell is an Asse</u>, V, vi, 25-26.
        As edited by Herford and Simpson, VI, p. 260, we find
        two lines, reminiscent of <u>TER</u>, in the mouth of Iniquity
        the Vice: "And in the meane time, to be greazy, and
        bouzy. / And nasty, and filthy, and ragged, and louzy,"
        as first noticed in no. 1953.4 below.

1651   CARTWRIGHT, WILLIAM. "Lesbia On her Sparrow" in <u>Comedies,
        Tragi-Comedies, with Other Poems</u>. Wing C709 (1651),
        pp. 225-226.
        As edited by G. Blakemore Evans in <u>The Plays and Poems
        of William Cartwright</u> (Madison, Wisconsin, 1951), p. 477,
        this poem, of 32 lines, combines the Catullan and Skel-
        tonic traditions, showing obvious echoes of <u>PS</u> (vv. 122,
        136, and 140) in lines 9, 14, and 11 respectively.

1655   HOWELL, JAMES. <u>Epistolae Ho-Elianae</u>. Wing H 3073 [3rd
        edn.] (1655), Bk. IV, no. xxvii.
        Howell refers to a copy of the 1568 <u>PPPW</u> which he
        found "pitifully totter'd [sic] and torn," "skulking in
        Duck Lane" [modern Duke St., West Smithfield], "not
        worth the labor and cost to put...in better clothes, for
        the Genius of the Age is quite another thing..."; closes
        with Skelton's "salutation," "Salve plus decies," found
        in <u>PPPW</u>.

1656   [HOLLAND, SAMUEL.] <u>Don Zara del Fogo</u>. Wing H 2437 (1656),
        reissued in same year as <u>Wit and Fancy in a Maze</u>, Wing
        H 2445.
            The hero, Don Zara, led by the sorceress Lancia to
        Elysium, finds the poets in contention for the laurel.
        Among the supporters of Chaucer, contesting for pre-
        eminence among the English poets with Spenser, Shake-
        speare, and Fletcher, he finds Skelton, Gower, and
        Lydgate. A marginal note explains that Skelton was
        "Poet Laureat" to Henry IV [<u>sic</u>] and "wrote disguises
        for the young Princes."

1660   [HOLLAND, SAMUEL.] <u>Romancio-Mastix, or A Romance of</u>
        <u>Romances</u>. Wing H 2443 (1660).
            A reissue of no. 1656 above; the romance was also re-
        printed in 1719 as <u>The Spaniard: or Don Zara del Fogo</u>.

1660.1 "The Old Gill."
            This parody of <u>TER</u>, beginning "If you will be still, /
        Then tell you I will / Of a lonely Old Gill / Dwelt under
        a Hill," first appeared in <u>J. Cleaveland Revised</u>, printed
        by Nathanial Brooks, 1660 (Cleveland having died in
        1658). It is rejected as spurious, however, by Brian
        Morris and Eleanor Withington (eds.), <u>The Poems of John</u>
        <u>Cleveland</u> (Oxford, 1967), p. xxxiii; it may be conveni-
        ently found in <u>The Works of Mr. John Cleveland</u>, Wing 4654
        (1687), pp. 306-307.

1660.2 <u>PANTAGRUEL'S PROGNOSTICATION</u>, Wing R 106 [where dated (<u>c</u>.
        1645), but <u>see</u> argument for <u>c</u>. 1660 advanced by F. P.
        Wilson, editor of the reprint for the Luttrell Society,
        no. 3 (1947)].
            A translation of Rabelaisian prognostications, it is
        dedicated to Lilly the Astrologer; Skelton is introduced
        in the Dedication as "Poet Laureat" and a "Merry Madcap,"
        who can "run a poor rhyme out of breath until it pant and
        expire, or hurling it on with such a strong gale, til it
        touch upon the coast of nonsense" yet has "some lucid
        intervalls of shrewd and poinant expressions."

1662   FULLER, THOMAS. <u>The History of the Worthies of England</u>
        [three volumes in one]. Wing F 2440 (1662).
            Fuller lists Skelton, very briefly under Cumberland
        (i, 221) as "a younger branch of the <u>Skeltons</u> of <u>Skelton</u>,"
        Cumberland, but cross-references to Norfolk (II, 257-258);
        he places Skelton in Norfolk on the double probability
        that a) the name had been "long fixed" there and b) Skel-
        ton had been beneficed at Diss in Norfolk. Fuller's com-
        mentary is more important for its judicious and elegant
        distillation of Bale than for its freshness or original-
        ity of documentation. He opines that Skelton had

"scholarship enough and wit too much," and fears that
his satiric wit unhappily fell on three "Noli me tan-
gere's: the rod of a Schoolmaster [William Lily], the
Couls of Friars [the Dominicans], and the Cap of a
Cardinal [Wolsey]. The first gave him a lash, the second deprived him of his livelyhood, the third almost
ousted him of his life." He cites Lily's epigram against
Skelton and nicely translates it.

1662.1   GRIM THE COLLIER OF CROYDEN: OR THE DEVIL AND HIS DAME.
          Wing G 1580. Printed in Gratiae Theatrales (1662) and
          reprinted in Tudor Facsimile Texts (? 1912).
              Resorts to scattered Skeltonics as in Act IV, 11.
          94ff.

1675   PHILLIPS, EDWARD. Theatrum Poetarum, or A Compleat Collec-
          tion of Poets. Wing P 2075 (1675), pp. 115-116.
              Phillips calls Skelton a "jolly English Rimer,"
          placing him in Edward IV's reign, now laid aside for his
          "miserable loos [sic] rambling style, and galloping
          measure of Verse"; he lists the following works, collec-
          ted out of "an old printed Book, but imperfect" (appar-
          ently, save for PS, a copy of CB): PS, SP, "Edw. IV,"
          "Ag Scottes," WH, "The Tunning of Eleanor Rumpkin."

1686   BUNYAN, JOHN. A Book for Boys and Girls: or Country
          Rhimes for Children. Wing B 5489 (1686).
              Poem II, "The Awakened Childs Lamentation," on pp. 2-7
          is in monorhyming quatrains with 2 or 3 stresses / line;
          Poem LXI, "Of Man by Nature," on p. 67 is written as 8
          lines of mono-rhyme with 2 or 3 stresses / line, both in
          a Skeltonical manner.

1687   WINSTANLEY, WILLIAM. The Lives of the Most Famous English
          Poets. Wing W3058 (1687), pp. 42-43.
              Winstanley bases his remarks on PHILLIPS, no. 1675
          above, including the comment on style quoted and the
          slightly varied spelling of "Elianer Rumpkin" in an iden-
          tical list of works cited. Available in the facsimile
          edition of Winstanley's Lives, edited by W. R. Parker in
          Scholars' Facsimiles and Reprints (Gainesville, Florida,
          1963), pp. 42-43.

1691   WOOD, ANTHONY À. Athenae Oxonienses. Wing W 3382 (1691);
          I, pp. 20-21.
              Wood condenses the biographical remarks of Bale (no.
          1559) and Pits (no. 1619) but notices in addition other
          Skeltons of early Tudor times, believing the poet to be
          descended from the Skeltons of Cumberland but distinguish-
          ing him from John Skelton, Vicar of Dultyng (1512) and
          Rector of Westquamtoked (1525). Although Englishing and

modernizing the titles of the items he cites, he bases
his list upon Bale and Pits, whose items he criticizes
as "slightly and unsatisfactorily set down," even though
he includes Good Order on Bale's word. In his own turn
he presents a selected bibliography, less than half the
length of Bale's and Pits', making no effort to list each
poem, but citing sixteenth or seventeenth century editions of the poet's works, e.g., "Elynour Rumpkin" from
no. 1624 above, Epitaphs from no. 1600 above, and noticing Weever, no. 1631 apparently, without mentioning
his name. In addition, he lists from Skelton's Garlande
of Laurell, 1. 1178, "Verses on the Creation of Arthur
Prince of Wales," a lost poem, and conjures out of thin
air, it would seem, a volume Poetical Fancies and Satyrs
of 1512.

    The second edition of Athenae Oxoniensis, 1721, makes
no changes; but see BLISS (ed.), Wood &c., no. 1813 below, for the third edition considerably revised.

1693   MS copy of "The Tunnyng of Elynour Rummyng--per Skelton
        Laureat to Henry VIII." In B.L. MS. Addit. 28504, fols.
        11 (c. 1693).
        This is a manuscript reproduction of the poem made by
        a William Daniel, probably taken from the sixteenth cen-
        tury printed text of TER, in one of the editions of
        Certayne Bokes, nos. 1545, 1554 and 1560.4 above.

1693.1   RYMER, THOMAS. A Short View of Tragedy. Wing 2429 (1693),
        p. 84.
        To give a notion of the secularization of religious
        drama "in the beginning of H. VIII. Reign," Rymer cites
        "the Laureat on Cardinal Woolsey: 'Like Mahound in a
        Play, / No man dare him with say.'" from WCY, 11. 594-
        595.

1716   [DAVIES, MILES.] Athenae Britannicae, sive Icon Libellorum
        or, A Critical History of Pamphlets. London and West-
        minster, 1716, pp. (28)-(30).
        Davies calls Skelton "One of the most notorious of
        all...Pamphlet-writers, both in Prose and Verse"; he
        draws on Bale, Pits, and Anthony à Wood (for Poetical
        Fancies and Satyres); he had apparently examined a copy
        of the 1624 edition of TER, for he describes her "por-
        trait" on the title page and cites the couplet printed
        beneath it.

1718   THE TUNNING OF ELINOR RUMMING. London: Printed for Isaac
        Dalton, and Sold by W. Bonham, 1718, sigs. [A]-E^4, pp.
        [12], 31.
        Contents: "To the Reader," a genial defense in prose
        of Skelton's tavern scenes, written for persons of "an
        extensive Fancy and just relish," and the poem proper.

1719   SWIFT, JONATHAN. "From Dr. Swift to Dr. Sheridan," in
            Swift, Poetical Works. Edited by Herbert Davis. Oxford,
            1967, pp. 177-178.
                 The three postscripts to Swift's letter of 14 December
            1719 are written in Skeltonic doggerel: [P.S. 1]: "I
            wish when you prated / Your Letter you'd dated / Much
            Plague it created, / I scolded and rated; / My soul it
            much grated, / For your Man, I long waited." &c., for a
            total of 15 lines; the other two postscripts are in
            short, irregularly cadenced couplets.

1720   J[ACOB], G[ILES]. An Historical Account of the Lives and
            Writings of Our Most Considerable English Poets....
            London, 1720, pp. 190-192.
                 A somewhat fanciful rewriting of Bale and Fuller in
            which Skelton is born in Dis, and during "his Restraint"
            at Westminster, adorns the monuments of "several great
            personages," Sigebert the Saxon and Chaucer among them!
            Lists as Skelton's chief works an elegy to Henry IV [a
            mistake for Edw. IV], SP, WH, and TER, "lately reprinted"
            (see no. 1718 above).

1736   DU RESNEL [DU BELLAY], ABBÉ [JEAN FRANCOIS]. Recherches sur
            les Poëtes Couronnez, in Mémoires de l'Académie des In-
            scriptions Mem. de Litt. 1736, X, p. 522.
                 The Abbé mentions letters patent now lost recognizing
            Skelton as poet laureate to Henry VIII; see no. 1512
            above.

1736.1   SKELTON, JOHN. PITHY PLESAUNT AND PROFITABLE WORKES OF
            MAISTER SKELTON, POET LAUREATE TO KING HENRY THE VIIITH.
            For C. Davis, London, 1736, pp. xiv, 294 [a reprint of
            PPPW, no. 1568 above].
                 Contents: The Editor's "Preface" intervenes between
            "Salve" and Churchyard's Commendary verses of 1568;
            otherwise the arrangement of the contents is precisely
            the same as in PPPW.
                 Notes: 1) A copy of this edition, with the autograph
            signature of Thomas Warton, critic and literary histori-
            an, is in the holdings of the Huntington Library, dated
            1753; see WARTON, no. 1778. 2) A copy of this edition
            much later prompted Southern's appreciative essay in the
            Retrospective Review, no. 1822.1 below. See also
            CHALMERS, no. 1810 below, for the next reprint of PPPW.

1737   [COOPER, ELIZABETH.] Editor of The Muses' Library or a
            Series of English Poetry from the Saxons, to the Reign
            of King Charles II. London, 1737, pp. 48-55.
                 "She" prints the "Prolog" to BC (18 stanzas). Con-
            trast "her" introductory remarks on Skelton with those
            of POPE, just below; "she" hails Skelton as "The

Restorer of Invention in English Poetry" and praises his
"Very rich Vein of Wits, Humor and Poetry, tho' much debased by the Rust of the Age he liv'd in." (The "her"
and "she" are placed in quotation marks because it seems
likely that William Oldys was the real editor, according
to D. N. Smith, Proc. Brit. Acad., XV (1929), p. 83.)

1737.1   POPE, ALEXANDER. The First Epistle of the Second Book of
          Horace Imitated (1737). As edited by John Butt, in
          Alexander Pope, Imitations of Horace with an Epistle to
          Dr. Arbuthnot and the Epilogue to the Satires, The
          Twickenham Edition of the Poems of Alexander Pope. Lon-
          don, 1939, IV, p. 197.
              In ll. 37-38, Pope charges that "Chaucer's worst
          ribaldry is learned by rote, / And beastly Skelton heads
          of houses quote." In his note to l. 38, Pope sets Skel-
          ton down as "Poet Laureate to Hen. 8, a Volume of whose
          Verses has been lately reprinted [see no. 1736 above],
          consisting almost wholly of Ribaldry, Obscenity and
          Scurrilous language" ["Billingsgate" substituted for
          "Ribaldry" in 2nd edn. of 1737]. Joseph Spence records
          in his Anecdotes, edited by S. W. Singer (1820), p. 87,
          that Pope believed that "Skelton's poems are all low and
          bad; there's nothing in them that's worth reading."

1739   BLOMEFIELD, FRANCIS. An Essay Towards a Topographical His-
          tory of the County of Norfolk. Fersfield, 1739, 2 vols.
          [vol. 3 continued by Charles Parkin (Lynn, 1769); vols.
          4 & 5 also written by Parkin (Lynn, 1775)].
              I draw upon the second edition, in 11 vols. (London,
          1805-10), I, p. 20. Blomefield draws on Bale, Weever,
          Fuller, à Wood, but unearths several new documents:
          e.g., a will proved 6 March 1504, for the funeral of
          Margery Cowper, the first witnessed in Diss by Skelton.
          Blomefield claims that among the "Evidences" of Mr.
          Thomas Coggeshall is evidence that the Rector's "mansion
          house" was in the tenure of "Master Skelton, Laureate"
          in 1504; further, he discovers a document showing that
          Thomas Clark was instituted rector of Diss 17 July 1529,
          following Skelton's death.

1744   ELYNOUR RVMMIN, THE FAMOUS ALE-WIFE OF ENGLAND. Reprinted
          in The Harleian Miscellany. London, 1744, I, pp. 402-
          410.
              The reprint is taken from Samuel Rand's edition of
          1624, no. 1624 above. See also no. 1808 below for the
          augmented reprint of the Miscellany where TER appears in
          I, pp. 415-422.

1748   TANNER, THOMAS (Bishop). Bibliotheca Britannico-Hibernica.
          London, 1748, pp. 675-676.

Tanner believes that Skelton is of a Cumberland
family; he notes the ordination records of 1498 and continues the legend that because of his marriage as priest,
quarrels with Dominicans and satires on Wolsey, Skelton
was forced into Westminster sanctuary where "humaniter a
Johanne Islip abbate exceptus"; cites Erasmus' praise,
no. 1499.1 above, and that of Caxton, no. 1490 above;
bases his comments and lists upon Bale, no. 1559, Pits,
no. 1619 and Wood, no. 1691; lists Wood's dubious Poemata
et Satyras, allegedly of 1512; locates MS. version of
"DEN" as Royal Library MS. 18. D. ii. 5; locates Methodos
[Spec Princ] in library of Lincoln Cathedral; prints 2
lines of dedicatory poem "I, liber" [?1512] and 2 lines
(plus) of dedicatory poem "Quamvis annosa est" both
prefaced Skelton's gift of De bellis contra Saracenos,
identifying the manuscript as a CCC Cambridge MS; more
precisely identifies Skelton's translation of DS as CCC
Cambridge MS viii. 5; falsely attributes to Skelton the
"Epitaph of Jaspar Duke of Bedford" and assigns to him
a volume not yet recovered, "Miseries of England under
Henry VII."

1749   AMES, JOSEPH. Typographical Antiquities.... London,
           1749, passim.
              Ames lists Rep without titlepage on pp. 128-129; Mag.,
           on p. 148; CB (Day), on p. 244; "general pieces compiled
           by master Skelton poet laureat," CC, PS, "&c" and PPPW,
           p. 300; mentions copies of WCY and CC bound together
           (Kytson), p. 304; also notes Merie Tales, p. 378, and A
           Skeltonical Salutation, on p. 453. See HERBERT, no.
           1790 below, for augmentation of AMES and the Skelton
           entries.

1752   "Elegia in serenissimae principis et dominae, Dominae
           Margaretae" [16 August, 1516]. In George Ballard,
           Memoirs of Several Ladies of Great Britain who have been
           Celebrated for Their Writings or Learning. Oxford: for
           the author, by W. Jackson, 1752, pp. 24-27.
              Reprinted with translation in heroic couplets.

1753   [SHIELS, ROBERT.] The Lives of the Poets of Great Britain
           and Ireland to the Time of Dean Swift...by Mr. Cibber.
           London, 1753, I, pp. 27-30.
              Although only the name of [Theophilus] Cibber (1703-
           58) appears on the t.p., this work was chiefly by Robert
           Shiels (d. 1753). Relying on Fuller, no. 1662, and
           Phillips, no. 1675, for biographical facts, Shiels adds
           a critical section on Skelton's verse ("cramped by a
           very short measure, and encumbered with...a profusion of
           rhimes"). He quotes the first two stanzas of BC and
           praises that poem as "of some merit," abounding with

"wit and imagination" and showing the poet to be well versed in human nature "and the insinuating manners of a court."

1755   JOHNSON, SAMUEL. "History of the English Language," in A Dictionary of the English Language. London, 1755, p. 9, col. 2.
        Although claiming that "[Skelton] cannot be said to have attained great elegance of language," Johnson nevertheless inserts the first 5 stanzas of BC as a sample, having incidentally devoted 7-1/2 pp. to a "larger specimen" of Sir Thomas More's writings.

1762   SHENSTONE, WILLIAM. Postscript to letter to William Percy (3 February 1762), in The Letters of William Shenstone. Edited by Marjorie Williams. Oxford: Basil Blackwell, 1939, pp. 618-619.
        Shenstone reports making boxes to hold books, to be lettered wittily or humorously, to replace the lack of wit or humor of the books within; one sort of a title he would draw from "Quaint & Antiquated" works, as afforded by "Skelton &c of old time," possibly an allusion to PPPW, no. 1736.1 or no. 1568?.

1765   PERCY, THOMAS (Bishop). "An Elegy on Henry, Fourth Earl of Northumberland," in Reliques of Ancient English Poetry. London, 1765, I, pp. 107-116.
        Percy reprints Skelton's "DEN" from PPPW, 1568. See also PERCY, no. 1794 below.

1776   [ANSTEY, CHRISTOPHER.] The New Bath Guide or, Memoirs of the B-R-D Family. London, 1776, pp. 38 and 99.
        Anstey makes use of Skeltonics as in Letter V, p. 38 and Letter XIII, p. 99.

1776.1 SKELTON, JOHN. "Manerly Margery." Skelton's poem, first printed by John Hawkins, in his History of Music. London, 1776, III, p. 2. Printed from B.L. MS. Addit. 5465 [c. 1504], fols. 96ᵛ-99.
        See also STEVENS, no. 1961.5 below.

1777   NASMITH, JAMES. Catalogus Librorum Manuscriptorum. Cambridge, 1777, p. 400.
        Nasmith prints 10 lines of Skelton's "I, liber," no. 1512.1 above.

1778   WARTON, THOMAS. The History of English Poetry. London, 1778, II, pp. 336-363.
        Warton presents a pungent and generally unsympathetic account of the range of Skelton's poetic writing. "If his whimsical extravagancies ever move our laughter, at

the same time they shock our sensibility. His festive
levities are not only vulgar and indelicate, but fre-
quently want truth and propriety. His subjects are
often as ridiculous as his metre: but he sometimes debases his matter by his versification.... It is supposed
by Caxton that he improved our language; but he sometimes
affects obscurity, and sometimes adopts the most familiar
phraseology of the common people" (II, 342). He does
find merit in BC, and praises Skelton's Latin elegiacs
as "pure, and often unmixed with monastic phraseology."
He discusses at length the moral interlude Nigramansir
which, he claims, the poet William Collins had shown him
a short time before his death in 1759, a play not since
recovered and whose very existence was questioned by
Ritson in his Observations of 1782 (below), and his
Bibliographia Poetica of 1802.

1782   RITSON, JOSEPH. Observations on the Three First Volumes of
        the History of English Poetry. In a Familiar Letter to
        the Author. London, 1782.
            "If the existence of this unheard of Morality [The
        Nigramansir] rest entirely upon the dictum of the author
        of the History of English Poetry, I had rather, if you
        please, withhold my belief till its production" (p. 26).

1789   [NEVE, PHILIP.] Cursory Remarks on Some of the Ancient
        English Poets.... Privately Printed, 1789, pp. 10-12.
            "...[Skelton] seems...remarkable, as he had suffi-
        cient confidence to satirize Wolsey, in the plenitude
        of his power."

1790   HERBERT, WILLIAM. Editor of augmented edition of Joseph
        AMES's Typographical Antiquities [no. 1749]. London,
        1785-90, 3 vols.
            Herbert adds reference to Nigramansir (see Warton, no.
        1778 above), I, 141; notes Wynkyn de Worde's [2nd] edition
        of BC, I, p. 227; notes [1st] edition of CC by T. Godfray,
        in "the possession of the Duke of Bedford," I, p. 325;
        wrongly records that GL was in possession of G. Steevens;
        notes editions of WCY (Toy) and CB (Marshe) not located
        by AMES. See DIBDIN, no. 1819 below, for further aug-
        mentation of Ames and Skelton entries.

1794   PERCY, THOMAS (Bishop). "An Elegy on Henry, Fourth Earl
        of Northumberland," in Reliques of Ancient English
        Poetry. Fourth edition. London, 1794, I, pp. 96-105.
            This time Percy prints Skelton's poem from the ms.
        version found in the B.L. MS Royal 18. D. II. See
        PERCY, no. 1765 above.

1794.1   "Portrait" of Elinour Rumming. Published by Richardson the
printseller of Castle Street, Leicester Square, London,
from the 1624 reprint of Elynovr Rvmmin.
     The "portrait" is commented on, by the book-collector
and antiquarian George Steevens, under the misleading
initials "G. R." in the European Magazine, XXV (May
1794), 334; his 16 lines of couplet are entitled
"Eleonora Rediviva" and begin "To seek this nymph among
the glorious dead"; they are reprinted by Dyce, II, pp.
153-154, no. 1843.1 below.

1797   "Portrait" of Skelton [Type 1]. Reproduced in Reverend
Daniel Lyson's Historical Account of the Environs of
London. Illustrated by Walter Wilson. London, c. 1797,
II, no. 192a.
     An engraving, half-length, of a young man, moustached
and bearded, looking to the left; but false, temp. Edward VI, from "an original picture in the possession of
a Mr. Richardson"; separately published 1 November 1797
by W. Richardson, New York House, 31 Strand; reprinted
by Alexander Chalmers, The General Bibliographical Dictionary, XXVIII (1816), facing p. 43, and by Thomas
Dibdin, Bibliomania (edn. of 1842), III, facing p. 386.
See O'DONOGHUE, no. 1914.4 below, for three "types" of
Skelton "portraits," none genuine.

1802   RITSON, JOSEPH. Bibliographia Poetica, A Catalogue of
Engleish [sic] Poets.... London, 1802, pp. 102-106.
     Ritson makes Skelton a "chaplain" to Henry VIII;
lists GL, BC (1 edition only), CC (notes Godfray's print
of it, among others), PS, SP (and notes ms. copy of SP
in Harley mss.), "Edw. IV," "Ag Scottes," WH, TER (all
from CB, as separately printed for Day, Kynge and Marche),
PPPW 1568 and reprint of 1736; gives title page of Rep
but states "no copy is known to be now extant"; doubts
that The Nigramansir described by Warton (II, 360), no.
1778 above, "ever existed."

1804   WORDSWORTH, WILLIAM. "With Ships the sea was sprinkled far
and nigh," in The Poetical Works of William Wordsworth.
Edited by E. de Selincourt and Helen Darbishire. Oxford,
1946, III, p. 18.
     A "Miscellaneous Sonnet," no. XXXII, it was found in
MS. M, transcribed before March 1804; to this sonnet
Wordsworth appended a note in 1807, about lines 5-8 as
taken from "a passage in Skelton which I cannot here insert, not having the Book at hand [BC, 36-39]." On May
21, 1807, in a letter to Lady Beaumont, Wordsworth wrote
an explication of the sonnet. See also WORDSWORTH, nos.
1833, 1833.1, 1843.2 and 1844.1 below, for additional
indications of his interest in Skelton.

1808 ELYNOUR RVMMIN, THE FAMOUS ALE-WIFE OF ENGLAND, reprinted
from S. Rand's edition of 1624, as found in The Harleian
Miscellany, no. 1744 above, in this the second and augmented edition of the Miscellany, I, pp. 415-422.

1810 CHALMERS, ALEXANDER (ed.). The Poems of John Skelton, in
The Works of the English Poets from Chaucer to Cowper.
London, 1810, II, pp. 227-310.
  Contents: "Salve"; Author's Life by Mr. Chalmers
[no new material]; Editor's preface from 1736 edition
(no. 1736 above); contents of 1736 edition reproduced in
precise order.
  Review by SOUTHEY, Robert, Quarterly Review, XI
(1814), 480-504, no. 1814 below.

1810.1 SOME ACCOUNT OF THE LIFE OF JOHN SKELTON [abridged from
Anthony à Wood's Athenae Oxonienses], B.L. 10855.aa.16
[6 copies only].

1813 BLISS, PHILIP (ed.). Anthony à Wood, Athenae Oxonienses...
a New Edition, with Additions, and a Continuation by
Philip Bliss. London, 1813, I, pp. 49-54.
  Bliss footnotes some of Wood's comments, no. 1691,
drawing on Warton's History of English Poetry, no. 1778,
Thomas Delafield's MS collections of Poets Laureate,
Gough's MSS in the Bodleian, and the Harleian Miscellany,
no. 1808 above; correctly identifies item no. 12 of Wood's
1691 list as WCY and cites undated sixteenth century edi-
tions of it; corrects Wood's 1691 entry no. 15, citing
Bale's mention of Veale's earliest printing (in Bale's
Actes, 1551); mentions Godfray's edition of CC and
Wyghte's printing of the poem; adds Nigramansir (from
Warton, no. 1778) CB, GL, Mag, REP. PS, SP; "Wofully
arayd" and "MM" (both from Hawkins, no. 1776.1) and "Ag
Garn" (B.L. MS. Harley 367) to Wood's 1691 lists of
printed editions and ms. material; adds the unknown
"Miseries of England under Henry 7th, 4°," "only known
from Tanner"; notices as Skelton's the non-canonical
"Epitaph of Jaspar, Duke of Bedford," "Image of Ypocres-
ye," and "Vox populi."

1814 BRYDGES, SIR SAMUEL EGERTON, and JOSEPH HASLEWOOD (eds.).
The British Bibliographer. London, 1814, IV, pp. 388-
390.
  The work provides a tracing of the "portraiɩ" of
Skelton (3), made by G. Steevens and found in GL, 1523
edition, together with title-page and colophon of GL; see
O'DONOGHUE, no. 1914.4 below.

1814.1 [SOUTHEY, ROBERT.] Review of "Chalmers' English Poets"
[1810], Quarterly Review, XI (1814), 484-485.

An influential review, prompting Alexander Dyce to
commence work on his edition of The Complete Poetical
Works, no. 1843; Southey criticizes Chalmers for failure
to "venture upon any emendation of a grossly corrupted
text," for failure to punctuate, to correct and also extend the canon in light of late eighteenth century and
early nineteenth century bibliographic scholarship, and
to provide a glossary; censures Chalmers for confused
critical opinions, "a tissue of inconsistencies"; calls
for a new edition "good, and complete" so as to display
the power, strangeness and volubility of Skelton's
language, that of "one of the most extraordinary writers
of any age or country." See also SOUTHEY, nos. 1820 and
1831.1.

1816   CHALMERS, ALEXANDER (ed.). The General Biographical Dic-
          tionary. London, 1812-17, XXVIII, pp. 43-48.
             Chalmers claims that Skelton came from Cumberland;
          discusses the laureateship as "a graduated rhetorician";
          draws on a transcription from Bp. Kennet's MSS. for
          Skelton's 1498 ordination; draws on Fuller for Skelton's
          three "foes" (Friars, Lily, Wolsey) in the treatment of
          whom the poet was "coarse enough in style, and perhaps
          illiberal in sentiment"; repeats Bale's story of Skel-
          ton's death-bed defense of his concubine and the legend
          that the poet was forced into sanctuary by Wolsey; men-
          tions "DEN" as having been "magnificently engrossed on
          vellum" and is aware that it lies in the British Museum.
          While not absolving Skelton of "indelicacies," he notes
          that they are no longer seductive since they are obscured
          by cant words and phrases not now intelligible. See also
          GORTON, no. 1851.

1816.1   GIFFORD, WILLIAM (ed.). The Works of Ben Jonson. London:
          Nicol, 1816, VIII, p. 77.
             Commenting on a passage in The Fortunate Isles and
          Their Vnion [1624], no. 1624.1 above, which is based on
          Skelton's TER, 80-84, Gifford digresses to defend Skelton
          from Warton and his school. Knowing Skelton only through
          the 1736 reprint of PPPW, a "stupid publication," he none-
          theless praises Skelton's "strong powers of description"
          and his "vein of poetry that shines through all the rub-
          bish that ignorance has spread over it." Notes that Skel-
          ton "flew at high game and therefore occasionally called
          in the aid of vulgar ribaldry to mask the direct attack
          of his satire." Declaims against the "process" that has
          set in against Skelton for "rudeness and indelicacy" and
          quotes from John Grange's Golden Aphroditis, no. 1577,
          in the poet's defense.

1819   DIBDIN, THOMAS FROGNALL. Editor of the third edition of
          AMES-HERBERT's TYPOGRAPHICAL ANTIQUITIES, nos. 1749 and
          1790 above. London, 1819, 3 vols.
               Corrects Ames-Herbert through Ritson (no. 1802) re
          statement that GL in Steevens' possession, correctly
          noting that it was purchased at the sale of Major Pear-
          son's library by John Brand, "who since sold it to the
          King's library" in III, p. 358; describes Rep fully from
          Heber's collection and prints excerpts from it, describ-
          ing the Skeltonic as "bastard Hudibrastic verses" in II,
          pp. 539-542.

1819.1   SANFORD, EZEKIAL, and ROBERT WELCH, JR. "Select Poems of
          John Skelton, with a Life of the Author," in The Works
          of the British Poets. Philadelphia, 1819, I, pp. [257]-
          282.
               Contents: "Prayer to Trinity" [doubtful], TER (11.
          1-159 only), PS (11. 1-186, 970-1209, omitting refrains
          in latter section); selections probably based on Chalmers
          text, no. 1810, for a note to TER is initialed "C."

1820   SOUTHEY, ROBERT. "The Cataract of Lodore, Described in
          Rhymes for the Nursery," in The Poetical Works of Robert
          Southey (Collected by himself). London, 1838, II,
          "Juvenile and Minor Poems," pp. 73-77.
               Written c. 1820, despite cross-rhymes, particularly
          noticeable in the first quarter of the poem, "Cataract"
          seems clearly to have been written under the conscious
          influence of Skelton's short lines, with feminine rhymes,
          shifting 2 or 3 beats, alliteration, and rhyme leash:
          e.g., "The Cataract strong, / Then plunges along, /
          Striking and raging / As if a war waging / Its caverns
          and rocks among / Rising and leaping, / Sinking and
          creeping, / Swelling and sweeping, / Showering and spring-
          ing &c." See also SOUTHEY, nos. 1814.1 and 1831.1.

1821   "Portrait of Skelton" [Type 2].
               An engraving of an academician, seated in a pew, the
          reproduction of the woodcut [Hodnett 229] on the title
          pages of ACC and DBDS, nos. 1527 and 1527.1 above; pub-
          lished by T. & H. Rodd, 17 Little Newport St., Leicester
          Square; reprinted by Sir Harris Nichols (ed.), "The Com-
          plete Angler" by Izaak Walton and Charles Cotton's "In-
          structions" (1831), 5th plate following p. 218. See
          O'DONOGHUE, no. 1914.4.

1821.1   SKELTON, JOHN. Magnyfycence. A reprint (1821) for Roxburghe
          Society of the first edition of the play, no. 1530.3; text
          taken from the imperfect B.L. copy; title-page and second
          leaf from Cambridge copy; pp. [8], fols. xxv [with some
          typographical errors]; 50 copies printed.

1822   SCOTT, SIR WALTER. <u>The Fortunes of Nigil</u>. Edinburgh,
            1822, I, p. 111.
                The introduction to chapter V, in which the author
            "Skeltonizeth" in 10 lines, is a brief imitation alluding
            to <u>WCY</u>, and begins, "Wherefore come ye not to courte?"

1822.1   SOUTHERN, H. "John Skelton's Poetical Works," <u>Retrospective
            Review</u>, VI (1822), 337-353.
                The review stems from an interest in "authors of ages
            gone by" and draws on the 1736 edition of <u>PPPW</u>; calls
            Skelton "a curious, able and remarkable writer"; notes
            that <u>TER</u> is "in Skelton's peculiar style--a style which
            is now generally described as <u>Skeltonizing...</u>," and
            quotes extensively from <u>WCY</u> where he finds "most inter-
            esting matter." Presents fresh evaluation of the poet,
            praising his command of the language but noting that his
            rhymes are often "spun out beyond the sense in the wan-
            tonness of power."

1822.2   STRYPE, JOHN. <u>Ecclesiastical Memorials</u>. 1822, I, ii,
            p. 59.
                Strype prints the record of Skelton's presence at the
            abjuration of Thomas Bowgas, May 4, 1528; <u>see</u> no. 1528
            above.

1824   WATT, ROBERT. <u>Bibliotheca Britannica</u>. Edinburgh, 1824,
            II, p. 859.
                Lists in an incomplete and uncertain manner certain of
            Skelton's published works but devotes one-half of its
            space to the <u>Merie Tales</u>, no. 1567 above.

1827   COLERIDGE, SAMUEL TAYLOR. "Notes on the History Plays,"
            in <u>Coleridge's Shakespearean Criticism</u>. Edited by
            Thomas M. Raysor. Oxford, 1930, I, p. 141.
                Coleridge commenting <u>c</u>. 1827 on Warburton's altera-
            tion of "Philip! sparrow" to "Philip, spare me" (<u>King
            John</u> I, i, 230-231), wishes that Warburton had read "old
            Skelton's 'Philip Sparrow,' an exquisite and original
            poem...." Raysor, in vol. II, cites Coleridge's "Table-
            Talk," March 12, 1827: "Pray look at Skelton's Richard
            [<u>sic</u>] Sparrow also."

1831   "Portrait of Skelton" [Type 3].
                The cut represents a young man standing, full length,
            holding a laurel branch, and is actually a tracing of
            the woodcut [Hodnett 2058] on the verso of title page
            to <u>GL</u>, no. 1523.3 above; reproduced in Sir Harris
            Nichols (ed.), <u>"The Complete Angler" by Izaak Walton and
            Charles Cotton's "Instructions"</u> (1831), as the sixth
            plate following p. 218; it is further reproduced in <u>An
            Elizabethan Garland</u>, privately assembled for E. D. Church,

n.d., at the Huntington Library. See O'DONOGHUE, no.
1914.4, for discussion of "portrait" types.

1831.1   SOUTHEY, ROBERT. "John Skelton," in Select Works of the
British Poets, from Chaucer to Jonson, with Biographical
Sketches. London, 1831, pp. 61-75.
  Contents: CC; PS, printed in 3 columns to the page,
70 lines/column.
  In his introductory commentary, Southey shows the
first real "modern" awareness of the difficulties in
Skelton's text and calls for a completely new edition of
his works, strengthening remarks made in his review of
Chalmers (1810), 1814.1 above.

1833   WORDSWORTH, WILLIAM. [Letter to Alexander Dyce, 7 January
1833], in The Letters of William and Dorothy Wordsworth.
Edited by Ernest de Selincourt. Oxford, 1939, II,
p. 678, no. 1036.
  Wordsworth commends Dyce for having "made such progress with Skelton, a Writer deserving of far greater
attention than his works have hitherto received."

1833.1   WORDSWORTH, WILLIAM. [Letter to Alexander Dyce, 4 December
1833], in Letters. Edited by de Selincourt, III, no.
1064.
  "How do you come on with Skelton?"

1837   "CHATEAUBRIAND ON THE CULTURE OF ENGLAND," Edinburgh Review,
LXIV (1837).
  After praising Chateaubriand for having undertaken
the task (p. 519), the reviewer goes on to give his own
historical account of English literature, mentioning
Skelton in brief on p. 526.

1837.1   HALLAM, HENRY. Introduction to the Literature of Europe in
the Fifteenth, Sixteenth and Seventeenth Centuries. [I
quote from the 4th edition, London, 1854, I, pp. 313,
423, 428-429.]
  In essence, disapproving; Skelton's longer works are
labelled "utterly contemptible."

1840   D'ISRAELI, ISAAC. Amenities of Literature. London, 1840.
The remarks below are based on the edition of 1880, I,
pp. 276-284.
  Disraeli writes a heightened appreciative essay praising the "fertility" of Skelton's conceptions and the
"velocity" of his verse: "the chimes ring in the ear,
and the thoughts are flung about like corruscations."
He bases his remarks on Puttenham, Warton, a reading of
TER in the Harleian Miscellany (1808), and George Ellis;
condensation of The Image of Hypocrisy [non-canonical].

1840.1   HOOD, THOMAS. "Miss Kilmansegg and her Precious Leg," New
          Monthly Magazine (September–November, 1840); reprinted
          in The Works of Thomas Hood. Edited with notes by His
          Son and Daughter. 1882, VII.
              We find Skeltonics in the section "Her Misery," VII,
          p. 446; the section "Her Moral" ends with Skeltonics,
          VII, p. 454.

1842   BROWNING, ELIZABETH BARRETT. Short essays on Skelton,
          originally printed in the Athenaeum, No. 763 (11 June
          1842), 520–521 and No. 765 (25 June 1842), 558.
              The first essay describes briefly but fervently Skel-
          ton's "wonderful dominion over language," the second
          advances Skelton as "almost the first English claimant
          of a dramatic reputation," referring to Magnyfycence and
          the lost, probably spurious Nigramansir. The essays are
          reprinted with others in her collection Greek Christian
          Poets and the English Poets (London, 1863).

1842.1   CHASLES, PHILARÈTE. "Du Mouvement Sensualiste avant la
          Reforme: Skelton, Rabelais, Folengo, Luther." Revue
          des deux mondes, 4th ser., XXIX (1842), 724–742, es-
          pecially 724–727, 737–742.
              With the other three priests of the time, Chasles
          argues, Skelton marks a revolt against the clergy, on
          the one hand, and a return to "sensualism" on the other.

1843   CHAMBERS, ROBERT (comp.). Cyclopedia of English Literature.
          1843, I, pp. 41–42.
              [This entry is taken from the 2nd edition, revised,
          of 1858]; Skelton is "more of a trivial than a heroical
          poet," "a sort of rhyming Rabelais"; Chambers praises
          his copiousness of language and his command of rhyme and
          gives brief excerpts from CC, and "Margaret Hussey" from
          GL.

1843.1   DYCE, ALEXANDER (ed.). The Poetical Works of John Skelton.
          London: Thomas Rodd, 1843, 2 vols., pp. i–xi [sic],
          1–427, 1–488.
              Contents: [vol. I]: Preface; "Lawde"; Some Account
          of Skelton and his Writings; Appendix I, Merie Tales of
          Skelton and Notices of Skelton from Various Sources;
          Appendix II, List of Editions; Appendix III, Extracts
          from, or Examples of "the metre called Skeltonical";
          [then follow the poems]: "Edw. IV"; "DEN"; "ACC";
          "Contra asinum"; "UDH"; "WW"; "MDD"; "Aunc Acq";
          "Knolege"; "Cuncta licet" (Lat. & Engl.); "Go"; "MM";
          BC; PS; TER; "Ag Garn"; "AVT"; "Tyme" [doubtful];
          "Prayers" [doubtful]; "Woffully Araid" [not Skelton's];
          "Vexilla Regis" [not Skelton's]; "I, liber"; "Maner of
          the World" [not Skelton's]; WH; "Dev Tr" & "Ep Adam";

"Diligo"; "Lamentatio"; "In Bedel"; "Salve"; "H VII";
"Eulogium"; "Tetr"; "Ag. Scottes"; "Chorus contra
Scottos"; "Chorus contra Gallos"; "VSD"; "El Marg";
"Calliope" (Engl. and Lat.); BTF [not Skelton's]; Rep;
Mag; CC; GL, [with "Frax. in silvis" and "En Parl"];
[vol. II]: SP; WCY; DDA; Notes; Poems (5 in number)
attributed to Skelton, Corrigenda and Addenda; Index to
Notes; Additional Notes; [further] Addenda.

Dyce's contributions to a "complete" Skelton: For
the first time Dyce prints the four "Flytings Agenst
Garnesche" from B.L. MS. Harley 367, fols. 101-109^V, and
"A Lawde and Prayse" from P.R.O. MS. (Tr). E. 36/288,
fols. 67-70, a holograph; first reprints the poems from
DBDS [c. 1527] ("Lullay," "Aunc Acq," "Knolege," "Cuncta
licet" [Lat. & Engl.], and "Go"), and first includes in
a collected works Mag, for the text of which he returned
to the first edition [c. 1530] rather than relying on
the inaccurate 1821 Roxburghe reprint; for the first
time reprints A Replycacion from the edition of c. 1528;
for the first time "restores" SP by a conflation of the
ms. version in B.L. MS. Harley 2252, fols. 133^V-140, with
the shorter printed version in CB [c. 1545], sigs. A2-A6,
and "recovers" the Latin poem closing CC from Harley
2252, fol. 153^V.

He made mistakes of his own, to be sure, printing BTF
again from PPPW although it was a redaction of chapters
49, 50 and 47, in that order, of Watson's 1509 translation of Brant's Shyppe of Fooles, and introducing as
canonical the unattributed "Woffully Araid" from B.L. MS.
Addit. 5465, fols. 63^V-67, "Vexilla Regis" from Christmas
Carolles [c. 1550, STC$^{2.2}$ 5204.5], and "The Maner of the
World Now-a-Dayes" (about which he later had doubts [II,
199-202] from a print (c. 1562), STC 17255. Like Stowe,
the probable editor of PPPW, no. 1568 above, Dyce was unaware of "BSK," no. 1513.4, not to be recovered until
1881.

Reviews of Dyce's edition: In GM, n.s. XXII, the
whole of No. CLXXVI (1844), 227-247 was devoted to his
work, with many emendations proposed, pp. 243-247; London Literary Gazette (1843), 805; QR, LXXIII (1844),
510-536; the remarks on Skelton and his writings contained in "Old Authors and Old Books," in Knight's Penny
Magazine, I (1846), 26-30, 49-53 were prompted by this
edition.

Reprinted by AMS Press, Inc., New York, 1965. See
also nos. 1855, 1856, 1864, and 1881.1.

1843.2   WORDSWORTH, WILLIAM. [Letter to Alexander Dyce, 6 June
          1843], in Letters. Edited by de Selincourt, III, no.
          1491.
              Wordsworth writes Dyce for information about the of-
          fice of Poet Laureate and the readiness of Dyce's edition
          of Skelton's works.

1844   STRICKLAND, AGNES. "Katherine of Arragon," in <u>Lives of the</u>
        <u>Queens of England from the Norman Conquest</u>. London,
        1844, IV, pp. 94-95.
            While commenting on Skelton's taunting of the dead
        James IV in "Ag Scottes," vv. 145-150, Strickland assails
        Skelton for his virulence and vulgarity: "the laureated
        bard of Henry knew well his sovereign's taste.... How
        probable it is that the corruption imparted by this
        ribald and ill-living wretch laid the foundations for
        his royal pupil's grossest crimes!"

1844.1 WORDSWORTH, WILLIAM. [Letter to Alexander Dyce, 5 January
        1844], in <u>Letters</u>. Edited by de Selincourt, III, no.
        1517.
            Thanks Dyce for his "very valuable" present of a copy
        of his edition of Skelton; compares the gift of an edition
        of Skelton to Pope's acquisition of a copy of Hall's
        <u>Satires</u> late in his career--he wished he had seen the
        book earlier.

1849   MELVILLE, HERMAN. <u>Mardi</u>. Written during 1847-48, first
        published 1849 in London by Bentley, March 16th; in New
        York by Harper & Bros., April 14th.
            For an opinion that Melville had drawn on <u>PS</u> for Chap-
        ter 50 of Mardi, involving Yillah and her enigmatic bird,
        <u>see</u> DAVISON, no. 1966.1 below; see <u>Mardi</u>, ed. Harrison
        Hayford, H. Parker and G. T. Tanselle (Evanston and
        Chicago: Northwestern University Press and the Newberry
        Library, 1970), p. 156.

1851   GORTON, JOHN. <u>A General Biographical Dictionary</u>. New edi-
        tion; London: [n.p.], 1851, III, "John Skelton."
            The entry is apparently a condensation of that found
        in Chalmers' <u>Dictionary</u>, no. 1817 above, or from an
        earlier edition of the <u>General Biog. Dict.</u>, 1st edition,
        1828, another issue, 1830; 2nd edition (to 1833), 1835,
        for Gorton is unaware of Dyce's edition of 1843.

1855   <u>THE POETICAL WORKS OF SKELTON AND DONNE, WITH A MEMOIR OF</u>
        <u>EACH</u>. Boston: Houghton, Mifflin and Co. [<u>c</u>. 1855],
        4 vols. in 2.
            Vol. I (Skelton), pp. cxlvii, [1], 250, [ii], 437 [3]
        [based on Dyce's edition of 1843, with textual notes
        dropped and some notes abridged or dropped]; [vol. II]
        (Donne) is printed from the same setting of type as for
        the separate edition edited by James Russell Lowell for
        F. J. Child's <u>British Poets</u> in 1855 [<u>see</u> Geoffrey Keynes,
        <u>A Bibliography of Dr. John Donne</u> (4th edition, Oxford:
        Clarendon Press, 1973), p. 211, nos. 89-90]. <u>See also</u>
        no. 1881.1 below.

1856   THE POETICAL WORKS OF JOHN SKELTON (with a memoir by
             Alexander Dyce). Boston: Little, Brown and Co., 1856,
             3 vols., pp. cxlvii; 250; 437; 453.
                Included in the series The British Poets, under the
             editorship of F. J. Child, it reproduces Dyce's text of
             1843 although dividing poems into two volumes, saving
             the 3rd for notes; it condenses Dyce's critical apparatus
             by minimizing variant readings; incorporates Dyce's cor-
             rections and proposes a few new readings, marked by as-
             terisks, chiefly in Mag.

1864   THE POETICAL WORKS OF JOHN SKELTON, WITH A MEMOIR. Boston:
             Little, Brown and Co., 1864, 3 vols.
                A reissue from the stereotypes of Works of 1856, with
             the same pagination; title pages in red and black, "One
             Hundred copies printed" on verso of title page of vol. I.

1866   "A Satirical Laureate of the Sixteenth Century." Dublin
             University Magazine, LXVIII (July-December, 1866), 603-
             618.
                Notes that Skelton raised the satire of his time to
             "intense poetry, melting and modelling with the fire of
             his original genius."

1866.1   SKEAT, W[ALTER] W. (ed.). The Romans of Partenay. EETS,
             XXII (1866), pp. ii-iii.
                Skeat prints a version of the non-canonical "Masteres
             Anne / I am your man" later claimed for Skelton by BRIE,
             no. 1907, and LLOYD, no. 1929.3 below, but see MAXWELL,
             no. 1950.3.

1868   WRIGHT, THOMAS. Caricature History of the Georges. London:
             John Camden Holton [1868], p. 406.
             Writes 5 lines of Skeltonics against Warton.

1871   SKEAT, W[ALTER] W. (ed.). Specimens of English Literature.
             Oxford, 1871, pp. 137-154.
                Includes excerpts from two of Skelton's poems, WCY,
             ll. 287-382, 396-575, 748-756; and PS 998-1193, 1219-
             1270.

1873   BIRCH, WALTER DE GRAY. "Peteuelly Constrayned am Y."
             Athenaeum (20 November 1873), 697.
                Prints as Skelton's the non-canonical poem "Peteuelly
             Constrayned" from a ms. version written inside a copy of
             the pseudo-Boethius De disciplina. See K&Y R68.

1873.1   "John Skelton." American Church Review, XXV (1873), 36-52.
                A general article on Skelton's life, works, and repu-
             tation, with a running, impressionistic commentary.

1876   LOWELL, JAMES RUSSELL. "Spenser," in the section "Literary
            Essays" in Among My Books, 2nd series. Works. Boston,
            1876, IV, pp. 273-274.
                 Lowell's essay had originally appeared in the North
            American Review, cxx (1875), 334-394, with 2 paragraphs
            on Skelton as Spenser's precursor, "an exceptional blos-
            som of autumn," praising his "vivacity, fancy, humor and
            originality."

1877   "Buried Poets: John Skelton." Dublin University Magazine,
            LXXXIX (January-June 1877), 640-644.
                 The article notes that Skelton could write Latin with
            purest elegance yet compose vernacular pieces of gross
            buffoonery; it opines that his TER was "undoubtedly one
            of the coarsest and most detestable pieces of vulgarity
            ever written in our language"; and believes that the
            poet should share a niche with the "degraded but talented
            Charles Churchill."

1879   HAMILTON, WALTER. The Poets Laureate of England, Being a
            History of the Office of Poet Laureate. London: E.
            Stock, 1879, pp. 22-30.
                 Adds nothing new to Skelton biography or criticism.

1880   A SKELTONICAL SALUTATION &c. Edited by Thomas Corser,
            Collectanea Anglo-Poetica, X, Chetham Society, CXVIII
            (1880).
                 Reprints no. 1589.1 above, accompanying it with a
            description and provenance.

1880.1   WARD, THOMAS [HUMPHREY] (ed.). The English Poets. Selec-
            tions with Critical Introductions by Various Writers and
            a General Introduction by Matthew Arnold. London:
            Macmillan & Co., [printed]. Oxford, 1880, I, pp. 186-
            191, with introduction by J. Churton Collins, pp. 184-
            185.
                 The selections from Skelton include "MDD"; 3 stanzas
            describing "Ryott" from BC; "Margaret Hussey" from GL;
            and 11. 287-375 from CC. The English Poets, Selections
            are later issued under the Macmillan imprint, London, in
            1885 with new material added to the later volumes and with
            subsequent reissues.

1881   KRUMPHOLZ, H[EINRICH]. "John Skelton und sein morality
            play, 'Magnyfycence.'" Prossnitz, 1881.
                 An "inaugural dissertation" of little value.

1881.1   THE POETICAL WORKS OF SKELTON AND DONNE, WITH A MEMOIR OF
            EACH. Boston: Houghton, Mifflin and Co., 1881, 4 vols.
            in 2: I (Skelton), pp. cxlii, [1], 250, [ii], 437 [3].
                 A reissue from stereotyped plates of the separate
            editions of the two poets published by Little, Brown and

Co., in 1856 and 1855 respectively; vol. I variously
dated 1881 and undated; vol. II undated; binding title:
"British Poets," "Riverside Edition."

1881.2   SMITH, G. BARNETT (ed.). "A ballade of the Scottysshe
          kynge," Athenaeum, no. 2790 (16 April 1881), 325.
              Reprints for the first time a version without com-
          mentary of Skelton's "BSK." See no. 1513.4 above and
          nos. 1882 and 1887 below.

1882   ASHTON, JOHN (ed.). "A ballade of the Scottysshe kynge."
          London: Elliot Stock, 1882, pp. iv, 96, limited to 500
          copies.
              Provides a facsimile text of Skelton's "ballade" with
          a historical and bibliographical introduction. See no.
          1513.4 above; see no. 1969 for a reissue of this edition
          and no. 1887 for Ashton's inclusion of the poem proper in
          a collection of "ballads."

1886   HERFORD, CHARLES H[AROLD]. Studies in the Literary Rela-
          tions of England and Germany in the Sixteenth Century.
          Cambridge: Cambridge University Press, 1886, pp. 350-
          357.
              Discusses somewhat inaccurately Skelton's use of
          Brant's "Ship of Fools" in BC and BTF [non-canonical].

1887   ASHTON, JOHN (ed.). "A ballade of the Scottysshe kynge,"
          in A Century of Ballads. London: E. Stock, 1887, pp.
          xiii-xvii.
              Reprints Skelton's "BSK," no. 1513.4, with a facsimile
          of the woodcut on the original title-page.

1887.1   CRESWELL, LIONEL G. "An Hour with old John Skelton."
          Book-Lore, V (1886-87), 153-159.
              A brief, chatty, "appreciation" of Skelton's verse.

1887.2   FITZGIBBON, H[ENRY] MACAULAY (ed.). Early English Poetry.
          London and Newcastle-on-Tyne: Walter Scott, 1887, pp.
          102-116.
              Presents selections from GL: "To Isabell," pp. 102-
          103 and "Margery Wentworth," p. 105; gives excerpts from
          "UDH," CC and PS. A second edition, 1888, London im-
          print only, presents the same excerpts on pp. 154-172.

1888   SCHÖNEBERG, G[EORG]. Die Sprache John Skeltons in seinen
          kleineren Werken. Marburg, 1888, 63 pp.
              An inaugural dissertation; includes discussion of short
          and long vowels, German and Romance; the consonants; the
          inflection of verbs, nouns and adjectives as found in the
          minor poems of Skelton including the doubtful pieces "Edw.
          IV," "Prayers," "Woffully Araid," "Vexilla Regis," "Maner
          of the World" and BTF.

1889   MINTO, WILLIAM. <u>Characteristics of English Poets from</u>
                <u>Chaucer to Shirley</u>. Boston, Massachusetts: Ginn & Co.,
                1889, pp. 85-91.
                "It wants some leniency in the definition of poetry
                to allow him the title of poet at all; he was not much
                more of a poet than Swift."

1890   POLLARD, A[LFRED] W[ILLIAM] (ed.). <u>Magnyfycence</u> (excerpted),
                in <u>English Miracle Plays, Moralities and Interludes</u>.
                Oxford: Clarendon Press, 1890, pp. 106-113.

1890.1   ZUPITZA, J[ULIUS]. "Handschriftliche Bruchstücke von John
                Skeltons 'Why come ye nat to courte?.'" <u>Archiv</u>, LXXXV
                (1890), 429-436.
                Zupitza prints Bodley MS. Rawlinson C. 813 [<u>c</u>. 1525-
                50], fols. 36-43^V, an imperfect version of Skelton's
                <u>WCY</u>, consisting of the incipit "All Noble" and vv. 838-
                1248 only, the incipit attached to provide an introduc-
                tion to the discussion of "grace" (838-879); ms. uniquely
                provides a heading after v. 1216 to separate the poem
                proper from a concluding invective against "suum
                calumpniatorem."

1891   MORLEY, HENRY. <u>English Writers</u>. London: Cassell & Co.,
                1891, VII, pp. 85-89, 180-203, 340-342.
                Morley provides well written appreciative comments on
                the range of Skelton's accomplishment, descriptive
                rather than analytical, to be sure.

1892   CLARK, J[OHN] SCOTT (ed.). <u>Selected Poems from Skelton,</u>
                <u>Wyatt and Surrey</u>. English Classics Series, No. 97.
                New York, 1892, pp. 5-19.
                Clark furnishes 2 pages of introduction based on
                D'Israeli, Minto and Taine; then prints "Margaret Hus-
                sey" from <u>GL</u>, and excerpts from <u>CC</u>, <u>WCY</u>, <u>BC</u>, <u>GL</u>, and <u>PS</u>.

1893   BRINK, BERNHARD TEN. <u>Geschichte der Englischen Litteratur</u>.
                Strassburg, 1893, II, pp. 460-473.
                Ten Brink gives a general review of Skelton's works
                and then on pp. 479-482 adds further comments on <u>Mag</u>.

1893.1   [GROLIER CLUB]. <u>Catalogue of Original and Early Editions...</u>
                <u>Langland to Wither</u>. New York, 1893, I, pp. 192-193,
                nos. 218 and 219.
                Provides descriptions of <u>WCY</u> (<u>STC</u> 22615), and of <u>PPPW</u>
                (<u>STC</u> 22608), with a reproduction of its title-page on
                p. 193.

1894   JUSSERAND, JEAN J[ULES]. <u>Histoire littéraire du peuple</u>
                <u>anglais</u>. Paris: 1894, Firmin-Didot et cie, II, pp.
                111-116.

Jusserand makes general remarks on Skelton's poetry; speculates interestingly on the origins of Skelton's rhyme-leash as derived from the fabliaux. His work is translated into English as A Literary History of the English People (New York: G. P. Putnam & Sons, 1931).

1895   COURTHOPE, W[ILLIAM] J[OHN]. "The Progress of Allegory," in A History of English Poetry. London and New York: Macmillan & Co., 1895, I, 382-386.
          Courthope is critical of Skelton's "short verses" as "...rude, anarchical, arbitrary...." His History has been reprinted 1906, 1911, 1919, 1926.

1895.1   FLÜGEL, EWALD (ed.). Neuenglisches Lesebuch. Halle, 1895, pp. 45-71.
          Includes the following selections: from GL 11. 323-434, 808-835, 1086-1586, the seven lyrics in the poem (11. 906-1085), "Frax in silvis"; and "En Parl"; from "Ag. Scottes" 11. 1-64; from WH 11. 1-83; from TER 11. 1-33, 91-132; from WCY "All Noble," 11. 1-64, 230-539, 1067-1249 plus Latin poems at end; and from PS 11. 1-67, 147-186, 788-844, 998-1256.

1896   BRADLEY, HENRY. "Two Puzzles in Skelton." The Academy, L (1896), 83.
          "Breaks" the numerical codes located in GL between 11. 751 and 752, and in WH, 238 and 239, where Arabic numbers equal the vowels in order (a, e, i, o, u) and also the order of consonants relative to the vowels in the alphabet: hence 1 = a or b, 2 = e or c &c. The Puzzle in GL = Rogerus Statham; in WH = Sceltonica. [Bradley refers to this article in his brief reply to THORNTON 1899, N&Q, 9th ser., III (1899), 498.]

1896.1   WÜLKER, RICHARD PAUL. Geschichte der Englischen Littera-tur. Leipzig and Wien, 1896, I, pp. 194-198.
          Presents chiefly a rehash, concentrating on CC = "Buch vom Bauern Lump," BC = "Der Freitisch am Hofe." 2nd, rev. & augmented edition, 1906; Skelton comments in I, 217-223.

1897   HOOPER, JAMES. "Skelton, Laureate." GM, CCLXXXIII (1897), 297-309.
          In examining the Norwich Diocesan Registers, Hooper noted that Skelton had followed Peter Greves to the living at Diss and was followed by Thomas Clark, 17 July 1529, facts previously noted by Blomefield in no. 1739 above.

1897.1   LEE, SIR SIDNEY. "Skelton, John (1460?-1529)." DNB (1897), LII, pp. 327-332.

Argues that Skelton was probably a native of Norfolk,
although Blomefield's claim that he was the son of Wm.
Skelton, whose will proved at Norwich 7 November 1512,
was ill-founded, notices another John Skelton in L&P,
H VIII, IV, i, no. 1235; notices DS from Nasmith no.
1777, but is unaware that Spec Princ is located in the
British Museum; wrongly ascribes to Skelton an epitaph
on Jaspar Tudor, and a second on H VII; mistakenly follows Herford in believing BC indebted to Barclay's
trans. of Ship of Fooles; dates "Dev Tr & Ep. Adam" 1517
instead of 1507 and "Lawde," 1516 instead of 1509; has
good summary of known facts of Skelton's life, although
he uncovers nothing new; believes the Skeltonic may have
sprung from French and low-Latin verse (330, col. 2);
brings bibliography up-to-date; knows of Ashton's edition of "BSK," no. 1882 above.

1899   REY, ALBERT. Skelton's Satirical Poems in Their Relation
        to Lydgate's "Order of Fools," "Cock Lorell's Bote,"
        and Barclay's "Ship of Fools." Berne: K. J. Wyss,
        1895, 59 pp.
            Claims that BC possibly indebted to Order of Fools
        for vices satirized, particularly "Dissimulation"; that
        "Harvey Hafter" derives from a character in Cock Lorell's
        Bote although this is unlikely, since the Bote was
        printed a decade after first edition of BC; argues the
        direct influence of Ship on BC, CC, and BTF (non-canoni-
        cal); misdates BC as coming after GL.

1899.1 THORNTON, RICHARD H. "Skelton's Cipher." N&Q, 9th ser.,
        III (1899), 386.
            Believes that the Latin jargon in WH probably delib-
        erate nonsense; but see no. 1896 above.

1899.2 WARD, [SIR] A[DOLPHUS] W[ILLIAM]. A History of English
        Dramatic Literature. "New & revised edn." London:
        Macmillan & Co., 1899, I, pp. 128-130.
            The entry on Skelton contains a brief presentation of
        Magnyfycence, an indication of a growing interest in the
        play that will culminate in Ramsay's edition of it in
        1908. See also nos. 1890, 1901, 1908.2, 1910.3, 1911,
        1911.1, 1913, 1914.2 and 1914.3

1900   ARBER, EDWARD (ed.). The Surrey and Wyatt Anthology.
        London: Henry Frowde, 1900, pp. 132-203.
            Offers selections from PS and WCY; reissued in 1901
        as a volume in Selections from the English Poets (with
        portraits). London: Henry Frowde.

1901   HOOPER, E. S. "Skelton's Magnyfycence and Cardinal Wolsey."
        MLN, XVI (1901), 313-315.

In essence claims that the character "Magnyfycence"
= Wolsey.

1902   POOLE, REGINALD LANE and MARY BATESON (eds.). <u>Bale's Index</u>
            <u>Britanniae Scriptorum</u>. Oxford: Oxford University Press,
            1902, pp. 252-255.
                 For Bale's list of Skelton's works, <u>see</u> no. 1556
            above.

1902.1   WILLIAMS, W[ILLIAM] H[ENRY] (ed.). <u>A Selection from the</u>
            <u>Poetical Works of John Skelton</u>. Isbister, 1902, pp. vi,
            268.
                 <u>Contents</u>: Introduction; from <u>BC</u>; from <u>PS</u>; from <u>CC</u>;
            and from <u>WCY</u>; with notes and glossary.
                 <u>Reviews</u>: "A Lippo Lippi of Poetry," <u>Academy</u>, LXIV
            (1903), 222-223; <u>Athenaeum</u>, pt. 2 (1903), 154.

1903   BATESON, MARY (ed.). <u>Grace Book B (Pt. I)...of the Univer-</u>
            <u>sity of Cambridge</u>. Cambridge: Cambridge University
            Press, 1903, pp. 54, 92, 148-149.
                 <u>See</u> nos. 1492, 1496 and 1501.1 above.

1904   KOELBING, ARTHUR. <u>Zur Charakteristik John Skeltons</u>.
            Stuttgart, 1904, 166 pp.
                 Despite his unquestioning acceptance of certain poems
            dubiously Skelton's ("Edw. IV," "Woffully Araid"),
            Koelbing provides still useful reminders of Skelton's
            position in the medieval traditions of the patriotic
            bard (cf. Minot), the parodist of the Mass, the courtly
            elegist, the anti-feminine and anti-ecclesiastical
            satirist, &c. <u>See also</u> KOELBING, no. 1908.1 below.

1905   GOODWIN, GORDON. "Commissary Court of Westminster." <u>N&Q</u>,
            10th ser., III (1905), 125.
                 Notes that Skelton's estate was administered by Wil-
            liam Mott (or Mote), curate of St. Margaret's Westmin-
            ster, on 16 November 1529 (6, Bracy).

1905.1   MANNING, C. U. "Master John Skelton, Laureate, Parson of
            Disse, 1504." <u>Antiquary</u>, XLI (1905), 383-386.
                 Manning, the rector of Diss at the time, briefly dis-
            cusses Skelton's poetry in relation to the local back-
            ground.

1905.2   THÜMMEL, ARNO. <u>Studien über John Skelton</u>. Leipzig: August
            Hoffman, 1905, 98 pp.
                 Presents a brief but alert examination of Skelton's
            academic career and of the meaning of "laureate" and
            "orator regius"; provides a close commentary on the back-
            ground for, and references in, Skelton's Latin court
            poetry; does early spade-work on Skelton's humanist

colleagues and Latin poets: Bernard André, Peter
Carmeliano, John de Giglis and Johannes Opicius.

1907   BRIE, FRIEDRICH. "Skelton-Studien." Engl. Studn., XXXVII
        (1907), 1-86.
            Brie's is the first attempt since Dyce's time (see
        no. 1843.1) systematically to determine the Skelton
        canon: identifies BTF, published by Dyce, as non-canoni-
        cal; rejects as non-canonical the poem "Petevelly con-
        strayned am Y," published as Skelton's, no. 1873 above,
        and by Flügel, without ascription, in Anglia, XII (1889),
        266-267 from a longer MS version; believes "Woffully
        Araid," "Vexilla regis," "Tyme," "Prayers," all printed
        by Dyce, to be non-canonical; lists as doubtful "Edw. IV"
        and "Qui trahis" (a poem he prints on p. 28), but ac-
        cepts the non-canonical "To Masteres Anne" (which he
        prints on pp. 29-31) and "How darest thow swere" (en-
        titled by Brie "The Recule against Gaguyne"); attempts
        a chronology of Skelton's works on pp. 84-86. See
        MAXWELL, no. 1950.3 for note that "Masteres Anne" printed
        by Skeat, in introduction to The Romans of Partenay,
        EETS (1866); see also LLOYD, no. 1929.3 for (1) rejection
        of Brie's attribution of "How darest thow swear" to Skel-
        ton and (2) acceptance of Brie's case for "Masteres
        Anne" (with correction of text); see also EDWARDS, no.
        1949, pp. 53 and 263 for rejection of "Masteres Anne"
        from canon.

1907.1 DUTT, WILLIAM [ALFRED]. Some Literary Associations of East
        Anglia. London: Methuen & Co., 1907, pp. 239-242.
            Presents a brief discussion of PS and WH as well as
        passing comments on Skelton's life.

1908   ASTLEY, HUGH J[OHN DUKINFIELD]. Memorials of Old Norfolk.
        London: Bemrose & Sons, 1908, pp. 315-321.
            Presents a biographical notice and a brief apprecia-
        tive essay of Skelton.

1908.1 KOELBING, A[RTHUR]. "Barclay and Skelton, Early German
        Influences on English Literature," in The Cambridge His-
        tory of English Literature. Cambridge University Press,
        1908, III, pp. 56-82, especially 67-79. [Reprinted 1918,
        1930, 1932, 1934, 1949, 1961, 1964 (text only, without
        notes)].
            Offers a brief life of Skelton, drawing on the tradi-
        tion of his quarrels with the Dominicans and his having
        to take refuge in sanctuary; relies on Brie, no. 1907,
        for the canon and dating; comments unevenly on the poems:
        e.g., GL shows Skelton's self-conceit unrelieved by
        humour; in PS, the second part of poem is only loosely
        connected to first, and the whole without any clear

design, a criticism that applies to <u>TER</u> as well; admits
that <u>BC</u> perhaps not directly indebted to Brant, but de-
tects strong resemblances, nonetheless.

1908.2   RAMSAY, ROBERT LEE (ed.). <u>Magnyfycence</u>. EETS (1908 for
          1906), XCVIII; pp. cxcvii, [1], 100; also issued as a
          Ph.D. thesis, The John Hopkins University, 1905, with a
          new cover as <u>Magnificence, a moral play</u>.
               <u>Contents</u>: Editions; Date, Plot, Dramatis Personae,
          Staging, Versification, Sources, Characterization,
          Satire, Background [here, in especial, Ramsay is still
          impressive, discussing the changes in moral plays, versi-
          fication, growth of morality plots and stages, general
          historical development of morality casts and characters,
          including fools and vices]; text; notes and glossarial
          index. <u>See</u> RAMSAY, no. 1925.3 for a reprint of this
          edition.

1908.3   SEARLE, WILLIAM GEORGE (ed.). <u>Grace Book Γ of the University
          of Cambridge</u>. Cambridge: Cambridge University Press,
          1908, p. 37.
               <u>See</u> no. 1504-05 above.

1908.4   TUCKER, S[AMUEL] M[ARION]. <u>Verse Satire in England before
          the Renaissance</u>. New York: Columbia University Press,
          1908, pp. 143-155.
               Discusses Skelton's major satires: <u>BC</u>, <u>SP</u>, <u>CC</u> and
          <u>WCY</u>.

1910   BASKERVILL, C[HARLES] R[EAD]. "Two Parallels to <u>Lycidas</u>."
          <u>The Nation</u>, XC, No. 2371 (8 December 1910), 546-547.
               Notes that "certain lines of Skelton's arraignment of
          prelates [<u>CC</u> 75-81 and 125-131] will bear...comparison
          with [Milton's] 'Lycidas' [114-118, 122-127]."

1910.1   FARMER, JOHN S. (ed.). <u>Magnyfycence</u>. In the Tudor Fac-
          simile Texts, XCIII (1910), pp. 3, 1, 58. This reprint
          was then reissued from Amersham, England, for subscribers,
          in Students' Facsimile Edition (1914).

1910.2   LEE, SIR SIDNEY. <u>The French Renaissance in England</u>. Ox-
          ford: Clarendon Press, 1910, pp. 100-107.
               Defines the Skeltonic as short lines of 4-6 syllables,
          with rhymes in couplets, "but at times...six times over";
          compares the form with the verse of Martial d'Auvergne,
          1440-1508.

1910.3   THOMPSON, ELBERT N. S. <u>The English Moral Plays</u>, in <u>Transac-
          tions of the Connecticut Academy of Arts and Sciences</u>,
          XIV (March 1910) bound separately (New Haven, 1910),
          pp. 346, 360, 361, 362, 383.

<u>Mag</u> indicative of the disintegration of religious drama in the new currents of thought.

1911   BASKERVILL, CHARLES R[EAD]. <u>English Elements in Jonson's Early Comedy</u>. Austin: University of Texas Studies, no. 178 (1911), pp. 172, 187-188, 248-253.
Examines, among other elements, Jonson's knowledge of Skelton's <u>Magnyfycence</u> and shows its influence on the construction of <u>Cynthia's Revels</u> in particular: "The striking kinship between the two plays lies in their similar modification of ethical conceptions derived ultimately from Aristotle, and in...the grouping of qualities of character in one class and qualities of conduct in another," pp. 252-253. <u>See</u> 1600.3 above.

1911.1   BROOKE, C. F. TUCKER. <u>The Tudor Drama</u>. Boston: Houghton, Mifflin, 1911, pp. 82-83.
Here mentioned as an indication of the interest in Skelton's play.

1912   HARVEY, H. "The Poetical Works of John Skelton, Laureate, 1460-1529." M.A. thesis, University of London [N/EX], listed in <u>RI</u>, I, p. 205.

1913   DODDS, M[ADELEINE] H[OPE]. "Early Political Plays." <u>Library</u>, 3rd ser., IV (1913), 393-394.
The character "Magnyfycence" = Duke of Norfolk.

1913.1   JAMES, M[ONTAGUE] R[HODES] (ed.). "<u>I, liber</u>," in <u>A Descriptive Catalogue of the Manuscripts in the Library of Corpus Christi College, Cambridge</u>. Cambridge: Cambridge University Press, 1913, II, pp. 338-339.
Gives the 10 lines of the poem plus 2 introductory hexameters and uncompleted 3rd line, identifying the poem as being in Skelton's own hand.

1913.2   SE BOYAR, G[ERALD] E. "Skelton's <u>Replycacion</u>." <u>MLN</u>, XXVIII (1913), 244-245.
Argues that <u>Rep</u>. dedicated to Wolsey because the poet was in need of Wolsey's help, having been accused by Bishop Nicke of "<u>gravia crimina et nephanda peccata</u>"; but there is little documentary indication that the poet is the man so accused.

1914   BERDAN, JOHN M[ILTON]. "The Dating of Skelton's Satires." <u>PMLA</u>, XXIX (1914), 499-516.
Dates <u>SP</u> earlier than later scholars will, as of 1517-18; places <u>CC</u> later than most recent scholars do, as of <u>c</u>. 1524-25.

1914.1 BISCHOFFBERGER, E[LSIE]. <u>Der Einfluss John Skeltons auf die Englische Literatur</u>. Freiburg, 1914, 80 pp.
A useful and relatively complete compendium in which mention of Skelton as a person or dramatic character, or imitation of his verse form, is listed; does not always use earliest edition or establish earliest date, however; arranged topically: Skelton and his contemporaries; Skelton's influence on later writers (reputation, citation, imitation in poetry, the Skeltonic in verse-drama, Skelton as a dramatic "character,"); the use of Skeltonic motives; Skelton among the critics.

1914.2 CAMPBELL, E[VA] M[ARIE]. <u>Satire in the Early English Drama</u>. Columbus, Ohio: University of Ohio Press, 1914, pp. 51-56.
Merely lists examples of "satire," relying on Ramsay's analysis of <u>Magnyfycence</u>.

1914.3 MACKENZIE, W[ILLIAM] ROY. <u>The English Moralities from the Point of View of Allegory</u>. Boston: Houghton, Mifflin, 1914, pp. 75-81.
Politics is an underlying current in <u>Magnyfycence</u>, not its main flow.

1914.4 O'DONOGHUE, FREEMAN (comp.). <u>Catalogue of Engraved English Portraits</u>. London: for the British Museum, 1912, IV, p. 114.
Classifies Skelton "portraits," none of them genuine, under three types: Type 1 "False" (<u>see</u> no. 1797); Type 2 "Imaginary" (<u>see</u> no. 1821.1); Type 3 "Imaginary" (<u>see</u> no. 1831) above.

1914.5 STOPES, C. C. "A Laureate Poem by Skelton." <u>Athenaeum</u>, no. 4514 (2 May 1914), p. 625.
Prints "Lawde" from P.R.O. Ms. (TR) E. 36/288, fols. 67-70, previously printed from same ms. by Dyce, I, pp. <u>ix-xi</u>, no. 1843.1.

1915 BERDAN, JOHN M[ILTON]. "The Poetry of Skelton: A Renaissance Survival of Medieval Latin Influence." <u>Romanic Review</u>, VI (1915), 364-377.
Argues that the "Skeltonic" is derived from secular, "Goliardic" Latin verse of the Middle Ages, itself related to Latin hymnody; seeks to demonstrate his argument by tracing the process through Caxton's modernization of the verse of Trevisa's translation of Higden's <u>Polychronicon</u>; but <u>see</u> PYLE, no. 1936.11 below.

1915.1 BERDAN, JOHN M[ILTON]. "'Speke Parrot': An Interpretation of Skelton's Satire." <u>MLN</u>, XXX (1915), 140-144.

Advances the view that Parrot represents the old conservative church of Warham and Fox, that the poem is a
running commentary on the events of 1517-18.

1915.2   GRAY, W[ILLIAM] FORBES. The Poets Laureate of England.
          New York: E. P. Dutton & Co., 1915, pp. 11-14.
          His discussion of Skelton is essentially a redoing of
          Hamilton's statements in his book on the Poets Laureate,
          no. 1879 above.

1915.3   KRAPP, GEORGE PHILIP. The Rise of English Literary Prose.
          Oxford and New York: Oxford University Press, 1915,
          pp. 280-286.
          Makes some brief comments on, and gives several cita-
          tions from Replycacion.

1916   COOK, ALBERT S[TANHOPE]. "Skelton's Garland of Laurel and
          Chaucer's House of Fame." MLR, XI (1916), 9-14.
          Establishes significant resemblances between the two
          poems: Eolus the trumpeter (GL 233-240, HF 1567-1573);
          Orpheus the harper (GL 269-273, HF 1193-1207); prevalence
          of rumor, similarity of decorations, 1000 gates in wall
          (GL), 1000 holes in roof (HF).

1916.1   GRAVES, ROBERT. "Free Verse," in Over the Brazier. London:
          The Poetry Bookshop, 1916, pp. 13-14.
          Despite irregular cross-rhyme, has the 2 to 3 beats /
          line and rhyme-runs of the Skeltonic whose forcefulness
          Graves fully acknowledges later; reprinted in Fairies
          and Fusiliers, no. 1917.1, pp. 82-84, and in 2nd edn.
          of Over the Brazier [1920], pp. 14-15. See also GRAVES
          nos. 1916.2, 1917.1, 1920.1, 1921, 1922.1, 1923, 1925,
          1925.1, 1927, 1927.1, 1927.2, 1934.11, 1955.2, 1961,
          1962.3, 1969.2 for other imitations of, or comments on,
          Skelton.

1916.2   GRAVES, ROBERT. David and Goliath. London: Chiswick
          Press [1916].
          The title poem, the second in the collection, pub-
          lished in late 1916, seems influenced by the longer Skel-
          tonic line of the Garnesche flytings iii and iv, for
          example.

1916.3   NEILSON, W[ILLIAM] A[LLAN] and K[ENNETH] G. T. WEBSTER
          (eds.). Chief British Poets of the Fourteenth and Fif-
          teenth Centuries. Cambridge, Massachusetts: Houghton,
          Mifflin, 1916, pp. 230-248 and 431, with glosses and
          notes at the foot of each page.
          Selections: PS (ll. 1-843); TER (from "Portrait" and
          Passus I, III, and V; CC (ll. 1-217, 288-375, 830-981,
          1097-1267); GL "Isabell Pennell"; "Lullay."

1917   DUNBABIN, R[OBERT] L[ESLIE]. "Notes on Skelton." MLR, XII
            (1917), 129-139, 257-265.
                Still a useful series of notes; suggests that Skelton
            is a Cumberland or Yorkshire name rather than a Norfolk
            one; argues that Skelton is not a humanist but, rather,
            a belated representative of medieval scholarship; pro-
            poses readings of specific passages and emendations of
            particular lines.

1917.1   GRAVES, ROBERT. Fairies and Fusiliers. London: W. Heine-
            mann, 1917.
                "John Skelton," on pp. 41-43, written in Skeltonics,
            beginning "What could be dafter / Than John Skelton's
            laughter"; "Free Verse," pp. 82-84 [as in no. 1916.1
            above]; "David and Goliath," pp. 11-13 (as in no. 1916.2
            above).

1919   BRIE, F[RIEDRICH]. "Zwei verlorene dichtungen von John
            Skelton." Archiv, CXXXVIII (1919), 226-228.
                Advances speculations on "The Tratyse of the Triumphes
            of the Red Rose" (GL 1223) and "Antomedon of Loves Medi-
            tacyoun" (GL 1181).

1920   BERDAN, JOHN M[ILTON]. Early Tudor Poetry. New York: The
            Macmillan Co., 1920.
                Still worth the reading for his views on Skelton as
            laureat and the meaning of the degree, pp. 92-95; on BC,
            pp. 95-102; on Skelton as an opponent of Humanism, pp.
            156-160; on Skelton's metrics, pp. 160-171; and on Skel-
            ton's stance as "a mighty warrior before the Lord." See
            also pp. 179-184, 194-201 for CC, and passim for obser-
            vations on other Skelton poems.

1920.1   GRAVES, ROBERT. Country Sentiment. London: M. Secker,
            1920.
                On p. 39, "Manticor in Arabia," with an epigraph from
            PS, "The mantycors of the montaynes &c.," vv. 294 ff.;
            or pp. 78-80, "A Rhyme of Friends (In a Style Skeltoni-
            cal)" in short 2 and 3 best lines although with occa-
            sional cross-rhyme.

1921   GRAVES, ROBERT. "The Finding of Love," in The Pier-glass.
            London: Martin Secker, 1921, pp. 15-16.
                The poem shows occasional irregular stresses within
            otherwise even trimeters, Skeltonical in rhythmic in-
            fluence.

1921.1   WESTLAKE, H[ERBERT] F[RANCIS]. "Skelton in Westminster."
            TLS (27 October 1921), p. 699.
                Cites Westminster Abbey Muniments Register Book II,
            fol. 146, in which Skelton mentioned as a tenant within

Westminster sanctuary, on the south side of the great
belfry "in quoquidem tenemento Johannes Skelton laureatus modo inhabitat"; see also WESTLAKE, no. 1923.3
below.

1922   GOLDING, LOUIS. "Merie Skelton." Saturday Review (London),
          CXXXIII (1921), 30-31.
              An enthusiastic essay, interesting in part for its
          attempt to define the "norm" of the Skeltonic line as
          "an anapaest and an iamb with either a masculine or
          feminine ending reduplicating its rhyme till the very
          invention of the poet is exhausted. The whole line may
          consist of one such abstract quality as 'equanimity'
          rhyming with 'uninterruptibility'...."

1922.1   GRAVES, ROBERT. On English Poetry, Being an Irregular
          Approach.... London: William Heinemann, 1922.
              As one of his two opening epigraphs, Graves includes
          Skelton's reference to the "Mustarde Tarte" [a lost
          piece, mentioned in GL, v. 1245] and indicates that he
          has had difficulty in restraining himself from the crea-
          tive capriciousness that Skelton's title represents in
          his essay "Spenser's Cuffs," p. 39. As a coda, he in-
          cludes "In Procession" (see no. 1923 below), a poem in
          Skeltonics, "written a few weeks after the remainder of
          the book," occupying pp. 137-142.

1922.2   HUGHES, RICHARD [A.W.]. Gipsy-Night and Other Poems.
          Waltham Saint Lawrence: The Golden Cockerell Press,
          1922.
              On pp. 32-33, "Poets, Painters, Puddings" in 32 lines,
          28 of which seem influenced by Hughes' knowledge of Skel-
          tonics [note his edition of Skelton, no. 1924 below],
          e.g., "Painters are gay / As young rabbits in May: / They
          buy jolly mugs / Bowls, pictures and jugs: / The things
          round their necks / Are lively with checks" &c. See also
          HUGHES, no. 1926 below for "carry-over."

1922.3   SALTER, FREDERICK M. "The Critical Ideas of John Skelton."
          M.A. thesis, Department of English, University of Chica-
          go, 1922, 57 pp. [2].
              Essentially argues that Skelton is a moderate, ap-
          proaching the humanists in thought, the medievalists in
          practice: conservative in religion, reformer from with-
          in, defender from without; conservative in educational
          ideals, leading him to oppose youthful study of Greek
          but encourage the vernacular; stout defender of his
          Juvenalian role as satirist, proud of his "sentens" yet
          conventionally disclaims his rhyme; early vaunter of di-
          vine inspiration. See also SALTER, nos. 1934.16, 1935.5,
          1936.12, 1945.2, and 1956.2+, 1959.4 (as co-editor).

1923   GRAVES, ROBERT. <u>Whipperginny</u>. London: William Heinemann,
        1923.
            On pp. 29-33 "In Procession," (<u>see</u> no. 1922.1) is in-
        cluded a redaction of the procession of the poets in
        Skelton's <u>GL</u> and the plight of the young poet in <u>BC</u>,
        written in Skeltonic short lines with some rhyme-leashes
        of 3-4 lines in duration but also with occasional cross-
        rhyme.

1923.1 HARRINGTON, KARL POMEROY. <u>Catullus and His Influence</u>.
        Boston: 1923, pp. 143-145.
            Argues that Skelton uses Catullus' two poems on Les-
        bia's sparrow, nos. ii and iii, as a basis for <u>PS</u>; but
        <u>see</u> MacPEEK, no. 1939.6 below.

1923.2 SITWELL, EDITH. <u>Bucolic Comedies</u>. London: Duckworth &
        Co., 1923.
            No. VI "Rose (Imitated from Skelton)" [cf. <u>PS</u>], pp.
        20-21 (stanzas 5 and 6): "Fly in my brain...those bright
        birds flock: / The butterbump, the urban / Ranee stork,
        the turkey cock" &c; no. VII "Gardener Janus Catches a
        Naiad" [despite some cross-rhyme shows Skeltonic short
        line], p. 22; "Clown Argheb's Song" on p. 28 [shows
        Skeltonic short lines]; <u>Facade</u>, "Facade no. II" on pp.
        53-54 [despite cross-rhymes, shows Skeltonic short line];
        "Facade no. IV" on pp. 56-57 [despite cross-rhymes, shows
        Skeltonic short lines, syncopation and rhyming]; and
        <u>Spleen</u>, no. II "Fantoches" (esp. 11, 13-18) shows in-
        fluence of Skeltonic line.
            <u>Bucolic Comedies</u> was issued in New Readers' Library in
        1927 then reprinted in 1928 (London: Duckworth); <u>see also</u>
        SITWELL, Edith, no. 1930.2.

1923.3 WESTLAKE, H[ERBERT] F[RANCIS]. <u>Westminster Abbey: The
        Church, Convent, Cathedral and College of St. Peter,
        Westminster</u>. London: P. Allan & Co., 1923, II, p. 426.
            Notes the institution of Skelton's successor at Diss,
        Thomas Clark, from Westminster Abbey Muniments, No.
        33325, fol. 17^v; also presents in greater detail than in
        no. 1921.1 above, the lease in which Skelton is mentioned,
        from W. A. Muniments, Register Book II, fol. 146.

1924   HUGHES, RICHARD [A.W.] (ed.). <u>John Skelton, Poems</u>. London:
        Heinemann, 1924, xvi, 208 pp.
            The edition is provided with glosses and notes at foot
        of the page, text from Dyce's edition of 1843, with a few
        editorial changes and emendations; and was limited to
        780 copies.
            <u>Contents</u>: <u>SP</u> (vv. 1-114, 209-233); "Woffully Arraid"
        [not Skelton's]; <u>PS</u> (vv. 1-614, 760-844); "Tyme" [doubt-
        ful]; "Prayers" [doubtful] <u>TER</u>; "UDH"; <u>BC</u>; <u>PS</u> ("Commenda-
        cions" vv. 998-1260); <u>CC</u>; <u>SP</u> (vv. 115-208); <u>WH</u> (vv. 29-

144); GL (vv. 1-1282), 1355-1518); "Peteuelly Constreynd"
[falsely ascribed]. Reprinted 1974 by Folcroft Press
(Folcroft, Pennsylvania).
   Reviews: Graves, Robert, Nation and Athenaeum, XXVI
(1925), 614-615; Spectator, CXXXIV (18 April 1925), 636-
639; TLS (1 January 1925), p. 6.

1925   GRAVES, ROBERT [under the pseudonym of "John Doyle"]. The
       Marmosite's Miscellany. London: Leonard and Virginia
       Woolf, 1925.
          The title-poem on pp. 7-17 is chiefly in rhyme royal
       as used by Skelton in SP; cf. stanza 36, vv. 5-7; "Mel-
       pomene, my favourite, finds me a chair. / She tempts me
       with titbits in / a tasty row. / I am like a learned
       parrot she loved long ago"; on p. 19n. a citation from
       SP (vv. 214-215). Reprinted in nos. 1927.1 and 1927.2
       below.
          [For GRAVES' review (publ. 1925) of Hughes' edition
       of Skelton's Poems, see under HUGHES, no. 1924 above.]

1925.1   GRAVES, ROBERT. Welshman's Hose. London: The Fleuron,
       1925.
          The first of two dedicatory epigraphs is taken from
       GL 1233-1239, beginning "Also the Tunnynge of Elinour
       Rummyng" and ending "It is no foly to use the Walshe-
       mannys hoos"; "Diversions: (I), To an Editor: A
       Satiric Complaint in the Old Style," pp. 15-19, beginning
       "John Cole, Esquire, / It is my desire," &c. is in 10
       line stanzas in short beat lines à la Skelton with oc-
       casional cross rhyme in variable positions, stanza to
       stanza; "Diversions: (II), The Kingfisher's Return,"
       on p. 20, is in short lines, 2-3 beats to line with
       couplets and triplets in the Skeltonic manner, with only
       one cross-rhyme (19 rhyming with 23, the last line).

1925.2   LLOYD, L[ESLIE] J. "John Skelton, A Forgotten Poet."
       Engl. Rev., XL (1925), 659-665.
          A brief, general, appreciative essay apparently writ-
       ten before the publication of Richard Hughes' edition of
       Skelton's poems (no. 1924); suggests that Skelton should
       be considered with Swift, Fielding and Smollett as one
       of the great English satirists.

1925.3   RAMSAY, ROBERT LEE (ed.). Magnyfycence. EETS, e.g. XCVIII.
          A reprint of the edition issued 1908 for 1900; see
       no. 1908.2 above.

1925.4   SKELTON, JOHN. [Bibliotheca Historica of Diodorus Siculus.]
          A photographic facsimile of Skelton's translation, no.
       1488 above, Corpus Christi College, Cambridge MS. 275.
       Made by the Modern Language Association of America (1925),

photographic facsimile no. 29, 225 sheets mounted in 128 leaves, negatives, deposited in Library of Congress. <u>See</u> SALTER and EDWARDS, nos. 1956.2+ and 1959.4 below.

1925.5   SKELTON, JOHN. [<u>Speculum Principis.</u>]
A photographic facsimile of Skelton's tractate, no. 1501.2 above, B.L. MS. Addit. 26787. Made by Modern Language Association of America (1925), photographic facsimile no. 27, 30 sheets mounted on 15 negatives, deposited in Library of Congress. <u>See</u> SALTER, no. 1934.16 below.

1926   HUGHES, RICHARD [A.W.]. <u>Confessio Juvenis, Collected Poems</u>. London: Chatto and Windus, 1926.
"Poets, Painters, Puddings" is included from <u>Gypsy-Night</u>, no. 1922.2, pp. 12-13; in 1st 10 lines of the "Epilogue" to "Lines, Written upon First Observing an Elephant Devoured by a Roc," p. 73, Hughes resorts to the abruptness of the Skeltonic couplet as in "The patient vole / Attained his hole, / The indolent hare / Sat up to stare / The beetle struggling in the cress / Has struggled none the less" (the poem had apparently been privately printed before its inclusion in this collection); "Unicorn Mad," pp. 77-81, shows Skeltonic terseness and economy of line as well as rhyme despite occasional non-rhyming lines).

1926.1   POLLARD, A[LFRED] W[ILLIAM] and G. R. REDGRAVE (principal comps.). <u>A Short-Title Catalogue of Books Printed in England, Scotland & Ireland and of English Books Printed Abroad 1475-1640</u>. London: The Bibliographical Society, 1926, pp. 526-527.
The Skelton items extend from nos. 22593, <u>Ballade of the Scottysshe Kynge</u> [<u>c</u>. 1513] through 22620, <u>A Skeltonicall Salutation</u> 1589 (anr. edn.); itemizes 15 works or collections of Skelton in 24 separate sixteenth and early seventeenth century editions: "BSK," <u>STC</u>, 22593; <u>PS</u>, 22594-22596; <u>BC</u>, 22597; <u>CB</u>, 22598-22600; <u>CC</u>, 22601-22603; <u>DBDS</u>, 22604; (<u>STC</u> 22605 <u>Epitaffe of Iasper Late Duke of Beddeforde</u> [non-canonical] = <u>STC</u>$^{2.2}$ (1976) No. 14477); (<u>STC</u> 22606 = a "ghost" of 22600); <u>Mag</u>, 22607; <u>PPPW</u>, 22608; <u>Rep</u>, 22609; <u>GL</u>, 22610; <u>ACC</u>, 22611; (<u>STC</u> 22612, an alleged 1609 <u>TER</u> really <u>Pimlyco or Runne Red-Cap</u> = STC 19936); <u>STC</u> 22613 = <u>STC</u> 22614, a 1624 printing of <u>TER</u>); <u>WCY</u>, 22615-7^a; (<u>STC</u> 22617^b = <u>STC</u>$^{2.2}$ (1976) No. 22615.5, a variant colophon); <u>Merie Tales...made by Master Skelton</u>, 22618; <u>A Skeltonicall Salutation</u>, 22619-22620]. <u>See</u> KINSMAN and YONGE, no. 1967.2, and <u>SHORT TITLE CATALOGUE</u> (Second Edition) Second volume I-Z, [<u>STC</u>$^{2.2}$], no. 1976.2 below.
<u>Supplements</u>: Finding-Lists locating <u>STC</u> items in as many British and North American libraries as possible,

well beyond the announced limits of Pollard and Redgrave, were published by William Warner Bishop in 1941 (a preliminary check list), and in 1944 (1st edn.) and 1950 (2nd edn.) as A Checklist of American Copies of "Short-Title Catalogue" Books (Ann Arbor); and by David Ramage as A Finding-List of English Books to 1640 in the British Isles (Excluding the National Libraries and the Libraries of Oxford and Cambridge) (Durham, England, 1958).

1927   GRAVES, ROBERT. John Skelton (Laureate) 1460?-1529 [with "Note (by R. G.)" on p. iii]. The Augustan Books of English Poetry, edited by Humbert Wolfe, Second Series, no. 12. London: Ernest Benn, 1927, pp. vi, 7-31; errata list tipped in.
Selections: "Jane Scroop's Lament" from PS; "Skelton's Address to Philip Sparrow"; from "Edw. IV" [doubtful]; "Mistress Isabel Pennell" GL; from "The Manner of the World Nawadays" [not Skelton's]; "Prayer to the Father" [doubtful]; from SP (1st 9 stanzas); "Lullay"; from TER ["Portrait"]; "To His Wife" [not Skelton's]; "Wofully Arrayed" [not Skelton's].

1927.1 GRAVES, ROBERT. Poems (1914-26). London: William Heinemann, 1927.
Epigraph on p. xii is a stanza from GL (vv. 1135-1141); includes "Free Verse" from nos. 1916.1 and 1917.1, entitled "In Spite," pp. 5-6; also includes "John Skelton" from no. 1917.1, pp. 6-8, and "The Finding of Love" from no. 1921, on pp. 42-43; adapts Skelton's version of rhyme royal in "Rocky Acres," p. 67; on pp. 181-199 reprints "The Marmosite's Miscellany," no. 1925 with its title-poem in imitation of SP; mentions Skelton in 1.4 of "Procession," from nos. 1922.1 and 1923 above, on pp. 102-107.

1927.2 GRAVES, ROBERT. Poems 1914-1927. London: William Heinemann, 1927.
In addition to the contents of Poems 1914-1926, this collection contained 9 additional poems, among them "The Philatelist Royal," which was written in Skeltonics: "The Philatelist-Royal / Was always too loyal" &c.

1927.3 RANSOM, JOHN CROWE. Two Gentlemen in Bonds. New York: A. A. Knopf, 1927.
For Skeltonics, see "In Mr. Minnit's House," in the section "The Innocent Doves," p. 19, vv. 5-14, 15-21; p. 21, vv. 11-14, "Anne with her bird, / Her bright yellow bird, / And Mortimer III, / With a cat that purred" (cf. PS in meter, rhyme and situation, the slaughter of a pet bird by Old Tom the cat); see "Our Two Worthies" in the section "The Manliness of Man," pp. 31-33 for a use of Skeltonic metrics.

1927.4   SITWELL, OSBERT. England Reclaimed. London: Duckworth,
          1927.
              On p. 23, "(3) In the Hothouses," ends with a short
          Skeltonic burst (4 lines): "With crimson and damson /
          The Nile and Am'zon / Emblazon / This halcyon / of grow-
          ing and blowing / Warm blossoms and leaves"; reprinted
          in The Collected Satires and Poems of Osbert Sitwell
          (1931), Book II, "Poems," p. 208. On p. 25 "Discordant
          Dawn": "Heavily / Warily / Ever / So cleverly / He
          treads through the garden"; reprinted in Collected
          Satires and Poems, no. 1931.2, pp. 210-211.

1927.5   SKELTON, JOHN. THE GARLAND OF LAURELL. In English Verse
          between Chaucer and Surrey. Edited by Eleanor Prescott
          Hammond. Durham, North Carolina: Duke University Press,
          1927, pp. 342-367.
              From incomplete ms. version, B.L. MS. Cotton Vitellius
          E.x; collated with edition of poem 1523 and as printed
          in PPPW 1568, with introduction, bibliography and selec-
          ted list of references, pp. 336-342; volume reprinted in
          1965 by Octagon Books (New York).

1928   ELYNOURE RUMMYNGE. Illustrated by Pearl Binder. London:
          Fanfrolico Press, 1928, 47 pp. (limited to 550 copies).
              See also nos. 1930.1 and 1953.5 for other limited edi-
          tions of TER, illustrated.

1928.1   NAYLOR, EDWARD W. The Poets and Music. London and Toronto:
          J. M. Dent & Sons; New York: E. P. Dutton, 1928, pp.
          142-147.
              Offers useful remarks on the role of music in "ACC."

1928.2   [SALE], HELEN STEARNS. "The Date of the Garlande of
          Laurell." MLN XLIII (1928), 314-316.
              Argues that the astronomical and biographical data
          point to April 1523 as the date of composition of GL.
          But see GINGERICH and TUCKER, no. 1969.1 below.

1928.3   [SALE], HELEN STEARNS. "John Skelton and Christopher
          Garnesche." MLN, XLIII (1928), 518-523.
              Sale expands the known background of the Garnesche
          family, meagrely given by Dyce: the father a member of
          the respected gentry of Norfolk; shows that Christopher
          probably served with Sir Thomas Brewse, an associate of
          his father, at Hasketon Hall; traces Garnesche's career
          from 1509-13 on, as compiled from L&P, H VIII.

1929   BLUNDEN, EDMUND. "John Skelton." TLS (20 June 1929),
          481-482.
              The leading article in memory of the 400th anniver-
          sary of Skelton's death, reprinted in Votive Tablets

(1932), pp. 11-23; rescues the "old author" from the
negligent reading of Pope and Warton; defends TER, which
was intended to show "in a more penetrative form than
sermons, the ruinous costliness of the tavern"; despite
the medieval spelling of his text, Skelton "lives in an
essential approachableness"; praises his metrical independence: "Skelton is rich in the tune and term of shop
door, ale bench, market place; quaintly learned and of a
wide-roaming fancy, he brings his subject home with the
sudden directness of language immediately conceived in
necessities."

1929.1   HEBEL, J. WILLIAM and HOYT H. HUDSON (eds.). Poetry of the
          English Renaissance. New York: Croft, 1929.
              This influential collection, freshly edited from
          early editions, had undergone 10 printings by 1945; it
          contained the following selections, all from PPPW, 1568:
          from PS (vv. 1-96, 115-146; 273-334); from CC (vv. 1-91,
          287-345); from GL "Mistress Isabel Pennell," "Mistress
          Margaret Hussey"; "Prayer" [doubtful]. The same selec-
          tions are contained in the revised edition by Francis R.
          Johnson, A. Wigfall Green, and Robert Hoopes (New York:
          Appleton, Century, Croft, 1953).

1929.2   LLOYD, L[ESLIE] J. "John Skelton and the New Learning."
          MLR, XXIV (1929), 445-446.
              While Lloyd believes that conclusive evidence is
          lacking to decide Skelton's attitude toward the New
          Learning, he indicates that Skelton's ability as a
          Latinist is demonstrable.

1929.3   LLOYD, L[ESLIE] J. "A Note on Skelton." RES, V (1929),
          302-306.
              Lloyd rejects Brie's ascription in no. 1907 of
          "Recule" but accepts his attribution of "Masteres Anne"
          and corrects Brie's text. But see MAXWELL, no. 1950.3,
          for rejection of "Masteres Anne" as Skelton's own.

1929.4   WOLFE, HUMBERT. Notes on English Verse Satire. New York:
          Harcourt, Brace & Co., 1929, pp. 42-48.
              Argues that no one, before or after Skelton, had mas-
          tered or could master his type of satiric verse.

1930   AUDEN, W[YSTAN] H[UGH]. Poems. London: Faber, 1930,
          pp. 49-50.
              Poem X, "Love by ambition," consists of 38 lines of
          Skeltonics as adapted by Auden ("Love by ambition / Of
          Definition / Suffers partition"); Poem XVIII, on pp.
          62-3, consists of 29 lines of Skeltonic rhyme and rhythm
          as adapted by Auden.

1930.1   ELYNOURE RUMMYNGE. Illustrated by Claire Jones. San Fran-
          cisco: Helen Gentry, 1930, 54 pp. [limited edition].
          Reviewed in TLS (7 January 1932), 9.

1930.2   SITWELL, EDITH. The Collected Poems of Edith Sitwell.
          London: Duckworth, 1930.
              Among the poems that Miss Sitwell at the time "cared
          to preserve" were all those of Skeltonic influence
          listed under Bucolic Comedies, no. 1923.2 above.

1931   HENDERSON, PHILIP (ed.). The Complete Poems of John Skel-
          ton, Laureate. London and Toronto: J. M. Dent & Sons,
          1931; New York: Dutton, 1932, pp. 1, 47.
              The edition is based on Dyce, no. 1843.1, but modern-
          ized in spelling, punctuation, and, upon occasion, in
          syntax and diction; translates Latin "inserts" in English
          poems, but places "Latin poems and Epitaphs," including
          Latin lines at end of WCY, in appendix without transla-
          tion; collated with Hughes' edition, no. 1924. For 2nd
          rev. edn. see HENDERSON, no. 1948; for 3rd edn., no.
          1959.2; and 4th edn. no. 1964.
              Contents: Introduction; General Note on Text; Bibli-
          ography; [Section on] Elegies and Prayers: "Edw. IV"
          [doubtful]; "DEN"; "Time" [doubtful]; "Woefully Arrayed"
          [not Skelton's]; "Prayer" [doubtful]; "UDH"; "To His
          Wife" [not Skelton's]; [Section on] Ballads and Ditties:
          "Now Sing We" [not Skelton's]; "Laud"; "Lullay"; "Anc
          Acq"; "Knoledge"; "Cuncta licet" (Lat.) and (Engl.);
          "Go"; "WW"; "Mistress Anne" [not Skelton's]; "Jolly Rut-
          terkin" [not Skelton's]; "MM"; BC; PS; TER; [Section on]
          Minor Satires: "ACC"; "Ag Garn"; "AVT"; "Recule" [not
          Skelton's]; "Manner of the World" [not Skelton's]; WH;
          "Ag Scots"; Mag; "Calliope"; [Section on] Major Satires:
          SP; CC; DDA; WCY; Rep; GL; [Appendix] Various Latin poems
          and epitaphs including "Dev. Tr. & Ep. Adam.," "H VII,"
          "In Bedel," "El Marg" and "Eulogium"; "Chorus contra
          Scottos"; "Chorus contra Gallos"; "VSD."
              Reviews: Auden, W. H., Criterion, XI (1932), 316-319;
          Benét, William R., SRL, VIII (1932), 831; Burdett, O.,
          Sat. Rev., CLII (1931), 239; Clarke, Austen, Spectator,
          CXLVII (1931), 648-649; Graves, Robert, "An Incomplete
          Complete Skelton," Adelphi, 3rd ser., III (1931), 146-
          159; (see also Henderson, Philip, "Skelton: A Reply to
          Robert Graves," Adelphi, 3rd ser., III (1932), 239-241
          [in defense of his editorial method]); Gregory, Horace,
          New Rep., LXXII (1932), 333-334; Schneider, Isidor, Nation,
          CXXXVI (1933), 153-154; Scovell, E. J., New Statesman,
          n.s. III (1932), 69-70; TLS (24 September 1931), p. 725;
          Warren, C. H., Fortnightly Rev., CXXXV (1931), 670.

1931.1   [SALE], HELEN STEARNS. "The Political Satires of John
           Skelton." Ph.D. dissertation, Yale University (1931),
           172 pp.
                Presents with brief prefaces and textual notes the
           critical texts of six of Skelton's later poems: SP, a
           conflation of B.L. MS. Harley 2252, fols. 133*v-140 with
           printed version in CB, STC 22598, sigs. A2-A6; WCY, based
           on STC 22615 but collated with later sixteenth century
           printed editions and with fragmentary text in Bodley MS.
           Rawlinson C. 813, fols. 36-43v; CC, based on manuscript
           version from BL MS. Harley 2252, fols. 147-153, as aug-
           mented by printed version in STC 22601 (collated with
           subsequent sixteenth century editions); DDA, from first
           printed version in PPPW, STC 22608, sigs. F2-G3v; and
           Rep, from STC 22609; has sections on Life of Skelton
           (pp. 1-51); Position of Churchmen in the State (pp. 52-
           59); and from pp. 156 ff. on composition of the poems,
           bibliographical descriptions of the texts; and nine
           brief appendices presenting legal proceedings that in-
           volve a John and Agnes Skelton over the years 1466-1485
           (from Early Chancery Proceedings C. I., bundles 60, no.
           15; 64, no. 332 and no. 333; 54, no. 226). Identifica-
           tion of these last with activities of the poet's family
           is uncertain.

1931.2   SITWELL, OSBERT. The Collected Satires and Poems of Osbert
           Sitwell. London: Duckworth, 1931.
                Book II, "Poems" no. 5, "Superstition," pp. 112-113,
           8 lines of Skeltonic refrain: "But, looking for eglan-
           tine / Columbine, celandine / [2 lines] Wortdragon,
           Snapdragon / Martagon, Campion / Tarragon, rampion /
           Rocambole, pompion / Deborah...wanders." See no. 1927.4
           for "Discordant Dawn" here reprinted, pp. 210-211.

1932   AUDEN W[YSTAN] H[UGH]. The Orators. London: Faber &
           Faber, 1932.
                Book III, "Six Odes": Ode IV, "To John Warner, Son
           of Rex and Frances Warner," p. 94, consists of 15 lines
           of Skeltonical couplets and triplets: "O my, what peeps /
           At disheartened sweeps-- / Fitters and moulders, /
           Wielders and welders...&c." See VINES, no. 1932.2 be-
           low, for republication of "Birthday Ode."

1932.1   SWAIN, BARBARA. Fools and Folly During the Middle Ages and
           the Renaissance. New York: Columbia University Press,
           1932, pp. 162-165.
                Briefly discusses the fool-figures of Mag.

1932.2   VINES, SHERARD (ed.). Whips and Scorpions. London:
           Wishart, 1932, pp. 11-20.
                Reprints the "Birthday Ode" to John Warner by W. H.
           Auden, in no. 1932 above.

1933   ARDAGH, J. "A Skelton Poem in Sloane MS 747, f88b." N&Q,
            CLXV (1933), 285.
                Ascribes to Skelton the non-canonical "nowe-a-dayes."

1933.1   AUDEN, W[YSTAN] H[UGH]. The Dance of Death. London:
            Faber & Faber, 1933, pp. 26-27.
                "A's song" in 22 lines, despite occasional cross-
            rhyme, seems based on Auden's adaptation of Skeltonics.

1933.2   DAY-LEWIS, C[ECIL]. The Magnetic Mountain. London: L. &
            Virginia Woolf, 1933.
                Poem no. 5, p. 13, "Let us be off! Our steam" shows
            Day-Lewis sharing his friend Auden's interest in the
            syncopation of the Skeltonic, as in the lines "The needle
            in the gauge / Points to a long-banked rage / And
            trembles there to show / What a pressure below."

1933.3   EDWARDS, H. L. R. N&Q, CLXV (1933), 228.
                A brief query that announces the start of Edwards'
            search for new biographical documentation of Skelton's
            life; see EDWARDS, no. 1935.3 below.

1933.4   GREGORY, HORACE. "Praise to John Skelton," in No Retreat.
            New York: Harcourt, Brace & Co., 1933.
                A poem of 42 lines which, despite occasional cross-
            rhyme and non-rhyming lines, clearly shows the influence
            of Skelton's rhyme and metrics: "John Skelton, laure-
            ate, / whose sun has risen late / never to close its
            eye / in our eternity..."; reprinted in Poems 1930-1940.
            New York: Harcourt, Brace & Co., 1941, pp. 74-75; in
            Selected Poems. New York: Viking Press, 1951, pp. 38-
            39; and in Collected Poems. New York: Holt, Rinehart
            and Winston, 1964, pp. 53-54.

1933.5   HALL, WILLIAM C. "John Skelton," in Papers of the Manches-
            ter Literary Club, LIX (1933), 119-138.
                Overlooking his pungent satires, sees in Skelton a
            writer of good narrative, a satisfactory allegorist, and
            a constant seeker after more efficient forms, a search
            that brings him to his own peculiar structure, a measure
            that can also be made delicately lyric.

1934   APPERSON, G. L. "English Epigrams." TLS (15 March 1934),
            p. 194.
                Points out the verse "When the rain raineth and the
            goose winketh, &c" is first found in Skelton (GL 1430),
            not in Herrick, as had been claimed.

1934.1   BENSLEY, EDWARD. "English Epigrams." TLS (2 August 1934),
            p. 541.

Indicates that Skelton was not the originator of the proverb "Well wotith the cat whose berde she likkith" (GL 1438), for it is found in Latin and French forms earlier.

1934.2   EDWARDS, H. L. R. "The Life and Works of John Skelton." M.A. thesis, University of Wales [N/Ex], listed in RI, I, 205.

1934.3   EDWARDS, H. L. R. "New Light on Skelton." TLS (27 September 1934), p. 655.
          Convincingly challenges findings of GORDON, no. 1934.7 below, that poem "Quod mihi dixisti" shows connections between Skelton and Bishop Stephen Gardiner.

1934.4   EDWARDS, H. L. R. "Pereles Pomegarnet." TLS (27 December 1934), p. 921.
          Notes that the phrase in SP 37, refers to Katherine of Aragon in a laudatory manner.

1934.5   EDWARDS, H. L. R. "Syr Capten of Catywade." TLS (9 August 1934), p. 553.
          The reference in "Ag Garn" i, 16, alludes to Cattawade, Suffolk; see no. 1934.15 below.

1934.6   EDWARDS, H. L. R. "Syr Capten of Catywade." TLS (30 August 1934), p. 589.
          Gives dates which render invalid REDSTONE's suggestions on the matter in 1934.15 below.

1934.7   GORDON, I[AN] A. "New Light on Skelton." TLS (20 September 1934), p. 636.
          Gordon (1) believes the reference in MS Egerton 2642 links Skelton with Bishop Stephen Gardiner; (2) "discovers" a poem to Skelton by Erasmus (summer 1499) in MS Egerton 1651; but see EDWARDS, no. 1934.3, for argument against (1), and LLOYD, no. 1934.13, for argument against (2).

1934.8   GORDON, I[AN] A. "Skelton's Phillip Sparrow and the Roman Service-Book." MLR, XXIX (1934), 389-396.
          While indicating that PS is not a strict parody of the Breviary and Missal of the Church as Dunbar's "Dirige to the King at Sterling" was, Gordon shows that the verses, antiphons and psalms incorporated from the Service for the Dead give a deeper, or paradoxically more personal tone to Skelton's half-serious lamentation, coming from the Officium Defunctorum (Breviary) 1-386; Missa pro Defunctis (Missal), 387-512; Absolutio super Tumulum (Missal), 513-570; Officium Defunctorum (Breviary) 571-602; Ordo Commendationis Animae (Breviary), 845-1260.

1934.9   GORDON, I[AN] A. "Skelton's <u>Speke, Parrot</u>." <u>TLS</u> (1 Febru-
          ary 1934), p. 76.
               Countering Berdan's dating of the poem as of 1517-18,
          Gordon points out that it is much more likely that Wol-
          sey's diplomatic mission to Calais and Bruges, August 2-
          November 28, 1521, and his establishment of a "chayre"
          in Greek at Oxford in 1520 indicate Skelton's points of
          reference in <u>SP</u>.

1934.10   GORDON, I[AN] A. "A Skelton Query." <u>TLS</u> (15 November
          1934), p. 795.
               Wonders if Stephen Hawes, the poet, is the "Gorbelyd
          Godfrey" referred to in "Ag Garn" ii, 29 and in "title"
          to that second flyting, the reference stemming from a
          character in Hawes' <u>Pastime of Pleasure</u>, vv. 3487ff.,
          especially 3547.

1934.11   GRAVES, ROBERT. "English Epigrams." <u>TLS</u> (19 July 1934),
          p. 511.
               Extends APPERSON's note, no. 1934, concerning Skel-
          ton's use of a proverb in <u>GL</u>.

1934.12   KERR, WILLIAM. "Skelton and Politian." <u>TLS</u> (20 December
          1934), p. 909.
               Inquires if attention has been directed to certain
          similarities between <u>PS</u> and Politian's "De angeli puel-
          la." <u>See</u> SCHULTE, no. 1963.6, where on pp. 78-82 the
          author argues that "De angeli puella," published in
          Poliziano's <u>Omnia Opera</u> (Venice: Aldus Manutius, 1498),
          influenced the description of Jane Scrope in "The Com-
          mendacions" section of <u>PS</u>.

1934.13   LLOYD, L[ESLIE] J. "New Light on Skelton." <u>TLS</u> (27 Septem-
          ber 1934), p. 655.
               Points out that the "<u>Carmen Extemporale</u>" by Erasmus,
          "discovered" by GORDON, no. 1934.7, is given in <u>toto</u> by
          Preserved Smith, <u>Erasmus</u> (1923), pp. 453-454, and that
          Skelton seems not to have seen the poem, nor Erasmus to
          have wished to publish it.

1934.14   PALETTA, GERHARD. "Das Problem des glückhaften Herrschers
          bei Skelton," in <u>Fürstengeschick und innerstaatlicher</u>
          <u>Machtkampf im englischen Renaissance-Drama</u>. Breslau,
          1934, pp. 3-16.
               <u>Mag</u>, he argues, is a dramatic mirror for princes:
          the ruler must beware lest worldly wealth decay and wis-
          dom vanish through wantonness.

1934.15   REDSTONE, B. "Syr Capten of Catywade." <u>TLS</u> (16 August
          1934), p. 565.

Believes the reference in "Ag Garn" i, 16 is connected with a bridge chapel; suggests that it may further
refer to the execution of R. Debenham, at Dovercourt.
But see EDWARDS, no. 1934.6 above.

1934.16   SALTER, FREDERICK M. "Skelton's Speculum Principis."
           Speculum, IX (1934), 25-37.
                Fully describes the manuscript copy, hitherto un-
           printed, of Skelton's Speculum, B.L. MS Addit. 26,787
           (leaves missing from first two quires), its history,
           date and collation; discusses Skelton as tutor to the
           young Henry and possibly also to Arthur; prints the text
           proper, some of it written in Latin rhyming prose.

1934.17   WEITZMANN, FRANCIS. "Philip Sparrow's 'Elegy.'" TLS (13
           December 1934), 895.
                Points out that the use of "elegy" in PS (824) is its
           first recorded use in English; = "epitaph," not "song of
           mourning," from the ancient practice of using a distich
           for sepulchral inscription(?).

1935   AUDEN, W[YSTAN] H[UGH]. "John Skelton," in The Great
           Tudors. Edited by Katherine Garvin. New York: E. P.
           Dutton & Co., 1935, pp. 55-67.
                A short but penetrating essay on Skelton as a metri-
           cal master; particularly incisive on Skelton's metrical
           variety in Mag.

1935.1   AUDEN, W[YSTAN] H[UGH] and JOHN GARRETT (comps.). The
           Poet's Tongue. London: G. Bell & Sons, 1935, 2 volumes
           in 1.
                On I, 37-38, English verses from "VSD"; on I, 120, 18
           lines from TER ("Margery Mylkeducke"); on II, 113, 2
           stanzas from SP, "Le dereyn Lenvoey."

1935.2   AUDEN, W[YSTAN] H[UGH] and CHRISTOPHER ISHERWOOD. The Dog
           Beneath the Skin. London: Faber & Faber, 1935, p. 134.
                "Voices from the Crowd," 15 lines of Skeltonics as
           adapted by Auden.

1935.3   EDWARDS, H. L. R. "John Skelton: A Genealogical Study."
           RES, XI (1935), 406-420.
                Suggests that the Skeltons had moved into Southern
           England by mid-fifteenth century; finds a possible con-
           nection between Edward Skelton, Sergeant-at-Arms to
           Henry VI and John Skelton (but does not push this point
           later in his 1949 Life and Times); see POLLET, no. 1952,
           for the Yorkshire origin of the Skeltons.

1935.4   GREENE, RICHARD LEIGHTON (ed.). The Early English Carols.
           Oxford: Clarendon Press, 1935, pp. 310-311.

Freshly edits Skelton's satiric carol "My Darling Dere, My Daysy Floure."

1935.5   SALTER, F[REDERICK] M. "New Light on Skelton." TLS (17 January 1935), p. 33.
          Rejects the poem on "Tyme," ascribed to Skelton in CB, no. 1545 above, as non-canonical.

1936   ABRAHAMS, PHYLLIS. "More on 'Pleris cum musco.'" TLS (3 October 1936), p. 791.
          Presents brilliant example from John of Garland to show that the mooted phrase "pleris cum musco," SP 185 = an electuary. See also 1936.1 and 1936.3 below.

1936.1   BUNYARD, EDWARD A. "Pleris cum musco." TLS (19 September 1936), p. 748.
          Relative to the phrase in SP 185, believes there were several varieties of pears that could fit the description given by Skelton. But see ABRAHAMS, no. 1936 above.

1936.2   EDWARDS, H. L. R. "Hermoniake." TLS (24 October 1936), p. 863.
          Argues that the word in CC 297, means "Armenian."

1936.3   EDWARDS, H. L. R. "Pleris cum musco." TLS (12 September 1936), p. 729.
          Relative to the phrase in SP 185, proposes that pleris = paeris (pears) flavored with musk; perhaps a pomand shaped like a pear." But see ABRAHAMS, no. 1936 above.

1936.4   EDWARDS, H. L. R. "A Skelton Emendation." TLS (19 December 1936), p. 1052.
          Would emend manuscript readings puevinate to pneumatisant, rare to bene in lines 2 and 3 of the Latin epilogue to CC; see SALTER and EDWARDS, no. 1959.4, however, vol. II, pp. 417-418 for second thoughts on the matter.

1936.5   FARNHAM, WILLARD. The Medieval Heritage of Elizabethan Tragedy. Berkeley: University of California Press, 1936, pp. 216-223.
          In Mag, Skelton is careful not to make the immediate political application of his play too exact; relies on Aristotle's "balanced worldly wisdom" to show that men can control material prosperity through reason but must remember wealth is transitory and not fix too strongly on it. Reprinted with corrections, in England by Blackwell, and in U.S.A. by Barnes and Noble, 1956.

1936.6   FRASER, G. S. "Skelton and the Dignity of Poetry." Adelphi, XIII (1936), 154-163.

Argues that Skelton is the one living poet of fifteenth century England because he managed without a tra-
dition--"an original artist." See, however, nos. 1949.2
and 1958.1 below.

1936.7   GORDON, IAN. "John Skelton and the Early Renaissance: A
           Biographical and Critical Study." Ph.D. dissertation,
           University of Edinburgh, 1936, 287 pp.
               See his published book, no. 1943.1 below, essentially
           derived, with little change, from the dissertation.

1936.8   LEVIN, HARRY. "Skelton and Oxford." TLS (9 May 1936), 400.
               Notes that a "John Skelton" is mentioned in Walter
           Paston's will, Norwich, June 18, 1479; but see SALTER,
           no. 1936.12 below.

1936.9   NELSON, WILLIAM. "Skelton's Quarrel with Wolsey." PMLA,
           LI (1936), 377-398.
               SP, CC, WCY, in that order, he argues are written
           1521-23; Skelton then made reconciliation with Wolsey;
           contains detailed analyses of particular passages: CC
           376-380 (pp. 383-384); GL (opening) (p. 387); GL 586-601
           (pp. 388-390).

1936.10   NELSON, WILLIAM. "Skelton's Speke Parrot." PMLA, LI
           (1936), 59-82.
               A careful examination of the poem to determine date
           (Fall 1521); contains detailed analyses of particular
           passages.

1936.11   PYLE, FITZROY. "The Origins of the Skeltonic." N&Q, CLXXI
           (1936), 362-364.
               In terms of metrical stress and line movement, he
           argues, the Skeltonic descends from the short rhyming
           couplet of post-Conquest popular verse, cf. "Les noms de
           un livre en Engleis" (temp. Reliq. Antiq. I, 133).

1936.12   SALTER, F[REDERICK] M. "John Skelton." TLS (16 May 1936),
           420.
               The "Skelton" mentioned in LEVIN's note, no. 1936.8
           above, was apparently neither don nor student, and
           originally from Cumberland, not Norwich.

1936.13   SUTTON, G. P. C. "Pleris cum musco." TLS (19 September
           1936), p. 748.
               The word may actually be "flouris" (in SP 185) as in
           a cinnamon flower. But see no. 1936 above.

1936.14   WILLIAMS, RALPH VAUGHAN. Five Tudor Portraits, A Choral
           Suite Founded on Poems by John Skelton (Laureate), 1460-

1529. London: Oxford: University Press [c. 1935],
125 pp.
The composition consists of "The Tunning of Elinor
Rummyng," a Ballad (for Contralto or Mezzo Soprano),
Chorus (S.A.T.B.) and orchestra; "Pretty Bess" [from SP],
an Intermezzo (for Baritone solo), Chorus (S.A.T.B.),
and orchestra; "An Epitaph for John Jayberd of Diss," a
Burlesca (for male chorus and orchestra); "Jane Scroop,
her Lament for Philip Sparrow," Romanza (for Mezzo-
Soprano (or Contralto) Solo), Chorus of women's voices,
and orchestra; "Jolly Rutterkin" (Scherzo) (for Baritone
solo), Chorus (S.A.T.B.) and orchestra. [This last "por-
trait" is based on a non-canonical poem, whose ascription
to Skelton was suggested by a reference to the song in
Mag, v. 747.] Sketches for the Portraits in B.L. MS.
Addit. 50455 according to P. J. Willetts, "The Ralph
Vaughan Williams Collection," BMQ, xxiv (1961), 9, show
that Williams' plans originally called for a solo for
'[Mistress] Margery Wentworth' from GL. The first performance of Five Tudor Portraits took place at the 34th
Norwich Triennial Festival, September 25, 1936, with
Astra Desmond and Roy Henderson as soloists, Vaughan
Williams conducting. Performances of the piece were
recorded in 1954 by Nell Rankin, mezzo soprano, and
Robert Anderson, bass-baritone, the Mendelssohn Choir
and the Pittsburgh Symphony Orchestra, William Steinberg,
conducting, on Capitol Records CTL 7047; and in 1969 by
Elizabeth Bainbridge, contralto, John Carol Case, baritone, The Bach Choir and New Philharmonia Orchestra,
David Willcocks, conducting, on Angel Records S-1-36685.
HMV ASD 2489 presents still another recording, unavail-
able for description. See also WILLIAMS, no. 1948.2 for
a second composition of his on a doubtfully "Skeltonic"
text.

1937   EDWARDS, H. L. R. "Robert Gaguin and the English Poets,
        1489-1490." MLR, XXXII (1937), 430-434.
            Includes brief speculation on Skelton's involvement
        in a literary quarrel between Gaguin, French humanist
        scholar and diplomat, spokesman for the French embassy
        at court of Henry VII, 1489-90, and the humanists in
        Henry's employ.

1937.1 EDWARDS, H. L. R. "Skelton at Diss." TLS (22 May 1937),
        p. 396.
            Traces will of John Clarke of Diss, proved 14 April
        1507; proposes emendations to lines 1, 3, and 9 of Latin
        mock-trental "In Bedel": El (Hebrew for "God"), "Nabal
        nebulo," and sit potus.

1937.2   [SALE], HELEN STEARNS. "The Date of Skelton's <u>Bowge of</u>
<u>Court</u>." <u>MLN</u>, LII (1937), 572-574.
    Demonstrates bibliographically that it was printed by
de Worde in 1499 just before he moved from Westminster
to London in 1500.

1938   AUDEN, W[YSTAN] H[UGH] (ed.). <u>The Oxford Book of Light</u>
<u>Verse</u>. Oxford: Clarendon Press, 1938, pp. 64-79.
    Contains selections from <u>PS</u>, <u>GL</u> (Isabel Pennell),
"VSD" (as "Gup, Scot"), and from <u>SP</u>.

1938.1   EDWARDS, H. L. R. "The Humanism of John Skelton, with
Special Reference to his Translation of Diodorus Siculus." Ph.D. dissertation, University of Cambridge,
1938, cxix, 452 pp.
    The introduction of 119 pp. is divided into 17 sec-
tions which describe the manuscript, discuss the author-
ship of the Diodorus, Skelton's scholarship, his
connection with the universities and his laureateship,
his years at Diss and later at Westminster and London,
his relationship to the New Learning and his views on
Greek, detail Skelton's Classical, Medieval and Renaissance Learning, analyze his use of the elements of the
Trivium (Logic, Grammar, Rhetoric), and rhetorical prose
in the Diodorus; the text of the Diodorus is then presented (pp. 1-378), followed by explanatory notes (pp.
379-414), and a glossary (pp. 415-452). <u>See</u> SALTER and
EDWARDS, nos. 1956.2 and 1959.4 for EETS edition of the
translation.

1938.2   EDWARDS, H. L. R. and WILLIAM NELSON. "The Dating of Skelton's Later Poems." <u>PMLA</u>, LIII (1938), 601-611, 611-614,
614-619, 620-622.
    On the basis of the "24º" found in a copy of the
<u>Chronique de Raines</u> given to Henry VIII by Skelton, Ed-
wards believes with Nelson that Skelton had a private
calendar which began 30 October-17 November 1488; dates
all poems signed "Orator Royal" from May 1512 or later;
Nelson agrees with Edwards about dating of poems signed
<u>orator regius</u> but raises questions on the dating of
parts of <u>SP</u> based on differences between manuscript and
printed version; Edwards then defends the unity of <u>SP</u>,
interprets certain lines in it and in <u>GL</u>; Nelson,
finally, reviews researches in the Norwich archives as
they bear on Skelton's residence at Diss and his activities in Norfolk, and defends his division of <u>SP</u> into 2
parts.

1938.3   LLOYD, L[ESLIE] J. <u>John Skelton: A Sketch of his Life and</u>
<u>Writings</u>. Oxford: Basil Blackwell, 1938, 152 pp. Re-
printed by Russell and Russell (New York, 1969), with

author's one page comment on his earlier deficiencies
and accomplishment.
  Contents: Early Years; Rector of Diss; Early Poems:
Beginning of a New Career; Phyllyp Sparowe; Words, Words,
Words [TER, "Ag Garn," WH]; Magnyfycence; The Satires
[SP, CL, WCY, the anti-Scottish poems]; A Poet's Faith
[GL, Rep]; Appendix I, Skelton's translation of DS: Ap-
pendix II, Skelton's Lost Works; Brief glossary; Index.
  Reviews: Davis, B. E. C., MLR, XXXIV (1939), 429-
430; D.F., SRL, XIX (1 April 1939), 18; Garnett, David,
New Statesman and Nation, n.s. XVI (1939), 1128; Hender-
son, Philip, "Beastly Skelton," Spectator, CLII (1939),
63; Koszul, A., Études Anglaises, III (1939), 265; London
Mercury, XXXIX (1939), 474; Salter, F. M., RES, XV (1939),
339-342; TLS (11 February 1939), p. 85. See Intro., xxxxv
for remarks on LLOYD's contribution.

1938.4   McCAIN, JOHN W. "Heywood's 'The Foure PP':· A Debt to
         Skelton." N&Q, CLXXIV (1938), 205.
           Heywood shows influence of Skelton's satiric spirit,
         word tricks and rhyme-leash in A Play of Love, and seems
         to have taken from CC the jest of the Friar and Dame
         Margery and worked it into the Foure PP.

1939   BERNARD, J[ULES] E[UGENE]. The Prosody of the Tudor Inter-
         lude. New Haven, Connecticut: Yale University Press,
         1939.
           Comments on Skelton's use of a 'rime royal of dipodes'
         in Mag but sees little connection between character or
         theme and verse treatment (pp. 10, 35-39, 207); notes
         dimeter couplets in Wit and Science, 11. 175-196, are
         Skeltonics (p. 61); "Skeltonics indicate a song in The
         Play of Love," vv. 425-464 (p. 63); notes that Skeltonics
         do not prominently appear in Tudor interlude after 1540
         and that they seem best suited for the zestful Vices
         (pp. 206-207 and n. 45 on p. 207).

1939.1   BROWN, CARLETON (ed.). Religious Lyrics of the Fifteenth
         Century. Oxford: Clarendon Press, 1939.
           Edits from mss. four poems doubtfully ascribed to Skel-
         ton and challenges those ascriptions: "A Lament of the
         Soul of Edward IV," from B.L. MS. Harley 4011 on pp. 250-
         253; "A Prayer to the Three Persons in the Trinity," from
         B.L. MS. Addit. 20059, on pp. 80-81; "Thou Sinful Man"
         ("Vexilla Regis"), from Arundel MS. 285, on pp. 151-156;
         and "Woefully Arrayd" from B.L. MS. Harley 4012, on pp.
         156-158.

1939.2   DALE, DONALD. "Editions of Skelton." TLS (18 February
         1939), p. 106.
           Brief, sketchy, mentions collections of Hughes 1924,
         Graves 1927, Henderson 1931; see also HAWKINS, no. 1939.4.

1939.3   EDWARDS, H. L. R. "Learning and John Skelton." <u>Life and</u>
          <u>Letters Today</u>, XXIII (1939), 41-52.
              While Skelton was not the most profoundly or widely
          learned man of his day, he nonetheless shows erudition
          on scholarly and ecclesiastical matters at salient points
          in his poetry.

1939.4   HAWKINS, DESMOND. "Editions of Skelton." <u>TLS</u> (4 March
          1939), p. 136.
              Asks for new edition of Skelton based on Dyce, no.
          1843.1, complete and in old spelling, not in "bastard
          dialect."

1939.5   HIBERNICUS. "Skelton's Reputation." <u>N&Q</u>, CLXXVII (1939),
          84.
              Writes a brief addendum to Nelson's chapter on Skel-
          ton's reputation; <u>see</u> no. 1939.8 below.

1939.6   MacPEEK, JAMES A. S. <u>Catullus in Strange and Distant</u>
          <u>Britain</u>. Harvard Studies in Comparative Literature, no.
          XV. Cambridge, Massachusetts: Harvard University Press,
          1939, pp. 55-61.
              Finds no clear evidence that Skelton knew Catullus'
          verse--"not one mention of Catullus amid a veritable
          host of authors" (in <u>PS</u>'s 1382 lines); believes Skelton
          relied on Ovid's "<u>In mortem psittaci</u>," <u>Amor</u>. II, vi, or
          some imitation of it such as Statius' "<u>Psittaci dux volu-</u>
          <u>crem</u>," <u>Silvae</u> II, iv.

1939.7   MUSSON, J. W. "William Dunbar and John Skelton." M.A.
          thesis, University of Bristol, 1939. [N/Ex], listed in
          <u>RI</u>, I, 205.

1939.8   NELSON, WILLIAM. <u>John Skelton, Laureate</u>. Columbia Univer-
          sity Studies in English and Comparative Literature, no.
          139. New York: Columbia University Press, 1939, 266 pp.
          Reprinted by Russell and Russell (New York, 1964).
              <u>Contents</u>: Introduction; The Scholars of Henry VII
          [the foreign humanists at court: André, Carmeliano,
          Opiciis]; John Skelton, Humanist [at Henry VII's court];
          Tutor to the Prince [the young Henry]; The Origin of
          Skeltonic Ryme [from tradition of rhyming Latin prose];
          Skelton at Diss; The Court of Henry VIII; The Grammari-
          ans' War (1519-21); <u>Speak Parrot</u>; The Quarrel with Wol-
          sey [<u>CC</u> and envoys to <u>GL</u>]; The Last Years (<u>DDA</u> and <u>Rep</u>];
          Reputation and Influence; Appendix I, Bernard André's
          Works; Appendix II, The Court of Requests [Ottey vs.
          Skelton, Bray vs. Prior of St. Bartholomew's]; Appendix
          III, John Skelton vs. Thomas Pykerell; Appendix IV, The
          King of England and The Scottish Herald [the exchange
          between Lyon, Scottish Herald and Henry VIII at Therou-
          anne, 1513]; Appendix V, Skelton's Handwriting ["Lawde,"

93

and Dedication (plus marginalia) to <u>Chronique de Rains</u>,
both in Skelton's holograph]; Appendix VI, Chronology of
Skelton's Works; Bibliography; Index.

    <u>Reviews</u>: Brie, Friedrich, <u>Engl. Studn.</u>, XXII (1940),
123-126; Heffner, Ray, <u>MLN</u>, LVII (1942), 72-74; Kane,
George L., <u>Catholic Historical Rev.</u>, XXVI (1940), 145-
146; Lloyd, L. J., <u>MLR</u>, XXXV (1940), 82-83; <u>N&Q</u>, CLXXVII
(1939), 53-54; Merton, Thomas, <u>NYTBR</u> (28 May 1939), p. 2;
Pollard, A. F., <u>EHR</u>, LV (1940), 124-128; Salter, F. M.,
<u>RES</u>, XVI (1940), 201-205; <u>TLS</u> (26 August, 1939), p. 499;
Warren, L. C., <u>Church History</u>, VIII (1939), 378-379;
Wright, Louis B., <u>AHR</u>, XLV (1940), 625-626.

    <u>See</u> Intro., pp. xxxxiii-xxxxiv for remarks on this
important book.

1939.9   [SALE], HELEN STEARNS. "Skelton's <u>Heare after Foloweth
    Certain Bokes</u>." <u>Yale University Library Gazette</u>, XIV
    (1939), 12.

    Provides a description of the Yale acquisition of a
copy of <u>STC</u> 22600.

1939.10   WHITMEE, DOROTHY EDITH. "Bibliography of John Skelton,
    Poet Laureat 1460?-1529." Handwritten thesis submitted
    in partial fulfillment of the requirement for the diplo-
    ma in Librarianship, University of London, 1939.

    The bibliography does not aim at completeness; it is
intended as a supplement to the list of works cited in
Henderson's edition of Skelton, no. 1931 above; it is
presented in four sections: I. Collected Works; II.
Individual poems; III. Selections; IV. Biography &
Criticism.

1940   BATESON, F[REDERICK] W. (general ed.). <u>The Cambridge Bib-
    liography of English Literature</u>. Cambridge: Cambridge
    University Press, 1940, Vol. I (600-1660), pp. 408-411.

    The Skelton entry is arranged under five headings:
1) Collected Works (4 entries); 2) Selections (2 entries); 3) Separate Works (13 entries, including "Edw.
IV" (doubtful) from <u>Myrroure for Magistrates</u> and "Vexilla
Regis" (non-canonical) from <u>Christmas Carolles</u> <u>STC</u>
5204.5); 4) Manuscripts (an especially valuable listing
of 21 items, some located in more than one ms.; includes
the doubtful "Edw. IV" in two ms. versions, the doubtful
"Tyme" from 1 ms., the doubtful "Prayers" from 1 ms.,
the doubtful "Qui trahis" from 1 ms., the doubtful "Salve
plus decies" from 1 ms., a non-canonical "Wofully Araid"
in 3 ms. versions; the non-canonical "How darest thow?"
in 1 ms., and the non-canonical "Petuelly constrayned"
in 2 ms. versions); and 5) Biography and Criticism (33
utens). <u>See</u> BATESON, no. 1957 below, for Supplement to
<u>CBEL</u> (Vol. V), and WATSON, no. 1974.5, for <u>The New Cam-
bridge Bibliography of English Literature</u>.

1940.1   JACKSON, WILLIAM A. and EMMA UNGAR. The Carl H. Pforz-
         heimer Library, English Literature 1475-1700. New York:
         Privately Printed, 1940, III, pp. 967-978, Pforzheimer
         nos. 940-948.
              Provide detailed descriptions of CB (STC 22598,
         22600); CC (STC 22601); PS (STC 22595a, 22596b); WCY
         (STC 22615, 22617a, 22617c); PPPW (STC 22608).

1941   ALDINGTON, JOHN (ed.). The Viking Book of Poetry of the
         English World. New York: Viking Press, 1941, pp. 26-32.
              Presents excerpts from PS, vv. 998-1040; from TER,
         vv. 91-132; from "Ag Garn," i (3 stanzas); from SP (3
         stanzas of concluding general indictment); from GL,
         "Margery Wentworth," "Isabell Pennell," "Margaret Hus-
         sey." [This same Skeltonic selection presented again
         by Aldington in Poetry of the English Speaking World
         (London: Heinemann, 1947), pp. 19-24.]

1941.1   HAMILTON, G[EORGE] ROSTROVOR. Apollyon and Other Poems of
         1940.
              In the title-poem, "Apollyon," certain passages have
         short, essentially two beat lines possibly influenced by
         the revival of interest in Skeltonic rhythms as well as
         rhymes; see p. 2 of that poem for an example.

1941.2   RUBEL, VERÉ LAURA. "Skelton, Hawes and Barclay," in Poetic
         Diction in the English Renaissance. New York: Modern
         Language Association, 1941, pp. 31-46.
              Rubel distinguishes three styles in Skelton's diction:
         "cacophonous distortion" and "ragged fluency" in the
         satires, "mellifluous sesquipedality" in his more formal
         verse; she gives a brief but precisely itemized cata-
         logue of Tudor rhetorical figures in Skelton's poetry.

1941.3   SWALLOW, ALAN. "Principles of Poetic Composition from Skel-
         ton to Sidney." Ph.D. dissertation, Louisiana State Uni-
         versity, 1941, pp. 61-111.
              Swallow's second chapter is devoted to John Skelton
         in two sections: 1) "the structure of the poem" (pp. 61-
         82) and 2) "metrics" (pp. 82-111). Swallow argues that,
         structurally, in poems like PS, TER, SP, CC, Skelton had
         arrived at a method "definitely not medieval"--direct,
         with central dramatic figure, inductive and "accumula-
         tive"; he demonstrates that Skelton relied where neces-
         sary on Romance pronunciation for rhyme, could write
         good iambic pentameter (66 of 1st 126 lines of BC), was
         aware of "sprung rhythm," but also chose to employ
         wrenched accent, and in non-lyrical verse incorporates
         the four-stress "broken back" line of older tradition;
         notes that the "Skeltonic" uses accumulative parallels
         and conversational accent in accord with Skelton's

general poetic method and the dramatic structure of his poem; see also SWALLOW, no. 1950.6 and SWALLOW, no. 1953.6 below.

1941.4   WORKMAN, SAMUEL K. "Versions by Skelton, Caxton, and Berners, of a Prologue by Diodorus Siculus." MLN, LVI (1941), 252-258.
Shows that Skelton's use of a highly paraphrastic style in his version of the prologue seems almost a parody of aureate phrasing and vocabulary.

1942   ANDREWS, H. C. "Baldock, Herts., and John Skelton." N&Q, CLXXXII (1942), 231.
Presents an explanation of the "jibbet of Baldock," SP (v. 75) and WCY (v. 953).

1942.1   UNTERMEYER, LOUIS (ed.). A Treasury of Great Poems English and American. New York: Simon and Schuster, 1942, pp. 176-184.
Presents excerpts from TER, from CC; and from GL, "Mistress Margery Wentworth," "Mistress Margaret Hussey," "Mistress Isabel Pennell."

1943   ATKINS, J[OHN] W[ILLIAM] H[EY]. "Native Literary Problems (continued): Caxton, Hawes, Skelton," in English Literary Criticism: The Medieval Phase. Cambridge: The University Press, 1943, pp. 173-181.
Notes Skelton's defense of poetry in Rep is based on St. Jerome's remarks, thus making the poet the mouthpiece of Divine Will, "guiding and reproving men for their good," and thus the first exposition by an English poet of the doctrine of poetic inspiration; presents Skelton's awareness in PS of the levels of diction in earlier English poets, and his appreciation of the plain and vernacular.

1943.1   GORDON, IAN A[LISTAIR]. John Skelton, Poet Laureate. Melbourne and London: Melbourne University Press, 1943, 223 pp. Reprinted by Octagon Books (New York, 1970).
Contents: The Age of Transition; The Career of John Skelton; Middle Ages and Renaissance; Woman and the Lyre [the early lyrics]; Skelton and the Humanists; The Faithful Son [CC, Rep]; The Goliard [PS]; Skelton and the Morality [Mag]; The Wolsey Group [CC, SP, WCY]; Poetry and Politics ["BSK," & Flodden Poems, DDA]; Skelton and the Court [minor poems, including Garnesche flytings]; the Re-discovery of Skelton; Appendix A, Chronology of Skelton's Poems; Appendix B, Editions of Skelton's poems; Appendix C, Bale's List of Skelton's Works; Bibliography (MSS and Printed Books); Index.
Reviews: C., A.M., "John Skelton, Poet Laureate," University of Edinburgh Journ., XII: 193-194; Esdaile,

Arundell, English, V: 56-57; Howarth, R. G., "Scholarship and Skelton," Southerly, VII, iii, 46-50; Pafford,
J. H. P., Library, 4th ser., XXV, 94-95; TLS (8 July
1944), p. 333.
　　See Intro., xxxxv for ed. comments on this major study.

1944　　ALGAR, F.　"More Conjectures and Comments on the Origin of
　　　　Who Killed Cock Robin?" N&Q, CLXXXVII (1944), 131.
　　　　　　Claims that there is no evidence for Skelton's author-
　　　　ship of the poem as claimed by C. K. R., no. 1944.2
　　　　below.

1944.1　FROST, GEORGE L. and RAY NASH.　"Good Order: A Morality
　　　　Fragment." SP, XLI (1944), 483-491.
　　　　　　The authors print as Skelton's a freshly recovered
　　　　fragment (132 lines) of a morality play printed by W. Ras-
　　　　tell, 1533, dealing with Old Christmas and oral prayer;
　　　　but see K&Y, p. 26, and GREG, no. 1956 below.

1944.2　R., C. K.　"Who Killed Cock Robin?" N&Q, CLXXXVIII (1944),
　　　　130-131.
　　　　　　Claims that Skelton's PS lies behind the origin of
　　　　the rhyme, but see ALGAR, no. 1944 above.

1944.3　TILNEY-BASSET, J. G.　"John Skelton and the Tilneys." TLS
　　　　(11 November 1944), p. 547.
　　　　　　Notes that of the 11 ladies celebrated by Skelton in
　　　　his lyrics to GL, four were members of the Tilney family:
　　　　Margaret, wife of Sir Philip Tilney of Shelley, Suffolk
　　　　(and grandmother of Sir Edmund Tilney of Queen Eliza-
　　　　beth's Revels Office); Lady Ann Dacres of the South,
　　　　Lady Elizabeth Howard, 3rd daughter of Agnes, sister to
　　　　Sir Philip Tilney, and second wife of Thomas Howard,
　　　　second Duke of Norfolk; Lady Muriel Howard, granddaugh-
　　　　ter of the Duke of Norfolk and Agney Tilney; draws on
　　　　Pishey Thompson's History and Antiquities of Boston
　　　　(1856) for pedigrees.

1945　　FISHER, A. S. T.　"Birds of Paradise." N&Q, CLXXXVIII
　　　　(1945), 95-98.
　　　　　　"Bird of Paradise," as used in the fifteenth and six-
　　　　teenth centuries, need not refer to the bird called by
　　　　that name today; Antonio Pigafetta's description of the
　　　　birds (Paris, 1525) was Englished by Richard Eden 1555
　　　　under term "Birds of God"; Skelton follows Lydgate and
　　　　the pseudo-Chaucerian Parliament of Birds in using the
　　　　phrase to refer to the parrot in SP; see SKEAT, no.
　　　　1945.3 below.

1945.1　HOWARTH, R[OBERT] G[UY].　"Scholarship and Skelton."
　　　　Southerly, VI, No. 2 (1945), 46-50.

A review of recent scholarship on Skelton, particularly of Ian Gordon's <u>John Skelton: Poet Laureate</u>, no.
1943.1 above.

1945.2   SALTER, F[REDERICK] M. "John Skelton's Contribution to the
English Language." <u>Transactions of the Royal Society of
Canada</u>, 3rd ser., sec. II, vol. XXXIX (1945), 119-217.
    A study of Skelton's diction and vocabulary in his
translation of the <u>Bibliotheca Historia of Diodorus Sicu-
lus</u> and in his poetry, wherein Skelton may have used up-
wards of 800 words 10-300 years earlier than the earliest
date recorded for them in the <u>OED</u>.

1945.3   SKEAT, W. W. "Birds of Paradise." <u>N&Q</u>, CLXXXVIII (1945),
210-211.
    Agrees that the "syncretism" noticed by FISHER (no.
1945 above), according to which several types of birds
were given the name "Bird of Paradise," was reflected in
West European terminology; notes that the Portuguese
traders called them "<u>Passaros da Sol</u>," the Dutch, "<u>avis
Paradiseus</u>."

1946   HARVEY, J[OHN] H. "Eleanor Rumming." <u>TLS</u> (26 October
1946), p. 521.
    Presents evidence from the Court Rolls of Pachenesham
Manor (which included Leatherhead), Surrey County Muniments S. C. 6/15, that on August 18, 1525 "Alianora
Romyng" was fined 2d for selling ale "at excessive price
by small measure."

1946.1   TILLEMANS, TH. "John Skelton, A Conservative." <u>ES</u>, XXVII
(1946), 141-149.
    Argues that Skelton was not strongly enough conserva-
tive to be inhibited in his use of conventional forms,
but too strongly conservative to side with the pioneers
of the new English verse.

1947   HEYWARD, JOHN. <u>English Poetry: A Descriptive Catalogue</u>.
Published for the National Book League by the Cambridge
University Press, 1947, pp. 5-6.
    Describes copies of <u>CB</u> (<u>STC</u> 22598) and <u>WCY</u> (<u>STC</u>
22615); (reissued 1950 with facsimiles of the title-pages
to these volumes, plates 9 and 10).

1948   HENDERSON, PHILIP (ed.). <u>The Complete Poems of John Skelton, Laureate</u>. Second, revised edn. London & Toronto:
J. M. Dent and Sons, 1948, xxii, 446 pp.
    <u>Contents</u>: [revised Intro. and Bibliog.]; [Poems, re-
arranged into a chronological sequence]; "Edw. IV"
[doubtful]; "DEN"; "Woefully Arrayed" [not Skelton's];
"Prayer" [doubtful]; "<u>Vexilla Regis</u>" [not Skelton's];

"UDH"; "Time" [doubtful]; "My Darling Dear" ["Lullay"];
"MM"; "Jolly Rutterkin" [not Skelton's]; "WW"; "Mistress
Anne" [not Skelton's]; "Anc Acq"; "Knoledge"; "Go";
"Though ye Suppose" ["Cuncta licet," Lat. & Engl.];
"ACC"; BC; "Dev Tr & Ep. Adam"; PS; WH; TER; "The Rose
both White and Red" [Lawde]; "Manner of the World" [not
Skelton's]; "Ag Scottes"; "VSD"; "Ag Garn" [4 poems];
Mag; "AVT"; CC; SP; WCY; "Calliope"; GL; DDA; Rep; Ap-
pendix (Latin poems); Glossary [added--no gloss in First
edn.]. See also HENDERSON, no. 1959.2 for 3rd edn. and
no. 1964 for 4th.

1948.1   HOWARTH, R[OBERT] G[UY]. "Notes on Skelton." N&Q, CXCIII
          (1948), 186.
                Argues that SP. 1. 18, directly taken from Ovid's
          elegy for Corinna's parrot, also helps link Parrot with
          Paradise, for in Ovid, the dead parrot is welcomed in
          Elysium by other birds, including the Phoenix; notes that
          the cipher in WH, between lines 239 and 40, may draw its
          content from Ovid, Amores, II, vi, 54.

1948.2   WILLIAMS, RALPH VAUGHAN. Prayer to the Father of Heaven,
          Motet for Chorus (Soprano, Alto, Tenor, Bass), A Capella.
          London: Oxford University Press [c. 1948], 11 pp.
                The text is doubtfully Skelton's.

1949   EDWARDS, H. L. R. Skelton: The Life and Times of an Early
          Tudor Poet. London: Jonathan Cape, 1949, 325 pp.
                Contents: Preface and Introduction; Book One, Tutor
          [Skelton as a "prentice poet" (Cambridge, Oxford and
          early service with court of Henry VII from ? 1488);
          "DEN," the quarrel with Gaguin, services to Cambridge
          University, anti-feminine poems, Royal Tutor, holy or-
          ders, BC]; Book Two, Parson [Diss and mock trental, the
          birth of the "Skeltonic"; WH, Jane Scrope of Carrow Ab-
          bey and PS; TER]; Book Three, Orator; Book Four, Satirist
          [Wolsey and "AVT"; Wolsey and Mag; Skelton, Abbot Islip
          and Sanctuary at Westminster (1518); SP; Skelton, the
          aristocracy and service as "the poet of the Howards";
          CC; WCY; "Defeat with Honour" (an understanding reached
          with Wolsey)]; Book Five, Courtier [GL, as poetic apolo-
          gia and as a quietly explicit olive-branch to Wolsey;
          Margaret Brews Tilney, sister-in-law of Jane Scrope, and
          Gertrude (Anstey) Statham, an acquaintance from Cambridge
          days, as two of the ladies of the Garland; Skelton's "re-
          alignment" with Wolsey as seen in the dedication to Rep,
          his "last satiric flight" directed against two heretical
          graduates of Cambridge]; Notes, Appendix I, Records
          [Cambridge and Oxford; Diocese of London; Court records;
          Court of Requests; Norwich Consistory records; Westmin-
          ster Abbey Muniments &c.]; Appendix II, Early Lives

[Horman and Braynewode's; Bale's; Gruffyd's]; Appendix
III [Latin Passages Translated in the Text]; Index.
  Reviews: Bullough, G[eoffrey], MLR, XLVI (1951), 261–
262; Fletcher, Iain, New Statesmen–Nation (21 January
1950), 72–74; Jones, T. H., Life & Letters, LXV (1950),
251–252; Kinsman, Robert S., JEGP, XLIX (1950), 400–401;
Langham, James, (London) Sunday Times (1 January 1950),
p. 3; Listener, XLIII (1950), 574; TLS (13 January 1950),
p. 23; White, Beatrice, RES, n.s. III (1952), 199. Reprinted by Books for Libraries (Freeport, Long Island,
New York, 1971).
  See Intro., pp. xxxxiv–xxxxv for comments.

1949.1   GANT, ROLAND (ed.). Poems by John Skelton. London: Grey
         Walls Press, Crown Classics Series, 1949, 64 pp.
           Contents: "UDH"; "WW"; BC ["Prologue and Dyssymula--
         tion" only]; PS (vv. 1–334); TER (vv. 1–243); "Woffully
         Araid" [not Skelton's]; "Ag Scottes" [brief excerpt];
         CC (vv. 1–74); from GL, "Mastres Margery Wentworth"; SP
         (vv. 442–511); WCY (vv. 1–165).

1949.2   KINSMAN, ROBERT S. "John Skelton, Satirist: The Tradition
         of Fifteenth Century Political Verse Satire." Ph.D.
         dissertation, Yale University, 1949, 284, iv, pp. [92].
           Discusses themes, attitudes, symbols (noblemen's
         badges, crests, and other heraldic devices), modes
         ("prophecy," "squibs" and "bills"), and "masks" (es-
         pecially that of "vox populi") found in fifteenth century
         verse satire; then seeks to trace Skelton's manipulation
         of them in his short satirical pieces as well as in "Ag
         Sc.," "BSK," "VSD," SP, CC, DDA, and WCY; appendix con-
         sists of translations of, and commentary on, Skelton's
         Latin verse; see KINSMAN, 1950.1 and 1950.2 for articles
         derived from the dissertation.

1950   AUDEN, W[YSTAN] H[UGH] and NORMAN HOLMES PEARSON (eds.).
         Poets of the English Language. New York: Viking Port-
         able Library, 1950, I, pp. 368–425.
           Selections: "Aunc Acq"; "Lullay"; PS (entire); SP
         (vv. 1–235); from GL, "Mistress Isabell Pennell," "Mis-
         tress Margaret Hussey."

1950.1   KINSMAN, ROBERT S. "Phyllyp Sparowe: Titulus." Stud. in
         Phil., XLVII (1950), 473–484.
           In the final line of the Latin elegiac couplet that
         concludes PS, Skelton refers to his poem as a titulus,
         thus relating it to medieval monastic memorial verse and
         a pattern of consolation.

1950.2   KINSMAN, ROBERT S. "Skelton's 'Colyn Cloute': The Mask of
         'Vox Populi,'" in Essays Critical and Historical

Dedicated to Lily B. Campbell. Berkeley and Los Angeles: University of California Press, 1950, pp. 17-23 and 260-261.

Argues that the deliberately rustic and ragged name Skelton gives his persona is reflected in the practice by leaders of anti-establishment movements (e.g., "Captain Cobbler") of taking "popular" names, and is further associated with the notion that the voice of the people is the voice of God.

1950.3   MAXWELL, J[OHN] C[OATTS]. "A Skelton Ascription." TLS (10 February 1950), p. 89.
The "Masteres Anne" poem ascribed to Skelton by BRIE (no. 1907) and LLOYD (no. 1929.3) was printed by W. W. Skeat in the introduction to The Romans of Partenay, EETS, XXII (1866), pp. ii-iii from an early ms. whose possible dating seems to render the ascription very doubtful.

1950.4   PINTO, VIVIAN DE SOLA (ed.). John Skelton: A Selection from his Poems. London: Sidgwick and Jackson; New York: Grove Press, 1950, viii, 127 pp.
Contents: Prefatory note, Introduction; "Edw. IV" [doubtful]; "UDH"; "Lullay" (burden and vv. 1-14); "Woefully Arrayed" [doubtful]; BC (vv. 1-364, 372-399, 414-539); PS (extract); TER (extracts); from "Ag. Scottes" and "Ag. Garn. (i)"; from Mag: "Fancy's Hawk," "Adversity Speaks" (3 stanzas), "Liberty's Song," "Goodhope and Magnificence" (25 lines); CC (14 lines); SP (extracts); WCY (extracts); from GL: "Countess of Surrey," "Margery Wentworth," "Isabel Pennell," "Margaret Hussey," "Isabel Knight"; DDA (70 lines), "A Defense of Poetry" (from Rep); Select Bibliography; Index of Words Glossed; [glosses, notes, and translations at the foot of page].
Reviews: Bullough, G[eoffrey], MLR, XLVIII (1953), 108-109; TLS (29 December 1950), p. 822; White, Beatrice, RES, n.s. III (1952), 199; see DEUTSCH, B[abette], no. 1953.2 below for poem occasioned by Pinto's selections.

1950.5   ROSSITER, A[RTHUR] P[ERCIVAL]. English Drama from Early Times to the Elizabethans. London, New York: Hutchinson's University Library, 1950, pp. 115-117.
Mag not entirely successful in its treatment of a contemporary political problem of "Sound Finance" vs. "Squandermania," although it successfully handles the moral problem of rule and misrule.

1950.6   SWALLOW, ALAN. "The Pentameter Lines in Skelton and Wyatt." MP, XLVIII (1950), 1-11; reprinted in An Editor's Essays of Two Decades. Seattle and Denver: Experiment Press, 1962, pp. 131-158.

Argues and demonstrates that Skelton capable of perfectly "regular pentameter lines in his rhyme royale
poems, side by side with 4-stress, hypersyllabic lines."

1951   FORSTER, E[DMUND] M[ORGAN]. "John Skelton," in Two Cheers
        for Democracy. New York: Harcourt, Brace and Co.,
        1951, pp. 135-153.
            This essay originally given at the Aldeburgh Festival
        of 1950; pleasant and charming yet not always well in-
        formed, it detects in Skelton an extraordinary character,
        at times coarse and merry, "enjoying itself under the
        guise of censoriousness."

1951.1 HUXLEY, H[ERBERT] H. "Philip Sparrow." N&Q, CXCVI (1951),
        17.
            Suggests that the pet's name of Philip [PS] derives
        from the Latin pipilabat, representing the sound pip or
        "peep."

1951.2 McMANAWAY, JAMES G. "An Uncollected Poem of John Skelton
        (?)." N&Q, CXCVI (1951), 134-135.
            Prints a non-canonical bawdy poem of 5 lines, ascribed
        to Skelton in Day's The English Secretorie, no. 1586
        above.

1951.3 McQUISTON, JAMES ROBERTSON. "The Satire of John Skelton's
        Poems in Skeltonic Verse." M.A. thesis, University of
        North Carolina, Chapel Hill, 1951, 221 pp.
            Discusses eleven Skeltonic "satires" written in the
        Skeltonic verse form: finds "Ep. Two Knaves of Diss"
        characterized by burlesque substitution of anathema for
        blessing and by repetitio; inspects "Commendacions" sec-
        tion of PS for burlesque of the equivalent religious
        office "in a fairly orderly procedure"; notes in WH that
        the hawking parson's lack of learning is both directly
        derided and indirectly scored by the use of macaronic
        verse and mock-latin cryptogram; comments that TER is a
        more skillful example than WH of Skelton's "concentric"
        method of satire, i.e., recurrent reproach progressively
        intensified, forming a narrative psychologically apt in
        breaking down "defense mechanisms" and "self-rationali-
        zations" of the types satirized; treats "Ag Garn," "Ag
        Dundas" and DDA as hubris punished, violations of Aris-
        totelean means (will over wit, rashness over caution);
        sees CC as "new satire" in converting "particulars" by
        apt phrase and characterization into "types" or "general-
        izations" again; holds that WCY fits together in Skel-
        ton's "orderly disorder" of "report" and digression,
        concentrically arranged to add and intensify, with Wol-
        sey the ultimate center of the remarks, "the representa-
        tive par excellence of the corruption of the church, the

oppression of the state, and the hypocrisy of the utterly damned soul"; completes his thesis by commenting less freshly and convincingly on DDA and Rep (not fully in Skeltonics).

1952   KINSMAN, ROBERT S. "The 'Buck' and the 'Fox' in Skelton's Why Come Ye Nat to Courte?." PQ, XXIX (1952), 61-64.
        Confirms Dyce's tentative query about the identification of the animals mentioned in vv. 118-119 of the poem: Buck = Edward, Duke of Buckingham; Fox = Richard Fox, Bishop of Winchester.

1952.1   PINE, EDWARD. "The Westminster Singing Boys." TLS (12 December 1952), p. 828.
        Mentions a scribbled couplet in Treasurer's accounts for 1530, on back page: "'Dame Elynour Rummyng / by her hummyng sunnyng [summyng]' / item paid to John Smythe....'" but already noted by Nelson, no. 1939.8, p. 120, although differently transcribed.

1952.2   POLLET, MAURICE. "Skelton et le Yorkshire." Études Anglaises, V (1952), 11-16.
        Argues from local distribution of family and place names that Skelton's family origin was in Yorkshire, close to city of York proper. For differing views, see EDWARDS, no. 1935.3 and JALAVA, no. 1965.2.

1953   BUDGEY, NORMAN F. "John Skelton, Dichter eines Uebergangszeitalters: Versuch einer neuen Wertung." Ph.D. dissertation, University of Marburg, 1953. [N/Ex], listed by Lawrence F. McNamee, Dissertations in English and American Literature, Theses Accepted by American, British and German Universities, 1865-1964 (1968), p. 193.

1953.1   DEUTSCH, BABETTE. "Homage to John Skelton." Poetry, LXXXII (1953), 95.
        Poem of 90 lines, with the middle section of 48 lines written in Skeltonics: "Verily, perroquet, / Your vivacious play / Should not a whit dismay / Maitre Mallormé; / Both sagacious birds / You both made poems with words" etc.; inspired by PINTO's selections from Skelton, no. 1950.4 above; poem reprinted in The Collected Poems of Babette Deutsch. Garden City, New York: Doubleday, 1969, pp. 102-104.

1953.2   KINSMAN, ROBERT S. "The Printer and Date of Printing of Skelton's Agaynste a Comely Coystrowne and Dyuers Balettys." HLQ, XVI (1953), 203-210.
        The printer is not Pynson as thought from the inclusion of ACC & DB in a bound volume with Rep. but John Rastell, c. 1527, as shown by examination of watermarks,

type-faces, woodcuts and printer's ornaments; evidence
further points to ACC's having been printed before DB.

1953.3   KINSMAN, ROBERT S. "Skelton's Uppon a Deedmans Hed: New
          Light on the Origin of the Skeltonic." Stud. in Phil.,
          L (1953), 101-109.
               Shows connection between medieval poems on the "Signs
          of Death" and verse form used in "UDH," arguing that the
          poem represents the earliest "Skeltonic" written, pre-
          sumably when Skelton was undergoing ordination or had
          been but recently ordained (1498).

1953.4   SERONSY, CECIL C. "A Skeltonic Passage in Ben Jonson."
          N&Q, CXCVIII (1953), 24.
               Shows that The Devil is an Ass, V, vi, 25 ff. offers
          language and verse strongly reminiscent of Skelton's TER.

1953.5   SKELTON, JOHN. A Poem Called The Tunnynge Of Elynour
          Rummynge, The Famous Ale-Wife of England, Written by
          John Skelton Poet Laureat to King Henry the VIII. Wor-
          cester, Massachusetts: the Gehenna Press, 1953, 34 pp.
               Illustrated with 12 engraved woodblock illustrations
          by L[eonard] Baskin, text from Dyce, limited to 118
          copies.

1953.6   SWALLOW, ALAN. "John Skelton: The Structure of the Poem."
          PQ, XXXII (1953), 29-42.
               Skelton arrives at a new poetic structure in his late
          satires, beginning with SP, by accumulating and accreting
          details and data, as rehearsed by a single dramatic ego
          (e.g., Parrot, Colin) through repetition and parallels,
          thus achieving a semblance of inductive thinking which
          leads to the reader's acceptance of the general state-
          ment; reprinted in An Editor's Essays of Two Decades.
          Seattle and Denver: Experiment Press, 1962, pp. 108-130.

1954   EVANS, ROBERT A. "Some Aspects of Wyatt's Metrical Tech-
          niques." JEGP, LIII (1954), 197-213.
               Comments on Skelton's and Wyatt's use of "-eth" in-
          flectional ending with optional syllabic value; of "-es"
          with metrical elision; of "-e" as a syllabic filler;
          agrees with Swallow, no. 1950.6, that in rhyme royal
          Skelton is in the decasyllabic tradition of the fifteenth
          century.

1954.1   LEWIS, C[LIVE] S[TAPLETON]. "The Close of the Middle Ages
          in England," in English Literature in the Sixteenth
          Century Excluding Drama. Oxford: Clarendon Press, 1954,
          pp. 133-143, especially 136-139.
               Points out affinities between contemporary Scottish
          popular verse and Skelton's poetry--"something faintly

like Skeltonics" in such Scottish poems as <u>Cowkelbie Sow</u>
[pre-1501] and "Lord Fergus' Gaist"; presents incisive
commentary on the effects of Skeltonics and stimulating
remarks on <u>PS</u> and <u>TER</u>; bibliography on pp. 674-675 (error
in listing Gant as Cant).

1954.2　LOMBARDO, AGOSTINO. "Morality and Interlude." <u>English</u>
<u>Miscellany</u>, V, 1954, 17-30.
　　Includes relatively conventional remarks on <u>Mag</u>; <u>see</u>
<u>also</u> LOMBARDO, no. 1957.2 below.

1954.3　RIBNER, IRVING. "Morality Roots of the Tudor History Play."
<u>Tulane Studies in English</u>, IV (1954), 23-30.
　　<u>Mag</u> is the first clear application of the morality
play to the problems of secular politics.

1954.4　ROLLINS, HYDER and HERSCHEL BAKER (eds.). <u>The Renaissance</u>
<u>in England</u>. Boston: D. C. Heath & Co., 1954, pp. 65-86.
　　<u>Contents</u>: [from 1568 <u>PPPW</u>]: "UDH"; "Edw. IV" [doubt-
ful]; <u>BC</u>, <u>PS</u>, [vv. 1-615, 709-833]; <u>TER</u>.

1955　CARPENTER, NAN COOKE. "Skelton and Music: Roty Bully
Joys." <u>RES</u>, ser. 2, VI (1955), 279-284.
　　In <u>ACC</u>, a dance song "Roty Bully Joys" is played by a
stableman upstart on a lute; the song title is used to
indicate his abuse of court privilege and ignorance of
courtly ideals. <u>See also</u> HOLLANDER, no. 1961.2 and
HEARTZ, no. 1966.4 below.

1955.1　EVANS, MAURICE. "John Skelton," in <u>English Poetry in the</u>
<u>Sixteenth Century</u>. London: Hutchinson's Home Library,
1955, pp. 47-64.
　　Presents a general discussion of the poet based on
recent scholarship; sees Skelton's poetic style as a
full realization of the vernacular in diction, idiom,
allusion and genre.

1955.2　GRAVES, ROBERT. <u>The Crowning Privilege, the Clark Lectures</u>
<u>1954-55</u>. London: Cassell & Co., 1955.
　　Written on "Professional Standards in English Poetry,"
the lectures contain many references to Skelton's standing and his poetry: pp. 4-5, 11-12 [["Edw. IV"]], 18;
21-22, 23, 24; 76, 79 [["Dev. Trent"]] and a chapter on
"Dame Occupaycyon" [from <u>GL</u>]. <u>Note</u> that Graves' Cambridge
Lectures <u>and</u> Oxford Addresses (no. 1961 below) are included in his collected volume <u>On Poetry: Collected</u>
<u>Talks and Essays</u>, no. 1969.2 below.

1955.3　KINSMAN, ROBERT S. "Eleanora Rediviva: Fragment of an
Edition of Skelton's <u>Elynour Rummyng</u> ca. 1521." <u>HLQ</u>,
XVIII (1955), 315-327.

TER perhaps written <u>c</u>. 1516; apparently printed by H.
Pepwell to judge from typefaces (but <u>see</u> SCHULTE, no.
1961.4 below); gives list of variant readings.

1955.4   LAMSON, ROY and HALLETT SMITH (eds.). <u>The Golden Hind</u>.
          Rev. edn., New York: W. W. Norton, 1955, pp. 17-26.
              <u>Selections</u>: <u>PS</u> (vv. 1-63; 769-833; 970-1237); from
          <u>GL</u>, "Mistress Margaret Hussey"; "MM"; <u>CC</u> (vv. 47-24,
          488-594, 637-672).

1955.5   POLLET, MAURICE. "John Skelton, Poète lauréat (1460-1529)."
          Doctoral dissertation, The Sorbonne, 1955, "Thèse dac-
          tylographiée," vi, 514 pp. [N/Ex].
              <u>See</u> POLLET, no. 1962.5 for finished book derived from
          this dissertation.

1955.6   WARREN, ROBERT PENN, and ALBERT ERSKINE (eds.). <u>Six Cen-</u>
          <u>turies of Great Poetry</u>. New York: Dell Press, 1955,
          pp. 21-28.
              <u>Selections</u>: "Second Person" [doubtful]; "UDH,"
          "<u>Vexilla Regis</u>" [non-canonical], "Lullay"; from <u>GL</u>,
          "Mistress Isabel Pennell," "Mistress Margaret Hussey."

1956   GREG, W[ALTER] W. (ed.). "<u>Old Christmas</u> or <u>Good Order</u>, A
          Fragment of a Morality printed by William Rastell in
          1533," in <u>Malone Society Collections</u>, IV (1956), pp.
          33 ff.
              Despite the argument of FROST and NASHE, no. 1944.1
          above, Greg does not believe that this is Skelton's work,
          as indeed both verse and content would seem not to indi-
          cate.

1956.1   RINGLER, WILLIAM. "John Stowe's Editions of Skelton's
          Workes...." <u>SB</u>, VIII (1956), 215-217.
              Argues that the "I.S." who "newly" collected the
          "workes" for the printer Thomas Marshe was John Stowe;
          attempts to establish the canon only incidentally.

1956.2+   SALTER, F[REDERICK] M. and H. L. R. EDWARDS (eds.). <u>The</u>
          <u>Bibliotheca Historia of Diodorus Siculus, Translated by</u>
          <u>John Skelton</u>. EETS, 2 vols. CCXXXIII (1956) [Text],
          pp. xvii, 395; and CCXXXIX (1959 for 1957), pp. liii and
          396-472 (<u>see</u> no. 1959.4).
              The first volume describes the manuscript from which
          it prints the text, notes Skelton's indebtedness to
          Poggio's Latin translation of Diodorus' Greek, comments
          on Skelton's prose style as translator and presents the
          text; the second volume presents notes on the text and
          contains useful appendices on Skelton's Greek, Skelton
          and the Latin Classics, his debt to Cato's Distichs, and
          a glossary; it also offers emendations to <u>SP</u> 270+, <u>Rep</u>

(Epit.) 8, and CC (Lat.) 2-3 on pp. 412, 413-414, and 417-418 respectively.
Manuscript Source: Corpus Christi College, Cambridge, MS 275, fols. 2, 268, 1, 13.
Reviews: Mustanoja, Tauno, Neophilologische Mitteilungen, LVIII (1957), 118-119; Nelson, William, RES, 2nd ser., X (1957), 192-193; Spencer, T. J. B., MLR, LII (1957), 247-248 [rev. of text]; Spencer, T. J. B., MLR, LIV (1959), 140-141, a brief review of the second volume (notes, gloss, and appendices).

1956.3   WILLS, FLOREID. "Skelton's Proverb Lore." M.A. thesis, Baylor University, 1956, 105 pp. [N/Ex], Howard no. 7588.

1957   BATESON, F[REDERICK] W. (general ed.). The Cambridge Bibliography of English Literature: Supplement (600-1900). Cambridge: Cambridge University Press, 1957, V, pp. 203-204.
Adds to section on Skelton's Biography and Criticism some 20 items from the years 1936-53. See WATSON, no. 1974.5 for The New Cambridge Bibliography of English Literature.

1957.1   HARRIS, WILLIAM O. "Theme and structure in Skelton's Magnyfycence." Ph.D. dissertation, University of North Carolina, 1957, iii, 231 pp.
Chap. I presents Skelton's unrecognized artistry in using soliloquies and monologues for structural effects, and in balancing contrasting and complementary scenes, fusing content and form into the older pattern of the morality and the Stoic-Christian concept of fortitude or moderation in both prosperity and adversity; Chap. II seeks to refute the notion that satire of Wolsey was the compelling purpose of Mag; Chap. III tries to refute the notion that the term "magnificence" was based on Aristotle's definition of liberality (substituting for it fortitude in the tradition of the four cardinal virtues); Chap. IV shows that the "dual conflict" pattern of the play is quite similar to that of Mankynde, a pattern supported by Skelton's use of a Horatian maxim on the conflict between prosperity and adversity; Chap. V develops the Stoic-Christian notion of "Fortitude" as the theme of Mag. See HARRIS, nos. 1960.4 (article, from Chap. II), 1963.3 (article, from Chap. IV), and 1965.1 (book, a complete reworking of Chaps. III-V, with new material added).

1957.2   LOMBARDO, AGOSTINO. Il Pre-Shakespeariano Drama. Venice: Neri Pozza, 1957, pp. 128-143.
Includes in his book article on Mag, no. 1954.2 above.

1957.3   PINTO, V[IVIAN] de SOLA and A. E. RODWAY (eds.). The
          Common Muse. London: Chatto & Windus, 1957, pp. 32-33.
             On these pages the editors present a reprint, with
          selected notes, of "A Ballade of the Scottysshe Kynge,"
          no. 1513.4 above.

1957.4   SCAMMELL, G. V. and H. L. ROGERS. "An Elegy on Henry VII."
          RES, VIII (1957), 167-70.
             A version from manuscript of a poem incorrectly
          ascribed to Skelton by seventeenth and eighteenth century
          bibliographers.

1958   CARRUTH, HAYDEN. "Anxiety." Nation, CXXXVI (26 April
          1958), 364.
             A poem in the Skeltonic manner, of 4 stanzas.

1958.1   PHILLIPS, NORMA ANNE. "John Skelton and the Tradition of
          English Realism." Ph.D. dissertation, Yale University,
          1958, 190 pp.
             Deals with the derivative nature of the "major realis-
          tic" poems of Skelton: (BC, Mag, TER) and the extent of
          the poet's dependence on Chaucer and Langland. While
          conceding that Skelton shows an "undeniable originality"
          in verbal and prosodic experimentation, argues that,
          contrary to "almost all existing opinion," in the so-
          called "realistic" aspects of his work he relies heavily
          on Chaucer and Langland for the form and substance of
          "real life." Dissertation not summarized in DA until
          XXVIII (1968), 2653A. See PHILLIPS, no. 1966.9 for
          article derived from dissertation.

1959   EMDEN, A[LFRED], B[ROTHERSTON]. "Skelton, John (Sceltonus,
          Schelton, Skeltonides, Skeltonus, Skelkonus)," in A
          Biographical Register of the University of Oxford to
          A.D. 1500. Oxford: Clarendon Press, 1959, III, pp.
          1705-1706; reprinted under same heading in A Biographi-
          cal Register of the University of Cambridge to 1500
          (Cambridge, 1963), pp. 529-530.
             The best "brief life" available; greatly expands the
          limited information given by John and J. A. Venn in
          Alumni Cantabrigiensis (Cambridge University Press,
          1927), Pt. I, vol. iv, pp. 82-83 [12 lines only]; and
          in effect corrects and updates Sir Sidney Lee's 1897 DNB
          entry on Skelton; bases new material on findings of
          William Nelson (1939) and H. L. R. Edwards (1949); still
          considers "Edw. IV" to be Skelton's earliest poem
          [doubtful].

1959.1   HEISERMAN, ARTHUR RAY. "John Skelton and Medieval Satire."
          Ph.D. dissertation, University of Chicago, 1959, 390 pp.
          plus bibliography.

Since this dissertation with the addition of a long chapter on <u>Mag</u> was published as a book in 1961, its description will be limited to the statement that it presents a background of Skelton criticism and presents its own examination, chronologically, of Skelton's major satires, defined as literary works which attack an object using certain structural conventions, personae and diction in a "manifest fiction," and analyzes <u>BC</u>, <u>SP</u>, <u>CC</u>, and <u>WCY</u> in these terms, each chapter following its analysis with a review of the earlier conventions drawn on; <u>see</u> HEISERMAN, no. 1961.1 below.

1959.2   HENDERSON, PHILIP (ed.). <u>The Complete Poems of John Skelton, Laureate</u>. 3rd edn. London: J. M. Dent, 1959, xxviii, 448 pp.
     Introduction revised, list of critical and biographical studies brought up-to-date, glossary expanded; otherwise texts unchanged from, and in same order as, the 2nd edn., no. 1948 above. <u>See also</u> HENDERSON, no. 1964.

1959.3   HOLLOWAY, JOHN. "Skelton." (The Chatterton Lecture on an English Poet, read 26 February 1958), in <u>Proceedings of the British Academy</u>, XLIV (1959), pp. 82-102.
     Considers <u>TER</u> the most significant "Skeltonic" poem, vitally and distinctively integrated by the single scene of the poem itself as it is brought progressively into focus; presents a provocative if brief discussion of Skelton's proverbial language and the Skeltonic meter; reprinted in his book, <u>The Chartered Mirror</u>, no. 1960.5 below.
     <u>Short Notice</u> of lecture by R. T. Davies, <u>MLR</u>, LVI (1961), p. 298.

1959.4   SALTER, F[REDERICK] M. and H. L. R. EDWARDS (eds.). <u>Bibliotheca Historia &c.</u>, vol. II. EETS, 1959 for 1957.
     Introduction, Notes, Appendices, and Glossary: <u>see</u> SALTER and EDWARDS, no. 1956.2+ above for fuller entry.

1960   BARNUM, PRISCILLA HEATH. "Skelton's <u>Magnificence</u> Reconsidered." M.A. thesis, Syracuse University, 1960, 120 pp.
     Sees the confessional monologues of Fansy and the four courtly vices as a reflection of the French <u>sottie</u> within a morality frame; notes Skelton's dependence on the general outlines of Thomistic theology for the elevation of reason over will, for his psychology of faculties, essences, virtues, vices and sins, and for keeping the roles of his fools and vices "firmly consistent with the theological definition of <u>vitia</u>"; observes that the concept of kingship implicit in the play reflects pre-Reformation ideas of the limited powers and moral

responsibilities of the office; argues that the action
of the play may be summarized in the infinitive phrase
"to become a king," a state not reached until Magnificence develops an inner strength (Perseverance), after a
lapse into prideful folly and a recovery through atone-
ment, at the end of which magnanimity is within reach
(v. 2492), and notes the "plot" may better be seen as an
analogue to the legend of Robert, King of Sicily, reduced
to the status of a fool but restored to kingship once his
pride has been humbled through suffering.

1960.1   CARMINATI, MARIA. "Magnyfycence by John Skelton." M.A.
         thesis, University of Foscari, 1960. [N/Ex], Howard no.
         7579.

1960.2   CHALKER, JOHN. "The Literary Seriousness of John Skelton's
         Speke, Parrot." Neophilologus, XLIV (1960), 39-47.
             Chalker advances 3 points to support view that despite
         its obscurities and apparent arbitrary development, SP is
         a serious literary achievement: 1) in the deliberate use
         of a late medieval fiction that speech is "but folly and
         sugared eloquence" as a deliberate and complex satiric
         instrument; 2) this tradition given tonal unity through
         the versatile and often ironic character of the Parrot;
         and in 3) the poet's shift of emphasis from a general to
         particular satire of the times, through a satire of po-
         litical acts, to an uncompromising attack on Wolsey,
         oblique in the first 21 stanzas, but increasingly direct
         in the envoys.

1960.3   GREEN, PETER [MORRIS]. "John Skelton," in Writers and
         their Work, no. 128. London and New York: published
         for the British Council and the National Book League by
         Longmans, Green and Co., 1960, 46 pp.
             A brief, popular discussion; includes selected bib-
         liography.
             Reviews: Hansen, Klaus, ZAA, XII (1964), 73-74;
         Zandvoort, R. W., ES, XLII (1961), 126-127.

1960.4   HARRIS, WILLIAM O. "Wolsey and Skelton's Magnyfycence: A
         Re-evaluation." Stud. in Phil., LVII (1960), 99-122.
             Argues that the date of the play (c. 1516), a review
         of the external facts of the mid-teens, and a comparison
         of the play with Skelton's other works indicate that
         Magnyfycence is not primarily an attack on Wolsey, if an
         attack on him at all.

1960.5   HOLLOWAY, JOHN. The Chartered Mirror. London: Routledge,
         Kegan Paul, 1960, pp. 3-24.
             Reprints his Chatterton Lecture, no. 1959.3 above.
             Review: Davies, R. T., MLR, LVI (1961), 298.

Annotated Bibliography c. 1488-1977

1960.6   HUGHEY, RUTH (ed.). <u>The Arundel Harington Manuscript of</u>
           <u>Tudor Poetry</u>. Columbus: The Ohio State University
           Press, 1960. 2 vols.
               <u>See</u> nos. 1536, 1560.2, 1566 above for poems derived
           from this manuscript, showing Skeltonic influence.

1960.7   KINSMAN, ROBERT S. "A Skelton Reference c. 1510." <u>N&Q</u>,
           N.S. VII (1960), 210-211.
               Skelton is mentioned in the <u>Great Chronicle of London</u>
           with Cornysh and More as poets for whose skill, even, the
           crimes of Grimaldis of Genoa (one of the tax collectors
           in the employ of Empson and Dudley) are too great to
           describe.

1960.8   O'CONNELL, RICHARD. "Variation on a Theme of <u>Maister Skel-</u>
           <u>ton, Poet Laureat</u>." <u>Botteghe Oscure</u>, XXV (1960), 198.
               A poem of 3 stanzas, six lines each of iambic pen-
           tameter, referring to <u>Speke Parrot</u>, and ending, "Here's
           not your habitat, squawk, parrot, squawk, / All men
           respect are the sparrow and hawk."

1961   GRAVES, ROBERT. "The Dedicated Poet: The Oxford Inaugural
           Lecture." <u>Encounter</u>, XVII (1961), 11-18.
               Includes translation of Skelton's Latin poem on Calli-
           ope; lecture is included in Graves' <u>Oxford Addresses on</u>
           <u>Poetry</u>, no. 1962.3 below as first chapter, pp. 3-25; <u>see</u>
           <u>also</u> GRAVES, no. 1969.2 below.

1961.1   HEISERMAN, ARTHUR R[AY]. <u>Skelton and Satire</u>. Chicago:
           University of Chicago Press, 1961, 326 pp.
               <u>Contents</u>: Chapter I, "History, criticism and conven-
           tion," presents the background of earlier Skelton studies,
           outlines the theory of his own book: that satire focuses
           on an <u>object</u> of attack, "a discernible historical par-
           ticular," using a <u>mixture</u> of <u>structural devices</u>, appro-
           priate <u>personae</u>, and selected levels of <u>diction</u> in a
           "<u>manifest fiction</u>" relying on conventions to control the
           response of the audience; Chap. II, "Shadow and Sub-
           stance," concentrates on <u>BC</u> with its attack on vices of
           court in the near-fatal voyage of "Drede," the fearful
           novice in poetry, and presents it against the background
           of earlier conventions of structure, character and alle-
           gorical action (<u>PP</u>, <u>H of F</u> and various anti-court com-
           plaints); Chap. III, "Measure is Treasure," presents as
           background to <u>Mag</u> the problems in 1516 of financial ex-
           cess in Henry VIII's foreign ventures, which had domestic
           overtones; traces the tradition of the medieval <u>Speculum</u>
           <u>principis</u> and problems of governance (measure) as trans-
           lated through dramatic plot with a <u>combination</u> of charac-
           ters (the proud prince and his wanton gallants); notes
           that the plot and "nowe-a-dayes" <u>topos</u> is Skelton's

111

admixture (as a survey of pertinent medieval moralities
shows); Chap. IV, "Above All Other Birds Alone," deals
with SP, a refashioning of the "complaints-against-the
times" in terms of the conventions of medieval political
prophecies, nonsense satire, and OT biblical allusions;
the apparent confusions in structure, character and
language are methodical, deliberate fictions, which,
when measured against a survey of medieval precedents,
shows Skelton's poem to be "a satire allegoria of un-
precedented richness and profundity," his theme and satiric method having pushed at the limits of satire, but
progressively failing in the envoys; Chap. V, "The Style
That's Plain and True," presents CC as well-organized,
"its objects, personae, structure and diction...of great
age" against a background of medieval attacks on the es-
tates, in plain diction and popular sayings; Chap. VI,
"Tudor Vates," deals chiefly with WCY, but includes DDA
and lesser invectives as written in the spirit of gross
invective and abuse, defensible as the work of a nation-
alistic court poet, who recounts recent events in the
style of the sirventes, with snatches of dialogue and
(occasional) recourse to the pattern of the love song
(as in incipit of WCY) or in style of personal debat of
the flyting ("Ag Garn"); Chap. VII, "That Supposicyon
that Callyd is Arte," summarizes the argument of the
book: Skelton is adept at mixing conventions drawn from
diverse literary sources but seldom able to blend them
harmoniously in terms of object, structure, personae in
diction, BC being his most successful poem, SP his most
interesting failure, CC less challenging and outreaching
in terms of total artistic endeavor. See HEISERMAN, no.
1959.1 above.

Reviews: Baker, Donald C., ELN, I (1963), 130-132;
Blissett, William, QQ, LXIX (Winter 1962-63), 647-648;
Craig, Hardin, Manuscripta, VI (1962), 112-114; K., R.E.,
College English (1963), pp. 328-329; Kinsman, Robert S.,
PQ, XLII (1963), 143-144; Nelson, William, RN, XV (1962),
137-139; Pollet, Maurice, Études Anglaises, XV (1962),
and also a notice in Med. Rev., XXXII (1963), 157-158;
Schirmer, W. F., Anglia, LXXX (1962), 468-470; Zandvoort,
R. W., ES, XLVI (1965), 422-424.
See Intro., xxxxvii-xxxxviii for comments.

1961.2   HOLLANDER, JOHN. The Untuning of the Sky, Ideas of Music
          in English Poetry, 1500-1700. Princeton: Princeton
          University Press, 1961, pp. 92-96.
          Offers an excellent analysis of Skelton's use of
          musical terms and concept in "ACC"; see also CARPENTER,
          no. 1955, and HEARTZ, no. 1966.4.

1961.3   KENDLE, BURTON STUART. "The Ancestry and Character of the Skeltonic." Ph.D. dissertation, University of Wisconsin, 1961, 226 pp.

          Reviews theories deriving the Skeltonic from Latin hymns, chants and sequences, and from the leonine hexameter, none of which he believes is a genuine progenitor, but all of which combine to provide a rich heritage of suggestive combinations; reviews theories connecting the Skeltonic with the secular Latin poetry of Middle Ages, certain types of French and Italian verse of the early Renaissance, Latin prose ornamented by internal rhyme and English prose derived from this practice, all of which, he finds, fail to furnish a direct ancestry but, again, provide a complex of possibilities out of which Skelton shaped his verse or which shaped his sensibility; traces the metrical patterns provided the poet in four stress alliterative verse (as in Mag) by the Alliterative Revival (with special indebtedness to PP) fused with rhythmical principles found in the syllabic and rhyming verse of medieval English romances and drama that reflected "continental" traditions; finally presents a detailed account of the interest generated by the Skeltonic in the twentieth century poetry of Graves, Hughes, Edith Sitwell, and Auden.

1961.4   SCHULTE, EDVIGE. "John Skelton nella tradizione poetica inglese." AIUON-SG, IV (1961), 149–171.

          In two sections: the first reviews Skelton scholarship, setting the poet into a late medieval and early humanist tradition in terms of diction, style and meter, and indicating his influence or effect on his successors; the second concentrates on TER and argues that the fragments of TER (c. 1521) described by Kinsman, no. 1955.3, were printed by Wynkyn de Worde, instead of Pepwell.

1961.5   STEVENS, JOHN [EDGAR]. Music and Poetry in the Early Tudor Court. London: Methuen, 1961, pp. 378–379.

          Edits freshly from the Fayrfax MS, B.L. MS. Addit. 5465, fols. 96ᵛ–99, Skelton's "Manerly Margery," no. 1495.1 above, as set to music by William Cornish, Jr.; provides brief commentary.

1962   BEVINGTON, DAVID M. "The Pioneering Contributions of Bale and Skelton," in From "Mankind" to Marlowe. Cambridge, Massachusetts: Harvard University Press, 1962, pp. 128–140.

          By arranging his play into 4 distinct phases--prosperity, conspiracy, overthrow, and restoration--Bevington demonstrates, Skelton forms a "new cast" for each phase so arranged that "their successive appearance is an expression of the homilectic aim of the play," structurally

relevant to a dramatic presentation of duplicity, and
conducive to an apprehension of the unseen world of in-
trigue.

1962.1   FISH, STANLEY E[UGENE]. "Aspects of Rhetorical Analysis:
          Skelton's Philip Sparrow," SN, XXXIV (1962), 216-238.
              PS is seen as a comparative study of innocence and
          experience reflected in Jane Scrope's reaction to the
          death of her sparrow and the poet's "commendation" of
          Jane's present beauty rather than the departed sparrow's
          "soul," and constructed upon a deliberate contrast in
          the rhetorical components used in the two parts of the
          poem.

1962.2   FISH, STANLEY E[UGENE]. "The Poetry of Awareness: A Re-
          assessment of John Skelton." Ph.D. dissertation, Yale
          University (1962), 239 pp.
              Argues that Skelton's poetry is the result of an in-
          tensely personal confrontation of experience, not a
          merely stereotyped response to a predetermined world-
          picture; believes the structural limitations and inade-
          quacy of personae in Skelton's poems of abuse and "proc-
          lamation" (WCY, "Ag Sc," DDA, "Ag Garn") also underlie
          the unsympathetic criticism accorded them; detects
          closer relationship between sophistication of language
          and rhetoric and level of awareness in the lyrics, and
          WH, PS; examines Skelton's aesthetic and poetic tech-
          niques as closely related to his philosophical awareness
          in BC, CC and SP. See FISH, no. 1965 for the book derived
          from this dissertation.

1962.3   GRAVES, ROBERT. Oxford Addresses on Poetry. London:
          Cassell, 1962, pp. 3-25.
              As the first chapter in the book, reprints "The Dedi-
          cated Poet," no. 1961 above; see also GRAVES, no. 1969.2
          for inclusion of the piece in a larger collection.

1962.4   LARSON, JUDITH S[WEETZER]. "What is 'The Bowge of Courte'?"
          JEGP, LXI (1962), 288-295.
              BC is not only an allegory itself but also a parody
          on the medieval form of allegory.

1962.5   POLLET, MAURICE. John Skelton (c. 1460-1529): Contribution
          à l'Histoire de la Prérenaissance Anglaise. Paris:
          Didier, 1962, 291 pp.
              Contents: Introduction, Epoque, origines et débuts;
          Un clerc-poète à la Cour d'Henri VII; Le Recteur de Diss;
          Orator Regius, ou le poète aux armées; Magnificence;
          Elynour Rumming, intermède profane; Franc Tireur, les
          satires contre Wolsey (SP, CC, WCY); La guirlande de
          laurier (GL); Les dernières annéees et la lutte contre

les Luthériens [C Mery Tales, Rep]; Légende et Réputation; L'Univers Skeltonien; La Satire; Conclusion; Appendice I [comparison of "BSK" and "Ag Scottes"]; Appendice II, Une Source inédite du poème Elynour Rummyng ["The Gossips' Song"]; Skelton apocrypha; Bibliographie; Index; [Table of Contents].

For translation of the book, see WARRINGTON, no. 1971.6.

Reviews: Chalker, John, SN, XXV (1963), 164-167; Heiserman, A. R., MP, LXI (1963), 127-128; Klein, Robert, RLC, XXXVIII (1964), 148-150; M., J., Bull. Assoc. G. Budé, 4º ser. (1963), 256-257; Marc'hadour, Germain, RN, XVI (1963), 122-124; Milligan, Burton, JEGP, LXII (1963), 367-369; Nelson, William, MAe., XXXII (1963), 242-244; Pinto, V. de Sola, MLR, LVIII (1963), 398-400; Robbins, R[ossell] H., Archiv, CCII (1965), 138-139; TLS (27 September 1963), p. 720; Watson, Curtis Brown, Études Anglaises, XVI (1963), 178-180.

See Intro., xxxxvi-xxxxvii for comments.

1962.6   SCHULTE, EDVIGE. "Skelton, Petrarca e l'amore della gloria nel The Garland of Laurel." AIUON-SG, V (1962), 135-163.
Argues 1) that Skelton follows Petrarch and More (see More's letters of 7 October 1517 and those of 1520) in valuing the "glory" acquired through literary works composed over a long and productive life, 2) that Skelton knew and drew on Petrarch's Africa and the Triumph of Fame (Chap. III, first version, redaction, and redaction re-elaborated), and Canzone CCXXIII, as well as Dante's Purgatorio for themes, situations and characters in the GL. Included in no. 1963.6 below.

1963   ANDERSON, M[ARY] D[ÉSIRÉE]. Drama and Imagery in English Medieval Churches. Cambridge: Cambridge University Press, 1963, p. 84.
The choice of knife or gallows offered by Despair to Magnificence in Skelton's play, is prefigured, so to speak, in a medieval trial scene as represented by small figures set in the mouldings of the chapter house door at Salisbury Cathedral (c. 1280, Plate 8a).

1963.1   DEYERMOND, A. D. "Skelton and the Epilogue to Marlowe's Doctor Faustus." N&Q, CCVIII (1963), 410-411.
Marlowe may have been familiar with Skelton's GL, 11. 15-21 (especially 18), which seem to be echoed in the epilogue to his play.

1963.2   FOSS, MICHAEL. "John Skelton." M.A. thesis, Temple University, 1963, 59 pp. [N/Ex], Howard no. 7580.

1963.3   HARRIS, WILLIAM O. "The Thematic Importance of Skelton's
          Allusion to Horace in Magnyfycence." SEL, III (1963),
          9-18.
               The allusion to Horace in v. 114 shows that Skelton
          is warning the king, Henry VIII, not to be proud in
          prosperity.

1963.4   KINSMAN, ROBERT S. "The Voices of Dissonance: Patterns in
          Skelton's Colyn Cloute." HLQ, XXVI (1963), 291-313.
               The structure of CC is based on the interplay of
          three "voices": those of the poet-prophet, Colyn as
          voice of the people, and the voice of a tyrannical
          churchman (Wolsey); restores readings from ms. in epi-
          logue to poem.

1963.5   MAXWELL, J[AMES] C[OATTS]. "Bone Ache." N&Q, CCVIII
          (1963), 13-14.
               Skelton's use of the phrase in Mag, 1. 1907 to denote
          venereal disease is earlier than the earliest citation
          for the term in OED; see ROWLAND, no. 1964.2 for differ-
          ent reading.

1963.6   SCHULTE, EDVIGE. La Poesia di John Skelton. Naples:
          Ligouri, 1963, 264 pp.
               Contents: Introduzione; Vita e Studi umanistici;
          L'accademia Fiorentina, Aldo Manuzio e gli umanisti
          Inglesi, La posizione di John Skelton; Le prime opere;
          The Bowge of Court e l'influsso di Brandt; Il Monologo
          Drammatico, La tradizione medievale e l'influsso
          rinascimentale nel Phillip Sparrow; Le opere drammatiche
          di John Skelton: Il Magnificence; La satira del tardo
          umanesimo e l'invettiva nelle opere di Skelton: Against
          Garnesche; L'Elinour Rummyng, La vecchia del Poliziano,
          e il Baldus del Folengo; Satira e allegoria nello Speak
          Parrot; Le ballate satiriche Colin Clout e Why Come Ye
          Nat to Court? e il Convocation Sermon di John Colet;
          Skelton, Petrarca e l'amore della gloria in The Garland
          of Laurel; L'ispirazione divina del poeta in A Replica-
          tion; Lingua, metrica e fortuna dello Skelton nel periodo
          rinascimentale; Osservazioni conclusive; Note bibliogra-
          fiche.
               Review: Chinol, Elio, Parole e le Idee, VII (1965),
          45-46; see also SCHULTE, no. 1962.4.
               See Intro., xxxxvii for ed. comment.

1963.7   STAHLMAN, W. D. and OWEN GINGERICH. "Introduction" to Solar
          and Planetary Longitudes for Years - 2500 to + 2000 by
          Ten-Day Intervals. Madison: University of Wisconsin
          Press, 1963, p. xii.
               Provides date of May 8, 1495 for GL; see GINGERICH AND
          TUCKER, no. 1969.1 for full argument on this matter.

1963.8   TAYLOR, WARREN and DONALD HALL (eds.). Poetry in English.
          New York: Macmillan, 1963, pp. 51-6. 2nd edn., see no.
          1970.6.
          Selections: from GL, "Isabell Pennell," "Margaret
          Hussey"; "UDH"; "Prayer to the Father" [doubtful];
          "Lullay."

1963.9   WILLIAMS, JOHN (ed.). English Renaissance Poetry. New
          York: Doubleday Anchor, 1963, pp. 1-10.
          Selections: "Woefully Arrayed" [non-canonical]; "Upon
          a Deadmans Head"; "My Darling Dear"; "To Mistress Anne"
          [non-canonical]; "Mistress Margery Wentworth"; "Go,
          little quair" [from WCY].

1963.10   ZALL, PAUL (ed.). "Merie Tales...Made by Master Skelton
          Laureat," in A Hundred Merry Tales and Other Jestbooks.
          Lincoln: University of Nebraska Press, 1963, pp. 326-
          348.
          See no. 1567 above.

1964   HENDERSON, PHILIP. The Complete Poems of John Skelton,
          Laureate. London: J. M. Dent; New York: E. P. Dutton,
          1964, 4th edn., xxviii, 448 pp.
          Prints a revised list of Critical and Biographical
          Studies; otherwise no change from 3rd edn., no. 1959.2
          above.

1964.1   MYERS, OLIVER T. "Encina and Skelton," Hispania, XLVII
          (1964), 467-474.
          While parallels or analogues cited, no actual influ-
          ence of one poet on the other shown.

1964.2   ROWLAND, BERYL. "'Bone Ache' in Skelton's Magnyfycence."
          N&Q, CCIX (1964), 211.
          Seeks to refute MAXWELL, no. 1963.5, by arguing that
          context supports the view that the "bone ache" of v.
          1907 means just that, not venereal disease.

1964.3   SWART, J. "John Skelton's Philip Sparrow," in "A Supple-
          ment" to English Studies, Presented to R. W. Zandvoort"
          (1964), pp. 161-164.
          In the epitaph with which he ends the first part of
          the poem, Skelton manages a double parallelism between
          the two parts of the poem: 1) Jane is to Skelton as
          Philip was to Jane: 2) Skelton's thoughts about Jane
          are as harmless to her as the sparrow's antics were.

1964.4   TUCKER, MELVIN J. "California MS. Ac 523, Formerly Phillips
          MS. 3841." N&Q, CCIX (1964), 374-376.
          The manuscript account book for the Howard family, 17
          April 1523-18 January 1524, makes no mention of Skelton,

and shows that the Countess of Surrey spent Christmas at
court with her husband; thus it may have been unlikely
that she was at Sheriff Hutton for the Christmas season
1522-23, as would have been necessary for the date ordinarily assigned GL. See TUCKER, nos. 1967.7 and
1969.7 below.

1964.5   TUCKER, MELVIN J. The Life of Thomas Howard, Earl of
         Surrey and Second Duke of Norfolk, 1443-1524. The
         Hague: Mouton, 1964.
             Table III shows the children by his first marriage,
         some of whom were mentioned, Tucker argues, in the lyrics
         to GL; note typo, Ann, daughter of Edward II, d. 1512
         not 1612. See also TUCKER, nos. 1967.7 and 1969.7 below.

1965   FISH, STANLEY E[UGENE]. John Skelton's Poetry. Yale
         Studies in English, CLVII. New Haven and London: Yale
         University Press, 1965, viii, 268 pp. Reprinted in
         Archon Books, Shoestring Press (Hamden, Connecticut,
         1976).
             Contents: Introduction [Skelton's poetry a verbal
         dramatization of the poet's problem of moral action];
         "This World is But a Cherry Fair" [The lyrics and BC];
         "Some Graver Subject" [Skelton and rhetoric: WH and PS];
         "The Poet as Hero" [SP, pts. i and ii; CC]; "Excess and
         Mean" [in WCY, Skelton lacks subtlety, is a single-toned,
         irresponsible voice, his accumulation of observation a
         dead weight; in GL, no longer troubled by the question
         of worldly fame, committed to a poetic vision that
         transcends this world, makes mock deference to the
         courtly lyric, and a poetic "surrender" to Wolsey "on
         his own terms"]; "Observations and Qualifications" [at
         the center of a Skelton poem is the psychological
         (spiritual) history of its protagonist, doubt-torn and
         questing, but returning to an order whose relevance is
         reasserted rather than weakened in the process].
             Reviews: Berry, Francis, Tablet, CCXX (1966), 644-
         645; Burke, Herbert G., LJ, XC (1965), 1721-1722; Craik,
         T. W., Anglia, LXXXIV (1966), 224-226; Fraser, Russell,
         So. Atlantic Quarterly, LXVI (1967), 491-494; Ingham,
         Patricia, RES, XVIII (1967), 308-310; Kinsman, R. S.,
         RN, XVIII (1965), 324-327; Milligan, Burton, JEGP, LXV
         (1966), 162-164; Nelson, William, MAe, XXXVI (1967),
         96-98 [includes remarks on William O. Harris' book on
         Magnyfycence]; Pollet, Maurice, Études Anglaises, XIX
         (1966), 285; Reiss, Edmund, Speculum, XLI (1966), 325-
         326; Smith, A. J., "Incumbent Poets," MLQ, XXIX (1968),
         341-350, especially 345-350 [also includes remark on Tom
         Scott's Dunbar (New York, 1966)]; TLS (11 November 1965),
         p. 1004; Thomson, Patricia, N&Q, N.S. XIII (1966), 38-39.
             See Intro., pp. xxxxvii-xxxxviii for comment.

1965.1   HARRIS, WILLIAM O[LIVER]. Skelton's 'Magnyfycence' and the
          Cardinal Virtue Tradition. Chapel Hill: University of
          North Carolina Press, 1965, x, 177 pp.
               Contents: "The Interpretive Choice" [Not Aristotelian
          opposition of moderation and prodigality, but late medie-
          val "fortitude" in mutability "Nowe all in welth; forth-
          with in Pouerte"]; "Wolseyan Satire Reexamined" [bulk of
          anti-Wolsey satires of period later (1522-28) making Mag
          (1517) suspect as an anti-Wolsey play, especially since
          Wolsey still in subordinate role, and Ramsay's equating
          of the vices with aspects of Wolsey's personality dra-
          matically unlikely anyway]; "The Meaning of 'Magnifi-
          cence' and Other Terms" [Mag related to "Fortitude"
          rather than to "Liberality"]; "Fortitude and the Two-
          Part Morality Structure [Temptation in Prosperity, and
          Fall; Struggle against Despair in Adversity, followed by
          Rescue and Regeneration]; "Three Interpretive Problems
          Solved" [(1) the theme of contemptus mundi, (2) the con-
          cept of measure, (3) the application of general prin-
          ciples specifically to kingly behavior]; "A Concluding
          Analogue" [cf. The Enterlude of the .iiii. Cardynal Ver-
          tues]; Index. See HARRIS, no. 1957.1.
               Reviews: Armstrong, W. A., English, XVI (1966), 62-
          64; Bevington, David, Speculum, (1966), 541-543; Burke,
          Herbert C., LJ, XC (1965), 4981; Clark, Larry D., QJS,
          LIII (1967), 209; Fish, Stanley E., MLR, LXII (1968),
          456-457; Habicht, Werner, Anglia, LXXXIV (1966), 438-
          439; Henry, A[vril] K., N&Q, N.S. XIII (1966), 306-308;
          Ingham, Patricia, RES, XVIII (1967), 308-310, particu-
          larly 310; Nelson, William, MAe, XXXVI (1967), 96-98
          [also reviews S. E. Fish's book on Skelton (1965)]; Pol-
          let, Maurice, Études Anglaises, XIX (1966), 283-284;
          Spivack, Bernard, RQ, (1968), 79-82.
               See Intro., p. xxxxvi for ed. comments.

1965.2   JALAVA, HILKKA. "The Language of John Skelton's Rhymes."
          Thesis submitted for the Licenciate in Philosophy, Uni-
          versity of Helsinki, 1965, 222 pp.
               Studies vowel sounds in rhymes used in Skelton's
          poems: short vowels in stressed syllables, long vowels,
          short diphthongs, long diphthongs; vowels and diphthongs
          in French loan words, low German and Dutch loans, Scan-
          dinavian loans, unstressed vowels; makes some technical
          remarks on Skelton's rhymes and versifications: "skilful
          variation," often serving "purely ornamental purposes,"
          but with large number of irregularities in rhyme in Mag
          from textual corruption; notes Skelton's tendency to give
          special stress to last syllable; cautiously concludes
          that the linguistic features revealed in the rhymes are
          predominantly East Midland, thus supporting the view of
          Fuller and Dyce that Skelton was a native of Norfolk.

1965.3   KANDASWAMI, S. "Skelton and the Metaphysicals," in <u>Critical</u>
          <u>Essays on English Literature</u>. Edited by V. S. Seturaman.
          Madras: Orient Longmans, 1965, pp. 157-169.
             Argues that Skelton anticipates the metaphysicals "by
          virtue of the fantastic strain in his poetry, his ques-
          tioning of the fundamental paradox of existence"; com-
          pares "Edw. IV," [a poem doubtfully Skelton's] with parts
          of Donne's "Nocturnal upon Saint Lucie's Day" and some
          lines from Vaughan's "To Amoret Weeping"; finds <u>PS</u> an
          anticipation of Dr. Johnson's pronouncement on the meta-
          physicals in his "life of Cowley": "as they sought only
          for novelty...they compared the little to the great, or
          the great to the little"; finds certain resemblances be-
          tween <u>GL</u> and Suckling's "Session of the Poets"; and makes
          comparisons between the young scholars of <u>Rep</u> with Samuel
          Butler's satire on the metaphysical sectarian in <u>Hudi-</u>
          <u>bras</u>.

1965.4   LAHIRI-CHOUDHURY, D. K. "Skelton and Aristotle: A Study
          of the Tragic View in <u>Magnyfycence</u>." Ph.D. dissertation,
          University of Leeds, 1965, 525 pp.
             Part I of the thesis deals with <u>Mag</u> and the Morali-
          ties: the problem, the <u>Poetics</u> (background), the <u>Poetics</u>
          (the texts), and <u>Mag</u> as compared with other moralities
          in terms of the hero, <u>hemartia</u>, <u>peripeteia</u> and <u>anag-</u>
          <u>norisis</u>, suffering, action, and <u>catharsis</u>; Part II deals
          with <u>Mag</u> and the Fall of Princes tradition, tracing "the
          tragic pattern," the notion of character and individual
          responsibility and ending with structure and miscellanea:
          structure, purgation, false identity; in essence Lahiri-
          Choudhury presents <u>Mag</u> as the product of a "new" notion
          of the tragic distilled and differing from the Aris-
          totelean and the Fall of Princes traditions.

1965.5   ROBBINS, ROSSELL HOPE [and] JOHN L. CUTLER (comps.). <u>Sup-</u>
          <u>plement to the Index of Middle English Verse</u>. Lexington:
          University of Kentucky Press, 1965.
             List by first line, alphabetically arranged, all of
          Skelton's canonical poems (30), noting their appearance
          in manuscripts or early prints and listing major eigh-
          teenth-twentieth century printings of them, in individual
          or collected form; also list 7 poems doubtfully Skel-
          ton's: "Elegy on King Henry the Seventh," no. 2578.5
          (in which they acknowledge Scammell and Rogers' discovery
          in <u>RES</u>, n.s. VIII (1957), 167-170 of Durham Cathedral
          ms.); "Edward IV," no. 2192, for which they locate a
          third ms., Corning Museum of Glass MS. 6 (<u>olim</u> Currer)
          fols. 131a-132b [<u>see</u> below KINSMAN, no. 1966.6]; "Maner
          of the World Nowadays," no. 3168.2 "possibly by Skelton"
          [but in the opinion of <u>K&Y</u> (1967), non-canonical];
          "Tyme," no. 2451.4 and "Prayers," no. 2546 [both doubt-
          ful]; "Hoyda Joly Rutterkyn," no. 2832.2 "perhaps" by

Skelton [but considered non-canonical by K&Y]; and
"Petyously constrayned," no. 2755.5, "sometimes ascribed"
to Skelton [but considered non-canonical by K&Y].

1965.6 SPINA, ELAINE. "Skelton's Achievement in The Tunnyng of
Elynour Rummyng." M.A. thesis, Columbia University,
1965, 120 pp. plus bibliography.
Examines the structure, genre and prosody of TER; in
chapters I and II argues that the poem shows sufficient
resemblances to the popular carol "The Gossips' Meeting"
[R. L. Greene EEC 419 Aa, 419 B] in gossips' names and
actions, and in the carol-like alternation of "soloist"
(ER) and "chorus" (the gossips) and use of "pseudo-
burdens" as to constitute Skelton's particular refine-
ment of the sub-genre "ale-wife and gossips-in-the-
tavern" (comparing the tavern scene of PP, Lydgate's
"Satirical Description of his Lady," Peblis to the Play,
Lorenzo de Medici's I Beoni, Villon's "Les Regrets de la
Belle Heaulmiere"); notes that Skelton differs more from
Dunbar than he compares with him in "Kynd Kyttok," "Twa
Cammeris" and "Tua Mariit Wemen and the Wedo"; in chapter
III analyzes Skelton's metrics, essentially the irregu-
larly spaced two-beat line in the opening and closing
fitts with a larger number of 4 stress lines (still in
the minority) in the middle "fitts" as the arrivals and
antics of the gossips increase; in chapter IV analyzes
rhyme and assonance in TER (one-fourth of the rhymes are
feminine, couplets and triplets constitute four-fifths
of the rhyme pattern, and "like-beginnings" of lines form
a significant bonding device). See SPINA, no. 1967.6
below for article based on chapter III of the thesis.

1965.7 TARGAN, BARRY. "Irony in John Skelton's 'Philip Sparrow.'"
URKC, XXXII (1965), 74-80.
The irony of the poem is keyed to Jane Scrope's "sin-
cere unawareness of her intense sexual concern."

1966   BERGER, JEAN. Skelton Poems; for Mixed Chorus, Baritone
Solo and Piano (Organ) Accompaniment. New York: A.
Broude, [1966].
1) "All Noble," 2) Interlude, 3) "The Manner of the
World Nowadays [not Skelton's], 4) Interlude, 5) "Fal-
coner, Thou art to blame" [not Skelton's], 6) "Justice
est morte" ("En Parl," from GL), 7) Interlude, 8) "Upon
a Dead Man's Head."

1966.1 DAVISON, RICHARD H. "Melville's Mardi [1848] and John
Skelton," Emerson Society Quarterly, no. 43, Second
Quarter, Part Two (1966), pp. 86-87.
Cites parallels in chapter 50 between Yillah and her
enigmatic bird and Jane Scrope and her sparrow.

1966.2   GLASSCO, WILLIAM G. "Against Wolsey: A Critical Edition
          of John Skelton's <u>Why Come Ye Nat to Courte</u> and <u>Colyn</u>
          <u>Cloute</u>." Ph.D. dissertation, University of Toronto,
          1966, 2 vols.
              Vol. I (texts) bases text of <u>WCY</u> on earliest printed
          edition, <u>STC</u> (<u>c</u>. 1545) with the exception of 11. 838-
          1248, which are based on Bodley MS. Rawlinson C. 813
          (<u>c</u>. 1537), fols. 36-43^v; bases text of <u>CC</u> on recently
          uncovered first edition, <u>STC</u>$^{2.2}$ 22600.5 (<u>c</u>. 1530), but
          with emendations and the addition of the concluding
          Latin Poem from B.L. MS. Harley 2252 (<u>c</u>. 1530), fols. 147-
          153. Vol. II (notes and commentary): dates <u>WCY</u> as
          September-November 1522, thus making it intervene be-
          tween <u>SP</u> and <u>CC</u>, Glassco dating the latter as having
          been written during the Spring and Summer of 1523, with
          interpolations, he argues, incorporated as late as
          1525-26; takes interesting side-glances at <u>GL</u>; cf. sum-
          mary in <u>DA</u>, XXVIII (September 1967), 1395A-1396A.

1966.3   GORDON, GARY D. "Point of View in the Poetry of John Skel-
          ton." M.A. thesis, Columbia University, 1966, 87 pp.
          [N/Ex], Howard no. 7581.

1966.4   HEARTZ, DANIEL. "A 15th Century Ballo: Rôti Bouilli
          Joyeux," in <u>Aspects of Medieval and Renaissance Music,</u>
          <u>A Birthday Offering to Gustave Reese</u>. Edited by Jan la
          Rue. New York: W. W. Norton, 1966, pp. 359-375.
              While no mention is made of "ACC," this article pro-
          vides valuable background to a song title mentioned in
          poem; <u>see also</u> CARPENTER, no. 1955 above.

1966.5   HENRY, C. J. "Skelton's Perspective: The Manner of the
          World." M.A. thesis, Rice University, 1966. [N/Ex],
          Howard no. 7583.

1966.6   KINSMAN, ROBERT S. "A Lamentable of Kyng Edward the IIII."
          <u>HLQ</u>, XXXIX (1966), 95-108.
              Prints for first time the full version of the elegy
          as found in Corning MS 7, Corning Museum of Glass (<u>olim</u>
          Miss Richardson Currer's ms.), and collates other texts
          of the poem in textual notes; <u>K&Y</u> consider poem non-
          canonical.

1966.7   KINSMAN, ROBERT S. "Skelton's <u>Magnyfycence</u> and the Strategy
          of the 'Olde Sayde Sawe.'" <u>Stud. in Phil</u>., LXIII (1966),
          99-125.
              An examination of Skelton's deployment of sententiae
          and proverbs or proverbial material shows that he builds
          his play upon a dialectic of prosperity beyond measure
          and adversity beyond moderation.

1966.8   MARING, DONALD. "John Skelton's <u>Garland of Laurel</u>." M.A.
          thesis, Rice University, 1966. [N/Ex], Howard no. 7583.

1966.9   PHILLIPS, NORMA ANNE. "Observations on the Derivative
          Method of Skelton's Realism." JEGP, LXV (1966), 19-35.
              Stresses Skelton's unexpected reliance on Chaucer and
          Langland in BC, Mag and TER for the so-called "realistic"
          aspects of his satire; see PHILLIPS, no. 1958.1 above for
          the dissertation on which this article is based.

1967   CARPENTER, NAN COOKE. John Skelton. Twayne's English
          Authors Series, No. 61. New York: Twayne Publishers,
          1967, 183 pp. [copyright 1967, publication [1968]].
              Contents: Preface; Chronology; Life c. 1460-1529
          (Laureate and Court Poet; Royal Tutor; Rector of Diss;
          Royal Orator, Westminster); Works (Westminster, Court of
          Henry VII: Prose Translations, Elegies, Early Lyrics,
          Court Satires, Religious Lyrics, Speculum Principis),
          (Diss: Mock Elegies, PS, WH), (Westminster, Court of
          Henry VIII: Political Poems, Flyting "Ag Garn"), Mag,
          "AVT," SP, CC, TER, WCY, GL, DDA, Rep); Essence (The Man,
          Humanist and Poet, Musician) [ed. note: throughout, in
          a most valuable way, Carpenter highlights Skelton's in-
          timate technical knowledge of music, dance-song and popu-
          lar song tags], Reputation and Influence; Notes and
          References.
              Reviews: King, Walter N., Georgia Review, XXIII
          (Winter 1969), 547-550; Kinsman, Robert S., RQ, XXII
          (1969), 281-284.
              See Intro., p. xxxxviii for ed. comments.

1967.1   HARRINGTON, DAVID V. "Skelton's 'Mannerly Margery Mylk and
          Ale.'" Explicator, XXV (1967), Item 42.
              The refrains as well as lines 8-9, 17 and 22-24 should
          be assigned to the wooing clerk, who pits self against
          two rustics with the hope that these less attractive
          swains will move "Mannerly Margery" to accept him; then
          having gained his end, the clerk callously rejects her.

1967.2   KINSMAN, ROBERT S. and THEODORE YONGE (comps.). John Skel-
          ton: Canon and Census. Bibliography and Index Series,
          Number Four. [New York: for the] Renaissance Society
          of America, 1967, xxv, 88 pp.
              Contents: Introduction [traces bibliographers, edi-
          tors and collectors who preserved or restored Skelton];
          Canon [presents sections on "Undoubted Pieces: Verse";
          "Undoubted Pieces: Prose"; "Doubtful Pieces"; "Rejected
          Pieces"; and "Lost Pieces"]; Census [of fifteenth and
          sixteenth century editions of Skelton's Works, including
          "Lost 16th Century Printings"]; Indexes [Printers and
          Stationers; Provenance Index].
              Review: Bennett, J. A. W., Library, 5th ser., XXVI
          (September 1971), 271-272.

1967.3   LUCIE-SMITH, EDWARD (ed.). <u>The Penguin Book of Satirical</u>
         <u>Verse</u>. Harmondsworth: Penguin Books Ltd., 1967, pp.
         45-54.
              <u>Contents</u>: from <u>SP</u> [first 20 stanzas]; from <u>WCY</u>, 11.
         396-575.

1967.4   MacDONALD, MARJORIE GRACE MADELEINE (Sister Maris Stella,
         CSSJ). "John Skelton, Living Man, Living Poet." Ph.D.
         dissertation, University of Ottawa, 1967, 266 pp.
              Arranged as a chronological study, this dissertation
         does not claim to contribute new knowledge about Skel-
         ton's life but does add to our understanding of his
         poetry and the poems doubtfully ascribed to him, particu-
         larly in terms of doctrinal or liturgical background:
         thus, the author notes the appropriate connection in
         "Edw. IV" [doubtful] with liturgy for Ash Wednesday-
         Easter-Feast of St. Justin Martyr; in "Prayers" [doubt-
         ful] makes connection with orthodox Trinitarianism and
         Council of Florence; connects "UDH" with the Offertory
         of the Daily Mass for the Dead, and indicates its ar-
         rangement as a meditation, beginning with "composition
         of place"; associates "ACC" and the Breviary (Compline),
         wherein Coystrowne "counters" "Custodi nos" rather than
         singing it <u>recto tono</u> or in plain chant; in <u>PS</u>, under-
         scores relationship of musical notes set in text with
         psalm tone endings, and notes the connection between the
         word <u>titulus</u> in the final Latin verse with the "titulus"
         of psalm "subtitles"; comments that while <u>WCY</u> relatively
         free of biblical allusions in contrast to <u>CC</u> and <u>SP</u>, v.
         1150 of the poem is nonetheless an ironic use of the
         opening line of the hymn "Ecce Sacerdos Magnus."

1967.5   REEVES, JAMES and MARTIN SEYMOUR-SMITH (eds.). <u>A New Canon</u>
         <u>of English Poetry</u>. London: Heinemann; New York: Barnes
         and Noble, 1967, pp. 3-7.
              <u>Contents</u>: "Knowledge"; "WW"; "Lullay"; "Go."

1967.6   SPINA, ELAINE. "Skeltonic Meter in Elynour Rummyng." <u>Stud.</u>
         <u>in Phil.</u>, LXIV (1967), 665-684.
              Suggests that Skelton constantly experiments with
         "Skeltonic meter" in a sophisticated way from poem to
         poem, particularly in its varied placement of accent
         within an irregular number of syllables (does not really
         consider such other features as sporadic rhyme runs, al-
         literation and assonance); demonstrates, nonetheless,
         that the two stress line is the norm in <u>TER</u>, established
         at the beginning, and re-established at the close of the
         poem, although significantly departed from in the 3rd,
         4th and 5th "fitts" of the poem, where three-stress lines
         are incorporated to signal the increasing number of gos-
         sips and their strange array, odd payments, and drunken

actions. <u>See</u> no. 1965.6 for thesis, from chapter III of which this article is taken and revised.

1967.7   TUCKER, MELVIN J. "Skelton and Sheriff Hutton." <u>ELN</u>, IV (1967), 254-259.
Presents a review of the evidence of occupancy of the castle which leads him to doubt that the Howards lived in Castle of Sheriff Hutton in 1523: "a more likely time is in the 1490s"; hence doubts that <u>GL</u> was written at Sheriff Hutton in late 1522 or early 1523. <u>See also</u> TUCKER, no. 1964.5 above and no. 1969.7 below.

1968   BEVINGTON, DAVID M. "Skelton and the Old Aristocracy," in <u>Tudor Drama and Politics, A Critical Approach to Topical Meaning</u>. Cambridge, Massachusetts: Harvard University Press, 1968, Chapter Four, pp. 54-63.
Skelton, responsive to the aristocratic claims of the old families, felt himself privileged as a result of his earlier connections with Henry as prince to criticize both Wolsey and Henry as the unscrupulous lieutenant and the impressionable young king, not as models but as the focus of concern; his great contribution to political drama (a problem of fiscal sanity) lies, however, "not [in] observation from...life but a closer application of old techniques to new realities than had heretofore been attempted."
<u>See</u> Intro., p. xxxxvi for ed. comments.

1968.1   BROWNLOW, F[RANK] W[ALSH]. "Speke, Parrot: Skelton's Allegorical Denunciation of Cardinal Wolsey." <u>Stud. in Phil.</u>, LXV (1968), 124-139.
Makes incidental judgments on the basic text, whose only authoritative basis he believes is to be found in the printed version of <u>CB</u> (<u>STC</u> 22598) yet believes the marginalia which is found only in MS. to have been Skelton's own; his major point is that <u>SP</u> incorporates "an allusive set of materials traditionally understood as revealing the doctrine of Anti-Christ," particularly Ps. 82 of the Vulgate Bible.

1968.2   COMMON, ROBERT MAGILL. "Skelton's Artistry: The Early Lyrics." M.A. thesis, Queen's University [Ontario, Canada], 1968, 231 pp.
In successive chapters discusses "Skelton Poeta" (Intro); Elegy ["DEN" in especial]; Secular Lyrics; The Emergence of the Skeltonic; Select Bibliography; the lyrics are examined for cohesiveness of structure, use of imagery and motif, rhetorical device and rhythm; they reveal, Common shows, a distinctly individual voice at times capable of an intensity which established Skelton unequivocally as "one of the brightest luminaries of the Tudor era."

1968.3   HAWKINS, RICHARD. "Structure through Irony in The Tunning
         of Elinour Rumming." URKC, XXXIX (1968), 199-203.
              The structural ironies are to be found in (a) the dis-
         crepancy between the character's illusions about herself
         and the poet's "realistic" presentation of her, and (b)
         allusive reference to an ideal festivity implicitly con-
         trasted with the "unsavory actuality" of ER's tavern.

1968.4   HELSLOOT, K. (trans.). "De Kroeg van Noortje Neut," Tirade,
         XII (1968), 299-316.
              A translation into Dutch of TER, with a two page in-
         troduction by the translator, the English text in a
         parallel column, taken from Henderson's modernized text
         · of the poem, no. 1948 or 1959.2 above.

1968.5   KINSMAN, ROBERT S. "Skelton Mocks the Muse: References to
         Romance Matters in his Poetry," in Medieval Epic to the
         "Epic Theater" of Brecht. Edited by Rosario P. Armato
         and John M. Spalek. University of Southern California
         Studies in Comparative Literature, I, 1968, pp. 35-46.
              In PS, Skelton blends the old and the new, the "his-
         torical" and "fictional," the "epical" and the amatory
         elements of romance in an attempt to convey the confusion
         and emotionality of Jane Scrope; in "Ag Garn" (a deliber-
         ate flyting), the poet draws on romance heroes and mat-
         ters, or their burlesqued images, to satirize the social
         pretentions of the newly-knighted Christopher Garnesche.

1968.6   KOZIKOWSKI, STANLEY J. "The 'Resydew' of John Skelton's
         Bowge of Courte." M.A. thesis, University of Massachu-
         setts, 1968, 53 pp. [N/Ex], Howard no. 7584.

1968.7   McGRATH, LYNETTE FAY. "Studies in the Norms and Techniques
         of Sixteenth Century English Satire from Skelton to
         Donne." Ph.D. dissertation, University of Illinois,
         1968, 625 pp. [N/Ex], summarized in DAI, XXX (1969),
         285A-286A.
              Explicates BC, SP, CC and WCY in terms of irony.

1969   ASHTON, JOHN (ed.). A Ballade of the Scottysshe Kynge. A
         reissue, by Singing Tree Press, Book Tower, Detroit,
         1969, of the edition by ASHTON, no. 1882 above.
              Occasion for review articles by G. Marc'hadour in
         Moreana, no. 35 (1972), 63-68; by M. J. Tucker in Moreana,
         no. 37 (1973), 15-23; see nos. 1972.2 and 1973.7 below.

1969.1   GINGERICH, OWEN and MELVIN J. TUCKER. "The Astronomical
         Dating of Skelton's Garland of Laurel." HLQ, XXXII
         (1969), 207-220.

126

The article expands the line of argumentation advanced by TUCKER in earlier notes (nos. 1964.4 and 1967.7) and illustrates from late fifteenth and early sixteenth century astrological texts the probability that an early version of GL had been completed in the Spring of 1495, perhaps specifically started on May 8th; see also TUCKER, no. 1969.7.

1969.2   GRAVES, ROBERT. <u>On Poetry: Collected Talks and Essays</u>. Garden City, New York: Doubleday and Co., 1969.
         The first six chapters are reissues of Graves' 1954-5 Clark Lectures at Cambridge, no. 1955.2 above, among which were two specifically on Skelton, "The Crowning Privilege" and "Dame Occupacyon," here pp. 11-31 and 107-126; and also includes Graves' addresses at Oxford, 1961-66, among which were "The Dedicated Poet," here pp. 279-300; see GRAVES, no. 1961 above.

1969.3   KINSMAN, ROBERT S. (ed.). <u>John Skelton: Poems</u>. Oxford: Clarendon Medieval and Tudor Series, 1969, pp. xxvi, 221.
         <u>Contents</u>: [Critical] Introduction; Biographical and Textual Notes; Select Bibliography, Texts: "Lullay," "Aunc Acq," "Knolege," "ACC," "WW," "UDH," BC; PS (vv. 1-845); TER; from Mag (scenes 16 and 17); SP, CC (vv. 1-719; 888-1095; 1118-1269, Epilogue); from GL "Margery Wentworthe," "Margaret Tylney," "Jane Blenner-Haiset," "Isabell Pennell," "Margaret Hussey"; Notes; Glossary.
         <u>Reviews</u>: Chalker, John, SN, XLIII (1971), 581-583; Ingham, Patricia, RES, XXII (1971), 185-187; Nelson, William, MAe, XL (1971), 208-210; Thomas, R. George, <u>Yearbook of English Studies</u> (1971), 225; Thomson, Patricia, N&Q (1971), 231-232.

1969.4   McGRATH, LYNETTE F. "'Speke Parrot' and Plautus." N&Q, CCXIV (1969), 452-453.
         Comments on SP, 11. 181-7 in light of the "Grammarians' War" of the years 1519-21 and indicates that the reference in them to Plautus may allude to a May 7, 1520 performance of a Plautine comedy at court.

1969.5   RANSOM, JOHN CROWE. "Agitato ma non troppo." <u>New York Review of Books</u>, XIII (23 October 1969), 5.
         A poem of 21 lines: shows a "return" to his earlier interest in Skeltonic rhythm and rhyme.

1969.6   SCHLAUCH, MARGARET. "John Skelton, Satirist and Court Poet, As Seen in the Light of Recent Studies." <u>Kwartalnik Neofilologiczny</u>, XVI (1969), 125-135.
         A review of Skelton studies, including articles as well as books, chiefly since the late 50's; advances the suggestion that one of the overlooked "sources" of Skeltonic meter was the <u>cursus</u>.

1969.7   TUCKER, M[ELVIN] J. "The Ladies in Skelton's <u>Garland of</u>
           <u>Laurel</u>." <u>RQ</u>, XXII (1969), 333-345.
                Identifies the Countess of Surrey mentioned in the
           poem as Elizabeth Howard (d. 1497) and furnishes care-
           fully researched and plausible identification for eight
           of her ten ladies-in-waiting (Margaret Hussey and Ger-
           trude Statham excepted) with documented dates to lend
           weight to the thesis that the poem in its first form can
           be dated 1494; <u>see also</u> GINGERICH and TUCKER, no. 1969.1
           above.

1969.8   WILSON, F[RANK] P. and G. K. HUNTER. <u>The English Drama</u>
           <u>(1485-1585)</u>. New York and Oxford: Oxford University
           Press, 1969.
                In the chapter "The Two 'Makers': Skelton and Lind-
           say," pp. 11-21, particularly 11-15, they comment that
           "Magnificence is not Mankind but 'a prince of great
           myght,' and thus the play is not so much a mirror for
           man as a mirror for princes, a lesson in the art of good
           government, but also a lesson in the art of preserving
           worldly prosperity."

1969.9   WINSER, LEIGH. "Skelton's <u>Magnyfycence</u> and the Morality
           Tradition." Ph.D. dissertation, Columbia University,
           1969, 186 pp.
                In chapter 1, Winser considers the nature of Magnifi-
           cence the protagonist; in 2, the range of meanings and
           hence the "moral dimensions" of "magnificence"; in 3,
           the figurative language of the play (medicinal, monetary,
           martial imagery) and metaphors from the chase (hawking,
           hunting, and riding); in 4, methods of satirical attack.
           In 5, questions the dating of <u>Mag</u> as of 1515-16 and very
           tentatively suggests a date late in Henry VII's reign,
           <u>c</u>. 1497; cf. summary in <u>DAI</u>, XXX (1969), 1154-A-B; <u>see</u>
           WINSER, no. 1970.9 for article based on part of disser-
           tation.

1970   BAINE, RODNEY M. "Warton, Collins and Skelton's <u>Necroman-</u>
           <u>cer</u>." <u>PQ</u>, XLIX (1970), 245-248.
                Argues that in the light of a neglected letter of
           11 February 1778 from Warton to David Garrick [in the
           <u>Private Correspondence of David Garrick</u> (1832), II, 286-
           287], Joseph Warton's confirmatory note [on another ques-
           tion, <u>Works of Alexander Pope</u> (1797), IX, 443-444n], and
           the recent identification of two books [<u>Aurelio and Isa-</u>
           <u>bella</u>, <u>El Vertadero Suceso</u>] suspected because mentioned
           by Warton, "an incredulous rejection of Skelton's <u>Necro-</u>
           <u>mancer</u>...is difficult to justify." <u>See</u> WARTON, no. 1778
           above.

1970.1 CARPENTER, NAN COOKE. "Skelton and Music: A Gloss on
        Hippates." ELN, VIII (1970), 93-97.
            Identifies this hitherto unglossed word in DS (Salter
        & Edwards, I, 303) as the name of the highest note in
        the last two of the interlocking tetrachords of the
        Greek scale called The Greater Perfect System; in modern
        terminology one of the lowest notes of the lyre.

1970.2 CARPENTER, NAN COOKE. "Skelton's Hand in William Cornish's
        Musical Parable." Comparative Literature, XXII (1972),
        157-172.
            Argues that Skelton may have contributed an occasional
        phrase or pun to Cornish's Treatise betwene trouth and
        Information (1504), finding certain similarities between
        the parable and Skelton's "AVT" (c. 1516).

1970.3 GRANDSEN, K[ARL] W[ATTS]. Tudor Verse Satire. London:
        Athlone Press, pp. 36-47, 163-164.
            Prints passages from CC, 11. 47-74, 287-330, 595-636,
        889-1183, 1236-1267; prints notes to excerpt on pp. 163-
        165.

1970.4 SKELTON, JOHN. Magnyfycence. Recording of First Part, a
        1970 reissue of recordings made for the BBC series "The
        First Stage," by Spoken Word Recordings, no. 99714-6.
        Jacket notes by David M. Bevington, University of Chi-
        cago; LC Cat. Card no. R68-3183.

1970.5 SKELTON, JOHN. Pithy, Plesaunt and Profitable Workes of
        Maister Skelton, Poete Laureate.... Menston, Yorkshire:
        Scolar Press, 1970.
            A facsimile reprint of PPPW, no. 1568 above; re-
        printed 1973.

1970.6 TAYLOR, WARREN and DONALD HALL (eds.). Poetry in English.
        2nd edn.
            For Skelton items, see TAYLOR and HALL, no. 1963.8
        above.

1970.7 TUCKER, MELVIN J. "Setting for Skelton's Bowge of Courte:
        A Speculation." ELN, VII (1970), 168-175.
            Speculates on a Skelton - Howard family association
        dating from c. 1490 on grounds of astronomical and as-
        trological "data" and on documentary evidence concerning
        ownership by 1st Duke of Norfolk of "Powers' Key."

1970.8 TYDEMAN, WILLIAM. "John Skelton," in English Poetry 1400-
        1580. New York: Barnes and Noble, 1970, pp. 66-90 and
        193-206.
            "Lullay"; "Aunc Acq"; from PS (182 lines); from TER
        (234 lines); from CC (219 lines); "Maystres Isabell

Pennell"; general notes and notes to individual lines
are placed in the rear of the book.

1970.9   WINSER, LEIGH. "Skelton's Magnyfycence." RQ, XXIII (1970),
          14-25.
              The article is a recasting of the fifth chapter of
          his dissertation, no. 1969.9 above, with a modified ar-
          gument: "I find much to suggest that Skelton conceived
          Magnyfycence before 1515-16; if not before he reached
          Diss in 1504, then perhaps shortly thereafter."

1971   [A Reply]. "STC 22606: A Bibliographical Ghost?" N&Q,
          CCXVI (December 1971), 465.
              An anonymous reader points out that Craig's identifi-
          cation of STC 22606 as a "ghost" (see no. 1971.2 below)
          had been made earlier by JACKSON, no. 1940.1 and had
          been elaborated on by KINSMAN and YONGE, C&C, no. 1967.2.

1971.1   BROWNLOW, F[RANK] W[ALSH]. "The Boke Compiled by Maister
          Skelton, Poet Laureate, Called Speake Parrot." ELR, I
          (Winter 1971), 3-26.
              Studies the relationship between the first printed
          edition ("Version I") and MS ("Version II" as augmented
          later); reads "Version I" as a logically developed, de-
          liberately arranged "ordered confusion," dating from
          after 1519.

1971.2   CRAIG, TIMOTHY. "STC 22606: A Bibliographical Ghost?"
          N&Q, CCXVI (June 1971), 212-213.
              Notes that STC 22606, lacking the title page, is ac-
          tually identical to STC 22600 [CB]; but see no. 1971
          above.

1971.3   FISHMAN, BURTON. "Recent Studies in Skelton." ELR, I
          (1971), 89-96.
              Covers the period 1950-70 with the exception of
          standard texts published earlier, arranges material un-
          der the headings General, Studies of Individual Works,
          Canon, Critique of Standard Edition (Dyce), Other Edi-
          tions.

1971.4   John Skelton and Early Lyric. Argo Stereo ZPL 1008 (Decca
          Record Co., 1971), Side 2.
              From CC, "Woefully Arrayed" [non-canonical], "Upon a
          Dead Man's Head" as read by David King; "MDD," "To Mis-
          tress Annie" [non-canonical] as read by Yvonne Bonnamy;
          from "The Manner of the World Nowadays" [non-canonical],
          "Calliope," from WCY, as read by David King; "Mistress
          Margaret Hussey," "Mistress Isabel Pennell" (from GL),
          as read by John Stride.

1971.5   ROBINSON, IAN. "The Last Chaucerians: Hawes, Skelton,
         Barclay, Wyatt," in Chaucer's Prosody: A Study of the
         Middle English Verse Tradition. Cambridge: Cambridge
         University Press, 1971, pp. 216-223.
              Deals with Skelton's treatment of rhyme royal; sug-
         gests that Skeltonics "are half lines of balanced pen-
         tameters made to stand independently."

1971.6   WARRINGTON, JOHN (trans.). John Skelton, Poet of Tudor
         England by Maurice Pollet, translated from the French.
         Lewisburg, Pennsylvania: Bucknell University Press,
         1971, 302 pp.
              See POLLET, no. 1962.5 above for original.
              Reviews: Richard Holmes, Times (London) (31 May
         1971), p. 5; TLS (9 April 1971), p. 415; M. J. Tucker,
         Moreana, no. 37 (1973), pp. 15-23; and Maurice Pollet,
         in passing, ibid., p. 97, f.n. 1.

1971.7   WEST, MICHAEL. "Skelton and the Renaissance Theme of
         Folly." PQ, L (1971), 23-35.
              While certain of Skelton's "fools" (as in WH, "ACC")
         show a close affinity with the Brantian fool, some show
         a kinship with the Renaissance fool "whose folly ap-
         proaches wisdom" (as Drede in BC, Colyn in CC, Foly in
         Mag and Parrot in SP); Skelton's own "antic disposition"
         in his practice of poetry reflects divinus furor, "in-
         spired folly."

1972   GARDNER, DAME HELEN (ed.). New Oxford Book of English
         Verse. Oxford: Clarendon Press, 1972, pp. 24-34.
              From PS, vv. 1-63, 108-146, 386-575; from GL, "Mis-
         tress Margery Wentworth," "Isabell Pennell," "Margaret
         Hussey."

1972.1   HOPE, A[LEC] D[ERWENT]. "Speak, Parrot." Meanjin Quarter-
         ly, XXXI (1972), 138.
              "Speak parrot, speak; flamboyant popinjay! / Speak,
         though like me you've nothing new to say. / ...A man
         like me / Grubbing in the dry springs of poetry, / ...I
         transmit what I scarcely apprehend."

1972.2   MARC'HADOUR, ABBÉ GERMAIN. "Croisade triumphale de l'Angle-
         terre: 1513. Réflexions en marge de John Skelton: 'A
         ballad of the Scottyshe Kynge.'" Moreana, no. 35 (1972),
         pp. 63-68.
              Examines the reactions of other contemporary poets to
         the 1513 wars on two fronts in France and the English
         border: Ammonius, Crétin and in particular Erasmus and
         More.

1972.3   McLANE, PAUL E. "Wolsey's Forced Loans and the Dating of
          Skelton's <u>Colyn Cloute</u>." <u>ELN</u>, X (1972), 85-89.
               Judging from 11. 346-375 of the poem and the use of
          the word "prestes" (forced loans) in 1. 1350 in particu-
          lar, McLane argues for a date as late as mid-1523.

1973   ATCHITY, KENNETH JOHN. "Skelton's Collyn Clout." <u>PQ</u>, LII
          (1973), 715-727.
               Skelton's satire is directed to three traditional
          levels of awareness--the individual, the generally human
          and the body politic, and the superhuman or cosmic--facts
          reflected in the Latin epigraphs at the beginning and the
          ending of the poem. The epigraph at the end indicates
          in its three lines that (1) the individual is incomplete,
          (2) man in society must seek greater completeness, and
          (3) beyond that must follow the impulse to imitate the
          perfection of God. The epigraph at the beginning, when
          placed in the full contexts of Psalm 94 and John 8 from
          which it is abstracted, anticipates the basic threefold
          tension of the poem.

1973.1   COLLEY, JOHN SCOTT. "John Skelton's Ironic <u>Apologia</u>: The
          Medieval Sciences, Wolsey and the <u>Garlande of Laurell</u>."
          <u>Tenn. Studies</u>, XVIII (1973), 19-32.
               <u>GL</u> is neither a capitulation to Wolsey nor a comic
          denial of Skelton's claim to poetic fame: through Skel-
          ton's careful use of astrological signs, dream lore,
          echoes from recent poems, and ironic misuse of poetic
          conventions, the reader is led to understand that Skel-
          ton's satiric mode is preferable to a conventional praise
          of ladies; he is also enabled to discover Wolsey, Skel-
          ton's foe, daringly alluded to in compromising situations.

1973.2   CROFT, P. J. (comp. & ed.). "John Skelton," in <u>Autograph
          Poetry in the English Language</u>. New York: McGraw-Hill
          Book Co., 1973, I, pp. 6-8 and facing plates.
               Reproduces, with headnote on the manuscript and hand,
          Skelton's "A Lawde and Prayse," written for Henry VIII's
          coronation, no. 1509.2 above.

1973.3   LYNN, KAREN. "Computational Prosodics: The Decasyllabic
          Line from Chaucer to Skelton." Ph.D. dissertation, Uni-
          versity of Southern California (1973), 2 vols., 381 pp.
               The first volume consists of her own text, the second
          volume of computer printouts; in I, 163-184, relying on
          the Halle-Keyser theory of the "stress maximum" in Eng-
          lish verse, Ms. Lynn analyzes Skelton's use of the de-
          casyllabic line in <u>BC</u> and <u>GL</u> in which he favors the 2nd
          and 4th positions as opposed to Chaucer's emphasis on
          the 2nd and 6th; Skelton's practice seems to reflect
          Lydgatian rather than Chaucerian influence, a conclusion

sustained on other counts as well. <u>See also</u> summary, <u>DAI</u>, XXXIV (1974), 4210A-B.

1973.4   McLANE, PAUL E. "Skelton's <u>Colyn Cloute</u> and Spenser's <u>Shepheardes Calendar</u>." <u>Stud. in Phil</u>., LXX (1973), 141-159.
Shows that Skelton's <u>CC</u> had a deeper influence on Spenser's <u>Shep. Cal.</u> than ordinarily conceded in the name of "hero," in tone and diction, and in devices and themes.

1973.5   NORTON-SMITH, JOHN. "The Origins of 'Skeltonics.'" <u>Essays in Criticism</u>, XXIII (1973), 57-62.
Believes that "Skeltonics" spring from the "rime doggerel" epistle of the late fifteenth century, apparently "a local East Anglian demotic form" and cites two such letters written by John Paston in 1465 and 1472.

1973.6   POLLET, MAURICE. [Remarks on Melvin Tucker's review, no. 1973.8 below], <u>Moreana</u>, no. 38 (1973), pp. 97-98.
Questions Tucker's assertion of an early association between Skelton and the Howards, repeats his own stand on the Yorkshire origin of the Skeltons, and on the date of writing of <u>GL</u>, 1523.

1973.7   SKELTON, ROBIN. "The Master Poet: John Skelton as Conscious Craftsman." <u>Mosiac</u>, VI (1973), 67-92.
The "master poet" is not merely a great poetic craftsman and moral teacher, but also one who adopts a "master poet persona" and uses it to lay down rules, or proclaims his views on his sources of inspiration or the proper models for the discipline, and speaks as spokesman for a culture. While Skelton is aware of his role as "Master Poet" in several other poems (in "AVT," for one example), it is in <u>GL</u> that he establishes his lineage, his control of the verse-forms and genres, and his kinship with the poets, rhetoricians, philosophers and historians of the past: "The Master-Poet, according to Skelton, must be omnicompetent, multi-lingual, and self-assertive."

1973.8   TUCKER, M[ELVIN] J. "Skelton's More-Howard Connections." <u>Moreana</u>, no. 37 (1973), pp. 15-23.
Reviews WARRINGTON's translation of Pollet, no. 1971.6, and the reissue of ASHTON's edition of Skelton's "BSK," no. 1969 above, reasserts early relationship between Skelton and the Howards in the 1480's and 90's, includes speculations on the lack of direct reference by More to Skelton and works in a brief review of Skelton scholarship between 1962 and 1972; <u>see</u> POLLETT, no. 1973.6 above, for remarks on "review."

1974   KIPLING, GORDON. "John Skelton and Burgundian Letters," in
        Ten Studies in Anglo-Dutch Relations. Edited by Jan van
        Dorsten. Leiden and London: for the Sir Thomas Browne
        Institute, 1974, pp. 1-29.
             Argues that (1) Skelton, at Henry VII's court, was in-
        volved in a "Burgundian" ambience (continued from Edward
        IV's court establishment) of principles, modes and books
        of princely instruction and of works of chivalric ro-
        mance, as assembled by the royal librarian (Quentin
        Poulet, a Fleming), and as illustrated by Flemish scribes
        and illuminators; (2) some of Skelton's stanza forms as
        in "Lawde" and "Calliope" are based on the Burgundian
        "vers septaine" and "vers brisiez" respectively, while
        the Skeltonic owes much to the "rhetorique batelée"
        (with its long mono-rhyme leashes of short lines, within
        eventual cross-rhyme, to be sure, and its parallel phras-
        al units) as well as the "rime rurale" (not recommended
        by the Burgundians--rhymes on the vowel only, in feminine
        endings); and (3) Skelton's concept of "Magnificence"
        originates in the Burgundian insistence that of the pair
        "magnificence/magnanimity," the former is the "architec-
        tonic virtue" on which magnanimity and fortitude depend.

1974.1 PROPPÉ, KATHERINE MILLER. "Reason, Sensuality and John
        Skelton: Patristic Psychology and Literary Attitudes
        in the Late Medieval Period." Ph.D. dissertation, UCLA,
        1974, 261 pp.
             Indicates that in metaphor and imagery from Patristic
        times down through the late middle ages, woman was used
        to represent sense perception, sensuality, fantasy,
        imagination, irrationality and those imperfect aspects
        of the human condition associated with the body, physi-
        cal inferiority and mortality. Despite very noticeable
        shifts in attitude towards the education of upper-class
        women displayed by the humanists in Early Tudor times,
        women were not deeply schooled in eloquence and their
        thoughts needed to be steadied by higher masculine
        reason: "embroidery and the dressing of wool hath ever
        been an honest occupation for a good woman" (Vives); in
        his lyrics on women, Skelton, save for three poems
        ("Knolege," "El Marg" and PS), stressed woman's sensual-
        ity, and in PS made use of the patristic notion that the
        "feminine" littera sola was a mere veil or husk for the
        "masculine" sententia or rational powers of the poet:
        PS was "ficta sub imagine texta"; similarly, GL finds
        Skelton abandoning Boccaccio's blending of "female" and
        "male" faculties in the latter's integration of Pallas/
        Minerva, by satisfying the "feminine" demands of the
        Queen of Fame that he praise ladies, in lyrics that range
        from pristine freshness for the young ladies-in-waiting
        through wary plurisignation (the Countess of Surrey),

sexual ambiguity (e.g., Elizabeth Howard, Lady Ann
Dakers), to ironic mock-encomium (Gertrude Statham);
see also summary in DAI, XXXV (1975), 5358A-5359B.

1974.2   SCATTERGOOD, V. J. "Skelton's 'Ryotte': 'A Rusty Gal-
         lande.'" N&Q, CCXIX (1974), 83-85.
              Ryotte's affinities as a stock character "are with
         the many impecunious but extravagantly dressed gallants
         who are frequent objects of mockery in late medieval
         satire."

1974.3   SYLVESTER, RICHARD S. (ed.). The Anchor Anthology of Six-
         teenth Century Verse. Garden City, New York: Anchor
         Press/Doubleday, 1974, pp. 1-104, 595-596.
              Contents: BC (complete); PS (complete); TER (com-
         plete); "UDH," "WW," "Lullay," "Aunc Acq," "Knolege,"
         "MM"; from GL, "Maystres Jane Blenner-Haiset," "Maystres
         Isabel Pennell," "Maystres Margaret Hussey."

1974.4   TIGGES, W[ILLEM]. "The Triumph of Skelton: The Garland of
         Laurel and the Tradition of Fame." M.A. thesis, Univer-
         sity of Leiden, 1974, 132 pp.
              Chap. III, "The Tradition," pp. 8-61 makes a genuine
         contribution to background studies of the poem, giving
         it a structure via the various rhetorical topoi of dream,
         debate (50-245), catalogue of poets (323-392), [a sub-
         division of enumeratio], Castle of Fame (459-490), the
         locus amoenus as rhetorical device (652-719), the as-
         sembly of ladies (769-1099), combined with complaint of
         ladies and example of good women, catalogue of works
         (enumeratio), and topic of affected modesty (822-835)
         "of which the whole poem is in a way the inversion";
         compares relationships of GL to Petrarch's Trionfi,
         Chaucer's H of F, Froissart's Temple d'honneur, Lydgate's
         T of G, Floure and Leafe, Molinet's Trosne d'honneur,
         Douglas' PH, More's "Nine Pageauntes," Hawes' P of Pl,
         Lemaire de Belges' Temple d'Honneur et de Vertus and
         Concorde des Deux Langages, Barclay's "Fourth Eclogue,"
         with the general conclusion that Skelton is little in-
         debted to fourteenth and fifteenth century authors
         (Chaucer excepted), but greatly influenced by the gen-
         eral tradition "to a very large extent free in its ulti-
         mate form and scope"; his remarks on verse-form and
         language plus general interpretation are too circum-
         scribed by the limits of a general essay to be anything
         more than interesting beginnings.

1974.5   WATSON, GEORGE (general ed.). The New Cambridge Bibliog-
         raphy of English Literature. Cambridge: Cambridge Uni-
         versity Press, 1974, vol. I (600-1660), pp. 1015-1019.
              The entry, in a volume that is a "total revision of
         the old volume I" (1940) and the appropriate section of

the 1957 supplement, adds under "Bibliographies" <u>K&Y</u>,
no. 1967.2 above, omits itemization of manuscripts given
in old <u>CBEL</u>; includes articles and books through 1970
bringing number of items in new § 2 to 133 (cf. with 33
items in § 5 of <u>CBEL</u>[1] "Biography and Criticism"). <u>Cor-
rections</u>: p. 1018, 4th item from bottom, read: "...
reference to Romance matters in his poetry. University
of Southern California Stud. in Comparative Literature";
p. 1019; "Thematic importance of Skelton's allusion &c."
should be credited to Harris, W. O.; correct spelling to
Heiserman, A. R.; clarify first two entries under
Schulte, E., by reading <u>Annali Istituto Universitario
Orientale</u>, <u>Napoli</u>, <u>Sezione Germanica</u> (AION-SG); under
Swart, J., read R. W. Zandvoort.

1975   CRISP, DELMAS. "Cardinal Wolsey in Skelton's Poetry."
           <u>Innisfree</u> [annual publication of the English Department
           of Southeastern Louisiana University], II (1975), 47-61.
             While centering in <u>SP</u>, <u>CC</u> and <u>WCY</u>, this article does
           glance at <u>Mag</u> earlier, envoys to <u>GL</u> and <u>DDA</u> and also the
           poem <u>Rep</u> later, then the three specifically anti-Wolsey
           satires; useful in summarizing differences in dating the
           various Wolsey poems but overly brief and derivative to
           be of vital use; errs in dating Wolsey's legateship 1524
           (made legate for life that year but first appointed
           legate-a-latere in 1518).

1975.1   POTTER, ROBERT. <u>The English Morality Play</u>. London and
           Boston: Routledge and Kegan Paul, 1975, pp. 67-77.
             Argues that <u>Magnyfycence</u> is more traditional than has
           been previously recognized in that its opening sequence
           establishes the "morality state of innocence"; the notes
           that protagonist's return to the stage at line 1375 be-
           gins the morality conversion of correct instruction into
           corrupted initiation into sex and other sins of the
           flesh and world, followed by adversity and fall, in turn
           bringing in figures of retribution which lead the hero
           to the brink of hopelessness, from which he is rescued
           by agents of repentence; believes the play is more revo-
           lutionary than previously acknowledged in that the
           Prince is made to represent the problem of human nature
           in terms of the question of wealth, so that <u>Mag</u> turns
           the attention of its audience to the duties of the earth-
           ly stewardship and guardianship that the Prince must as-
           sert over the collective destiny of his subjects in a
           commonwealth, rather than concentrating the audience's
           moral attention on problem of salvation.

1976   LEE, JOHN MAYNARD. "A Critical Edition of John Skelton's
           <u>Garlande of Laurel</u>." Ph.D. dissertation, University of
           Wisconsin, 1976.

Bases text on B.L. MS. Cotton Vitellius E. x., fols. 208–225^V for the lines of the poem it contains (1–245, 721–1135 [out of a total of 1610 lines]), then draws on edn. of 1523 (STC 22610) for 246–336, 344–406, 414–720, 1136–1586, and on version in PPPW (1568) [STC–22608] for two dropped stanzas 337–343, 407–413 and for "L'autre Envoy," 1587–1602. In commentary divides poem into three major sections: a) 1–245, treating Honor as contemptible because it consists only of specious acclaim; b) 246–765, distinguishing between Fame's definition of Honor and a concept of poetic honor based on the writing of allegorical poetry in the tradition of orators and poets from Quintilian, Cicero and Homer through Chaucer, Gower and Lydgate, thus making Skelton reject Aquinas' notion that Honor is desirable only when men honor excellence given by God as a means of honoring God through men; and c) 716–1079, 1080–1610, demonstrating Skelton's claim to Honor as an inspired moral poet via his inset lyrics and his catalogue of works. See also summary in DAI, XXXVII (1976), 2838A–2839A.

1976.1   PSILOS, PAUL D.   "'Dulle' Drede and the Limits of Prudential Knowledge in Skelton's Bowge of Courte." Journal of Medieval and Renaissance Studies, VI (1976), 297–317.
          Presents BC as a significant anticipation of "picaresque satire" in England, i.e., uses self-exposing first person persona "Drede", who dramatizes the social organization and value of court by accepting and misunderstanding the very values he attacks; notes that BC uses basic picaresque pattern of victimization (satiric observer exposed, and knave-fool punished by other knaves), Drede's dramatically distorted moralizing not only revealing his moral obtuseness but suggesting by implication proper time-tested moral norms, rather than momentary prudential rationalizations; explores the duplicity of the poem's action and symbols in the two part structure of a static, but self-incriminatory Prologue and the dramatically revealing "colloquy" of Drede and double-edged allegorical personifications.

1976.2   A SHORT-TITLE CATALOGUE OF BOOKS PRINTED IN ENGLAND, SCOTLAND & IRELAND AND OF ENGLISH BOOKS PRINTED ABROAD 1475–1640.   First Compiled by A. W. POLLARD and G. R. REDGRAVE.   Second Edition Revised and Enlarged, Begun by W[ILLIAM] A. JACKSON & F[RANCIS] S. FERGUSON, Completed by KATHERINE F. PANTZER.   London: Bibliographical Society, 1976, Volume Two, I–Z.
          The Skelton entry adds variant colophons PS 22595.5, CC 22602.5, WCY 22615.5, 22617a.5; locates editions missed in 1926 First edition of STC: BC 22597.5 [2nd edn., de Worde, [c. 1510], CUL), CC 22600.5 (1st edn.

137

Godfrey, [c. 1530], Woburn Abbey), TER 22611.5 (fragments of 1st edn., de Worde [c. 1521]); lists the non-
canonical Old Christmas after Mag 22607 with x-ref. to
18793.5; identifies as non-canonical Epitaffe of Iasper
Duke of Beddeforde (old STC 22605) by x-ref. to 14477,
and x-refs. non-canonical Elegy H VII to 13075; notes
that old STC 22606 a "ghost" of 22600, and that old STC
22612 (TER) = part of 19936; identifies old STC 22613
with STC 22614 (anr. edn. TER of 1624; establishes old
STC 22617b as variant colophon of earlier edition of
WCY = 22616.5.

1976.3   SPEARING, A[NTHONY] C. "Skelton: 'The Bowge of Court'"
and "Skelton: 'The Garland of Laurel,'" in Medieval-
Dream Poetry. Cambridge: Cambridge University Press,
1976, pp. 197-202 and 211-218.
    Notes Skelton's innovations to dream-poetry in BC: a
real place related to the significance of the dream, the
narrator acquiring the identity of a personification, and
the setting aboard a ship; shows that life on the ship
is an emblem of court-life, itself a special case of
life in the world; indicates that the Dreamer is not a
complete innocent but nonetheless sufficiently inexperi-
enced and paranoia-inclined as to flounder in a sense of
unreliability of things and persons to a nightmarish ex-
tent--"a new and frightening use for the dream-poem."
In GL, compares Skelton to T. S. Eliot in his conscious
invoking of a tradition while making it serve his individual talent; notes Skelton's deliberately self-mocking
and ironic use of dream as a wish-fulfilling self-justi-
fication and his defense of the poet as seer and vision-
ary, as seeker after fame, deserved on this earth, and
as conferrer of fame good or bad on others, as they de-
serve--as exemplified in the lyrics integrally set into
the main body of the poem; notices Skelton's ingenious
twist of the tradition that the dreamer be awakened by
some physical sensation within the dream in the firm
shutting of Occupation's book [containing Skelton's long
bio-bibliographical listings]: "it is the book of the
dream as well as the book within the dream that is to be
shut fast."

1976.4   WILLIAMS, FRANKLIN B. JR. "Alsop's Fair Custance: Chaucer
in Tudor Dress." ELR, VI (1976), 351-367.
    For details on the envoy written in Skeltonics, see
ALSOPPE, no. 1525 above.

1976.5   WINSER, LEIGH. "The Bowge of Courte: Drama Doubling as
Dream." ELR, VI (1976), 3-39.
    Argues that BC was conceived as a dramatic entertain-
ment, combining "elements of the Disguising, the Farce,

the Morality Play and even the Pageant," and intended
for performance rather than solely for reading.

1976.6   WINSER, LEIGH. "The Ornamental Compartment of _Magnyfycence_,
          1530." _Library_, 5th ser., XXXI (1976), 136.
              Notices the compartment, described by McKerrow in his
          book on title-page borders as no. 12, in two books un-
          listed by McKerrow, Lily's _De generibus nominum_ (n.d.,
          B.L. 625 d. II), and Whittinton's _De octo partibus ora-_
          tionis (_STC_ 25507 [?1530], "per me Petrum Treueris"); and
          identifies a similar, earlier compartment used by
          Thierry Martens, Louvain, 1523, of which Treveris' block
          is a close but coarse copy.

1977   KOZIKOWSKI, STANLEY J. "Lydgate, Machiavelli, and More and
          Skelton's _Bowge of Courte_," _American Notes & Queries_, XV
          (January, 1977), 66-7.
              Lydgate's "Mumming at London," Machiavelli's "Capitolo
          di Fortuna," More's "Fortune," like Skelton's _Bowge_, por-
          tray Fortune in a court setting, attended by a train of
          appropriate personifications. Like Skelton, Machiavelli
          and More suggest that Fortune is fearsome in her own
          variability and in the individual menace of her followers.
          Like Lydgate, Skelton allegorically depicts a series of
          conversations (between the hero and virtues in Lydgate,
          between the hero and vices in _Bowge_), suggesting that
          Skelton's poem, like Lydgate's Mumming, may have been
          intended as a pageant (cf. _BC_ 1. 574).

1977.1   WINSER, LEIGH. "'The Garlande of Laurell': Masque Spec-
          tacular." _Criticism_, XIX (1977), 51-69.
              In a not always persuasive manner or absolutely con-
          vincing way, Winser "tentatively" proposes that _GL_ is
          "the narrative account of a complex entertainment, an
          early Tudor Disguising, designed by Skelton for perform-
          ance at a splendid Christmas fête"; argues that the _time_
          indicated in the poem is that of the mid-winter feast of
          peace (12 days of Christmas); the _locus_ that of a ban-
          quet hall; the _action_ that of a "process" or onward
          movement in space, _presented_ within 4 mobile or fixed
          spectacular pageant structures: (a) the movable forest,
          (b) the pavilion of Dame Pallas, (c) the palace of Fame,
          the "chief set" (within whose compartments are located
          the Countess of Surrey's chamber, and a battlement from
          which the poet watches the assault on the "English gate,"
          and (d) a simulated arbor or garden; an _action marked by_
          dramatic entries of masqued noblemen (orators, poets-
          laureate), a "mumming disguising" in which the men are
          joined by a second set, the gentlewomen disguised as
          goddesses and the Muses, to dance about the Laurel-tree;
          an _action_ further characterized by four central events

presented "dramatically"--(a) the debate between Pallas
and Fame, (b) the dramatic reading by Occupation of Skelton's "boke of remembrance (perhaps itself to be a royal
gift)," and the poet's recitation of presentation of
poems to the Countess of Surrey and her ladies-in-wait-
ing, (c) the presentation of the garland, and (d) the
approval by the noble audience of his standing as a poet;
suggests that as in seventeenth century masques of Jonson, some disorder is present but is subjected to the
order of the masque, and that, as in Jonson, darkness as
a fully developed anti-masque for a brief while "engulfs
the hall."

Indices

Author Index

(Authors of reviews are listed separately under Subject Index: "Reviews")

A

Abrahams, Phyllis, 1936
Aldington, John, 1941
Algar, F., 1944
Allen, Don Cameron (ed.); see under 1598.1 (2x)
Allen, P. S. (ed.); see under 1499.1
Alsoppe, Thomas, 1525; see also 1976.4 Williams
Ames, Joseph, 1749
Anderson, M[ary] D[ésirée], 1963
Andrews, H. C., 1942
[Anstey, Christopher], 1776
Apperson, G[eorge] L., 1934
Arber, Edward (ed.), 1900; see also under 1528.1, 1530
Ardagh, J., 1933
Ashmole, Elias (ed.), 1557
Ashton, John (ed.), 1882, 1887, 1969
Astley, Hugh J[ohn Dukinfield], 1908
Atchity, Kenneth John, 1973
Atkins, J[ohn] W[illiams] H[ey], 1943
Auden, W[ystan] H[ugh], 1930, 1932, 1933.1, 1935, 1938
_____ (co-author) 1935.2; see also Isherwood, Christopher
_____ (co-ed.) 1935.1; see also Garrett, John

_____ (co-ed.) 1950; see also Pearson, Norman Holmes
Avale, Lemeke, 1569

B

Baine, Rodney M., 1970
Baker, Herschel (co-ed.) 1954.4; see also Rollins, Hyder
Baldwin, William, 1553
Bale, John, 1548, 1549, 1556, 1559
Ballard, George, 1752
Barclay, Alexander, 1509, 1514, 1515
Barlowe, William, 1528.1; see also Roy, William
Barnes, -----, 1548.1
Barnum, Priscilla H., 1960
Baskervill, Charles R[ead], 1910, 1911
Baskin, Leonard (illus.), 1953.5
Bateson, F[rederick] W. (general ed.), 1940, 1957
Bateson, Mary (ed.), 1492-3, 1496, 1501.1, 1903
_____ (co-ed.), 1556, 1902
Bensley, Edward, 1934.1
Berdan, John M[ilton], 1914, 1915, 1915.1, 1920
Berger, Jean (composer), 1966
Bernard J[ules] E[ugene], 1939
Bevington, David M., 1962, 1968, 1970.4 (recording)
Binder, Pearl (illus.), 1928
Birch, Walter de Gray, 1873

_____ (co-ed.), 1956.2+, 1959.4;
see also Salter, F[rederick] N.
Emden, A[lfred] B[rotherton],
1959
Erasmus, Desiderius, 1499,
1499.1
Erskine, Albert (co-ed.),
1955.6; see also Warren,
Robert Penn
Evans, Maurice, 1955.1
Evans, Robert A., 1954

F

Farley, Henry, 1616
Farmer, John S. (ed.), 1523.1,
1534, 1591, 1910.1
Farnham, Willard, 1936.5
Ferguson, Francis (co-comp.),
1976.2
Fish, Stanley E[ugene],
1962.1, 1962.2, 1965
Fisher, A. S. T., 1945
Fishman, Burton, 1971.3
Fitzgibbon, H[enry] Macaulay
(ed.), 1887.2
Florio, John, 1611
Flügel, Ewald (ed.), 1895.1
Forster, E[dmund] M[organ],
1951
Foss, Michael, 1963.2
Foulface, Philip [pseud.],
1593
Fraser, G. S., 1936.6
Frost, George (co-author),
1944.1; see also Nash, Ray
Fuller, Thomas, 1662
Furnivall F[rederick] J[ames]
(ed.); 1534.1, 1547.3, 1548.1,
1560

G

Gant, Richard (ed.), 1949.1
Gardner, Dame Helen (ed.),
1972
Garrett, John (co-ed.), 1935.1;
see also Auden, W. H.
Garvin, Katherine (ed.), 1935
Gascoigne, George, 1575
Germann, Friedrich (ed.); see
under 1547.1, 1548.3

Gifford, William (ed.), 1816.1
Gingerich, Owen (co-author),
1963.7, with Stahlman; 1969.1,
with Tucker
Glassco, William G., 1966.2
Golding, Louis, 1922
Goodwin, Gordon, 1905
Gordon, Gary D., 1966.3
Gordon, I[an] A[listair],
1934.7, 1934.8, 1934.9, 1934.10,
1936.7, 1943.1
Gorton, John (ed.), 1851
Grandsen, K[arl] W[atts], 1970.3
Grange, John, 1577
Graves, Robert, 1916.1, 1916.2,
1917.1, 1920.1, 1921, 1922.1,
1923, 1925, 1925.1, 1927,
1927.1, 1927.2, 1934.11,
1955.2, 1961, 1962.3, 1969.2
Gray, W[illiam] Forbes (comp.),
1915.2
Green, Peter M[orris], 1960.3
Greene, Richard Leighton (ed.),
1935.4
Greene, Robert, 1594
Greg, Sir W[alter] W[ilson] (ed.),
1561, 1593.2, 1956
Gregory, Horace, 1933.4
Grosart, Alexander (ed.), 1592,
1593.1, 1597
Gryffyd, Elis, 1560.1

H

Hall, Donald (co-ed.), 1963.8,
1970.6; see also Taylor, Warren
Hall, Joseph, 1598
Hall, William C., 1933.5
Hallam, Henry, 1837.1
Halliwell, James O. (ed.), 1620
Hamilton, G[eorge] Restrevor,
1941.1
Hamilton, Walter, 1879
Hammond, Eleanor Prescott (ed.),
1927.5
Harrington, David V., 1967.1
Harrington, Karl Pomeroy, 1923.1
Harris, William O[liver], 1957.1,
1960.4, 1963.3, 1965.1
Hartshorne, Charles H. (ed.),
1550

Harvey, Gabriel, 1573, 1574,
1577.1, 1578.1, 1592, 1593.1
Harvey, H., 1912
Harvey, J[ohn] H., 1946
Haslewood, Joseph (co-ed.), 1814
Hathway, Richard (co-author),
1600.2; see also Rankins,
William
Hawkins, Desmond, 1939.4
Hawkins, John, 1776.1
Hawkins, Richard, 1968.3
Hazlitt, W[illiam] C[arew] (ed.);
see under 1547, 1548.4, 1567
Heartz, Daniel, 1966.4
Hebel, J. William (co-ed.),
1929.1; see also Hudson,
Hoyt H.
Heiserman, Arthur R[ay],
1959.1, 1961.1
Helsloot, K. (trans.), 1968.4
Henderson, Philip (ed.), 1931,
1948, 1959.2, 1964
Henry, C. J., 1966.5
Herbert, William (ed.), 1790
Herford, C[harles] H[arold],
1886; (co-ed.), 1600.3 &c.,
see note under 1600.3
Heron, John; see under 1498.1
Heyward, John, 1947
Heywood, John, 1523, 1523.1,
1534
Heywood, Thomas, 1638
"Hibernicus," 1939.5
Holden, William P. (ed.), 1553
Holinshed, Raphael, 1577.2
[Holland, Samuel], 1656, 1660
Hollander, John, 1961.2
Holloway, John, 1959.3, 1960.5
Hood, Thomas, 1840.1
Hooper, E. S., 1901
Hooper, James, 1897
Hope, A[lec] D[erwent], 1972.1
Howarth, R[obert] G[uy], 1945.1,
1948.1
Howell, James, 1655
Hudson, Hoyt H. (co-ed.),
1929.1
Hughes, Richard A. W., 1922.2,
1924, 1926
Hughey, Ruth (ed.), 1560.2,
1566, 1960.6; see also under
1536
Hunter, G. K. (co-author),

1969.8; see also Wilson,
F[rank] P.
[Huntingdon, John], 1542
Huth, Henry (ed.); see under
1530
Huxley, H[erbert] H., 1951.1

I

I. C., Gent, 1579
Isherwood, Christopher (co-
author), 1935.2

J

Jackson, William A. (co-comp.),
1940.1, 1976.2; see also under
1624
J[acob], G[iles], 1720
Jalava, Hilkka, 1965.2
James, M[ontague] R[hodes] (ed.),
1913.1
James, Richard, 1625
Johnson, Samuel, 1755
Jones, Claire (illus.), 1930.1
Jonson, Ben, 1600.3, 1621, 1624.1,
1624.2, 1633, 1640, 1640.1,
1641
Jusserand, J[ean] J[ules], 1894

K

Kandaswami, S., 1965.3
Kendle, Burton Stuart, 1961.3
Kerr, William, 1934.12
King, Humphrey, 1613
Kinsman, Robert S., 1949.2,
1950.1, 1950.2, 1952, 1953.2,
1953.3, 1955.3, 1960.7, 1963.4,
1966.6, 1966.7, 1968.5, 1969.3;
(co-comp.), 1967.2; see also
Yonge, Theodore (co-comp.)
Kipling, Gordon, 1974
Koelbing, A[rthur], 1904, 1908.1
Kozikowski, Stanley J., 1968.6,
1977
Krapp, George Philip, 1915.3
Krumpholz, H[einrich], 1881

L

Lahiri-Choudhury, D. K., 1965.4
Lamson, Ray (co-ed.), 1955.4;
see also Smith, Hallett

Laneham, Robert, 1575.1
Larson, Judith S[weetzer],
 1962.4
Lee, John Maynard, 1976
Lee, Sir Sidney, 1897.1,
 1910.2
Leland, John; see Bale, John,
 1549
Levin, Harry, 1936.8
Lewis, C[live] S[tapleton],
 1954.1
Lily, William, 1520
Lloyd, L[eslie] J., 1925.2,
 1929.2, 1929.3, 1934.13,
 1938.3
Lodge, Thomas, 1594.2
Lombardo, Agostino, 1954.2,
 1957.2
Lowell, James Russell, 1876
Lucie-Smith, Edward (ed.),
 1967.3
Lynn, Karen, 1973.3

M

McCain, John W., 1938.4
MacDonald, Marjorie Grace
 Madeleine (Sister Maris
 Stella), 1967.4
McGrath, Lynette Fay, 1968.7,
 1969.4
MacKenzie, W[illiam] Ray,
 1914.3
McKerrow, R[oland] (ed.);
 see under 1560.3, 1600.5
McLane, Paul E., 1972.3,
 1973.4
McManaway, James G., 1951.2
MacPeek, James A. S., 1939.6
McQuiston, James R., 1951.3
Manning, C. U., 1905.1
Marc'hadour, Abbé Germain,
 1972.2
Mardelay, John, 1548.2
Maring, Donald, 1966.8
Maris, Stella, Sister (C.S.J.);
 see MacDonald, Marjorie
 Grace Madeleine, 1967.4
Markham, Gervase, 1613.1
Mauritius, Johannes (Morris,
 John), 1605
Maxwell, J[ohn] C[oatts],
 1950.3, 1963.5

Meagher, John C. (ed.); see
 under 1601.1, 1601.2
Melville, Herman, 1849
Meres, Francis, 1598.1
Minto, William (ed.), 1889
Mish, Charles C. (ed.); see under
 1590.1, 1630.1
Morley, Henry, 1891
Morris, John; see Mauritius,
 Johannes
Muir, Kenneth (co-ed.); see under
 1594.1; see also Wilson,
 F[rank] P.
Munday, Anthony, 1601.1, 1601.2,
 1615
Musson, J. W., 1939.7
Myers, Oliver T., 1964.1

N

Nash, Ray (co-author), 1944.1;
 see also Frost, George
Nashe, Thomas, 1600.5
Nashe, Thomas (of the Inner
 Temple), 1633.1
Nasmith, James, 1777
Naylor, Edward W., 1928.1
Neilson, W[illiam] A[llan]
 (co-ed.), 1916.3; see also
 Webster, K. G. T.
Nelson, William, 1936.9, 1936.10,
 1938.2, 1939.8
[Neve, Philip], 1789
Norton-Smith, John, 1973.5

O

O'Connell, Richard, 1960.8
"Orpheus Junior," see Vaughan,
 Sir William, 1626.1

P

Paletta, Gerhard, 1934.14
Pantzer, Katharine (co-comp.),
 1976.2; see also Jackson,
 William A. and Ferguson,
 Francis S.
Parkhurst, John, 1573.1
Peacham, Henry, 1621.1
Pearson, Norman H[olmes] (co-ed.),
 1950; see also Auden, W. H.

Peele, George, 1593.2
Percy, Thomas, 1765, 1794
Phillips, Edward, 1675
Phillips, Norma Anne, 1958.1,
  1966.9
Pine, Edward, 1952.1
Pinto, Vivian de Sola (ed.),
  1950.4; (co-ed.), 1957.3;
  see also Rodway, A. E.
Pits, John; see Pitseus,
  Ioannis
Pitseus, Ioannis (John Pits),
  1619
Pollard, A[lbert] F[rederick]
  (ed.); see under 1548.5
Pollard, A[lfred] W[illiam]
  (ed.), 1890; (co-comp.),
  1926.1; see also Redgrave,
  G. R.; see further Jackson,
  W[illiam] A., Francis Fer-
  guson and Katherine Pantzer,
  1976.2 (2nd edn., 2nd vol.
  of STC)
Pollet, Maurice, 1952.2,
  1955.5, 1962.5, 1971.6,
  1973.6
Poole, Reginald Lane (ed.),
  1902; see also under 1556
Pope, Alexander, 1737.1
Potter, Robert, 1975.1
Proppé, Katherine Miller,
  1974.1
Prynne, William, 1633.2
Psilos, Paul D., 1976.1
Puttenham, George, 1589
Pyle, Fitzroy, 1936.11

R

R., C. K., 1944.2
Ramsay, Robert Lee (ed.),
  1908.2, 1925.3
Rankins, William (co-author),
  1600.2; see also Hathway,
  Richard
Ransom, John Crowe, 1927.3,
  1969.5
Redford, John, 1531.1
Redgrave, G. R. (co-comp.),
  1926.1; see also Pollard,
  A[lfred] W.

Redstone, B., 1934.15
Reeves, James (co-comp.),
  1967.5; see also Seymour-Smith,
  Martin
Rey, Albert, 1899
Ribner, Irving, 1954.3
Riche, Barnaby, 1581
Ringler, William, 1956.1
Ritson, Joseph, 1802
Robbins, Rossell Hope (co-comp.),
  1965.5; see also Cutler,
  John L.
Roberts, Henry, 1600.6
Robinson, Ian, 1971.5
Robinson, Richard, 1574.1
Rogers, H. L. (co-author),
  1957.4; see also Scammell, G. V.
Rodway, A. E. (co-ed.), 1957.3;
  see also Pinto, V[ivian]
  de Sola
Rollins, Hyder (co-ed.), 1954.4;
  see also Baker, Herschel
Rossiter, A[rthur] P[ercival],
  1950.5
Rous, John, 1640.2
Rowland, Beryl, 1964.2
Rowlands, Samuel, 1612
Rowley, Samuel, 1605.1
Roy, William (putative author),
  1528.1; see also Barlowe, Jerome
Rubel, Veré Laura, 1941.2
Rymer, Thomas, 1693.1

S

[Sale], Helen Stearns, 1928.2,
  1928.3, 1931.1, 1937.2, 1939.9
Salter, F[rederick] M., 1922.3,
  1934.16, 1935.5, 1936.12,
  1945.2
_____ (co-ed.), 1956.2+ and
  1959.4; see also Edwards, H. L.
  R., 1956.2+ and 1959.4
Sanford, Ezekiel (co-ed.), 1819.1;
  see also Welch, Robert, Jr.
Scammell, G. V. (co-ed.), 1957.4;
  see also Rogers, H. L.
Scattergood, V. J., 1974.2
Schlauch, Margaret, 1969.6
Schöneberg, G[eorg], 1888
Schulte, Edvige, 1961.4, 1962.6,
  1963.6

Scott, Sir Walter, 1822
Searle, William George (ed.),
 1908.3; see also under 1504–05
Se Boyar, G[erald] E., 1913.2
Seronsy, C[ecil] C., 1953.4
Seturaman, V. S. (ed.), 1965.3
Seymour-Smith, Martin (co-
 comp.), 1967.5; see also
 Reeves, James
Shakespeare, William, 1602.1
Shenstone, William, 1762
Shepherd, Luke, 1547, 1547.1,
 1547.2, 1548.3, 1548.4,
 1548.5
[Shiels, Robert], 1753
Sidney, Sir Phillip, 1583,
 1583.1
Sitwell, Dame Edith, 1923.2,
 1930.2
Sitwell, Osbert, 1927.4, 1931.2
Skeat, W. W., 1945.3
Skeat, W[alter] W. (ed.),
 1866.1, 1871
Skelton, Robin, 1973.7
Smith, G. Barnett (ed.),
 1881.2
Smith, Hallett (co-ed.), 1955.4;
 see also Lamson, Roy
Southern, H., 1822.1
Southey, Robert, 1814.1, 1820;
 (ed.), 1831.1
Spearing, A[nthony] C., 1976.3
Spence, Joseph; see under
 Pope, 1737.1
Spenser, Edmund, 1579.1
Spina, Elaine, 1965.6, 1967.6
Stahlman, W. D. (co-author),
 1963.7; see also Gingerich,
 Owen
Steevens, George; see under
 1794.1
Stevens, John [Edgar] (ed.),
 1961.5
Stopes, C. C., 1914.5
Strickland, Agnes, 1844
Sutton, G. P. C., 1936.13
Swaen, A. E. H. (ed.); see
 under 1602
Swain, Barbara, 1932.1
Swallow, Alan, 1941.3, 1950.6,
 1953.6

Swart, J., 1964.3
Swift, Jonathan, 1719
Sylvester, Richard S. (ed.),
 1974.3

T

Tanner, Thomas, 1748
Targan, Barry, 1965.7
Taylor, John, 1630
Taylor, Warren (co-ed.), 1963.8,
 1970.6; see also Hall, Donald
Thomas, A. H. (co-ed.); see
 under 1510.2; see also
 Thornley, I. D.
Thompson, Elbert N. S., 1910.3
Thornley, I. D. (co-ed.), see
 under 1510.2; see also Thomas,
 A. H.
Thornton, Richard H., 1899.1
Thümmel, Arno, 1905.2
Thynne, Francis, 1598.3
Tigges, W[illem], 1974.4
Tillemans, Th., 1946.1
Tilney-Basset, J. G., 1944.3
Tucker, M[elvin] J., 1964.4,
 1964.5, 1967.7, 1969.7, 1970.7,
 1973.8; (co-author), 1969.1;
 see also Gingerich, Owen
Tucker, S[amuel] M[arion], 1908.4
Twyne, Brian, 1608
Tydeman, William, 1970.8

U

Ungar, Emma (co-ed.), 1940.1;
 see also Jackson, William A.
Untermeyer, Louis (ed.), 1942.1

V

Van Dorsten, Jan (ed.); see
 under 1974
Vaughan, Sir William ("Orpheus
 Junior"), 1626.1
Vines, Sherard (ed.), 1932.2

W

W. R., 1570
Ward, [Sir] A[dolphus] W[illiam],
 1899.2

Ward, Thomas [Humphry] (ed.),
1880.1
Warren, Robert Penn (co-ed.),
1955.6; see also Erskine,
Albert
Warrington, John (trans.),
1971.6
Warton, Thomas, 1778
Watson, George (general ed.),
1974.5
Watt, Robert, 1824
Webbe, William, 1586.1
Webster, K. G. T. (co-ed.),
1916.3; see also Neilson,
W[illiam] A[llan]
Weever, John, 1631
Weitzmann, Francis, 1934.17
Welch, Robert Jr. (co-ed.),
1819.1; see also Sanford,
Ezekiel
West, Michael, 1971.7
West, Richard, 1606.1
Westlake, H[erbert] F[rancis],
1921.1, 1923.3
White, Beatrice (ed.); see under
1514
Whitmee, Dorothy Edith, 1939.10
Whittinton, Robert, 1519
Williams, Franklin B., Jr. (ed.),
1976.4; see also under 1525
Williams, John (ed.), 1963.9
Williams, Ralph Vaughan,
1936.14, 1948.2
Williams, W[illiam] H[enry]
(ed.), 1902.1

Wills, Floreid, 1956.3
Wilson, F[rank] P. (co-author),
1969.8; see also Hunter, G. K.
_____ (co-ed.); see under 1594.1;
see also Muir, Kenneth
Winser, Leigh, 1969.9, 1970.9,
1976.5, 1976.6, 1977.1
Winstanley, William, 1687
Wolfe, Humbert, 1929.4
Wood, Anthony à, 1691, 1813
Wordsworth, William, 1804, 1833,
1833.1, 1843.2, 1844.1
Workman, Samuel K., 1941.4
Wright, Thomas, 1868
Wülker, Richard Paul, 1896.1
Wyatt, Sir Thomas, 1536

Y

Yonge, Theodore (co-ed. and
comp.), 1967.2; see also
Kinsman, Robert S.

Z

Zall, Paul (ed.), 1963.10; see
also under 1567
Zupitza, J[ulius] (ed.), 1890.1;
and see under WCY, no. 1545.3

Subject Index

Fuller, Thomas, 1662
Goodwin, Gordon, 1905
Gordon, I[an] A[listair], 1934.7,
1934.10
Gorton, John, 1851
Gray, W[illiam] Forbes, 1915.2
Hamilton, Walter, 1879
Hooper, James, 1897
J[acob], G[iles], 1720
Lee, Sir Sidney, 1897.1
Levin, Harry, 1936.8
Lloyd, Leslie J., 1934.13
Manning, C. U., 1905.1
Phillips, Edward, 1675
Pollet, Maurice, 1952.2, 1973.6
Poole, Reginald Lane and Mary
Bateson, 1556, 1902
[Sale], Helen Stearns, 1928.2,
1928.3
Salter, F[rederick] M., 1936.12
Searle, William George, 1504–05,
1908.3
[Shiels, Robert], 1753
Some Account of the Life of
Skelton, 1810.1
Tucker, M[elvin] J., 1973.8
Warton, Thomas, 1778
Weever, John, 1631
Westlake, H. F., 1921.1, 1923.3
Winstanley, William, 1687
Wood, Anthony à, 1691, 1813

BIOGRAPHY: LIFE RECORDS &
CONTEMPORARY REFERENCES

1490   Caxton's preface to
Eneydos (late June,
1490), refers at some
length to Skelton, no.
1490
1492-3 Grace Book B (Laureation
at Cambridge, 1492–3),
no. 1492–3
1496   Grace Book B (Meals in
London, after Pente-
cost, 1496), no. 1496
1498   Register 'Hill' 31 March,
14 April, 9 June, 1948,
process of ordination
to priesthood, no. 1498
1498   Account Book of John

Heron, 11 November,
1498; Henry VII's offer-
ing at Skelton's mass,
no. 1498.1
1499 Mentioned by Erasmus, no.
1499
1499 Mentioned by Erasmus, no.
1499.1
1501 PRO Court of Requests,
Skelton as defendant in
Otty case, no. 1501
1501 Grace Book B (Meals at
Westminster), no. 1501.1
1502 PRO Court of Requests,
Skelton as surety, 10
June, 1502, no. 1502
1504 Norwich Consistory Court
Register R, Skelton wit-
nesses will of Margery
Cowper of Diss, no. 1504
1504 Blomefield, Topographical
History of Norfolk,
Skelton succeeds Peter
Graves as Rector of
Diss, before 10 April
1504, no. 1504
1504-5 Grace Book Γ, Skelton
granted grace for in-
corporation from Oxford,
with privilege of wear-
ing the habit granted
him by the king, 1504–
05, no. 1504–05
1509 Mentioned by Alexander
Barclay, Shyp of Folys,
c. 1509, no. 1509
1509 PRO Supp. Patent Rolls,
Skelton granted routine
royal pardon, 21 Octo-
ber, 1509, no. 1509.2
1509 Consist. Court Act Bk.,
Norwich Cathedral, 3
December, 1509, Skelton
involved in case against
a parishioner, Thomas
Pykerell, no. 1509.3
1510 Continuation of Pykerell
case, 14 January, 4
February 1510, nos.
1510 and 1510.1
1510 Mentioned in The Great
Chronicle of London, c.
1510, no. 1510.2

1511   Westminster Abbey Muni-
        ments, 5 July, 1511,
        Skelton dines with Ab-
        bot Islip, no. 1511.2

1511   Institution Book XIV, Nor-
        wich Cathedral, Skelton
        appointed an arbitrator
        in Nick vs. Dale, 11
        Nov. 1511, no. 1511

1512   du Resnel, Recherches
        sur les Poètes Couron-
        nez (1736), Skelton
        apparently granted let-
        ters patent recognizing
        him as poet laureate to
        Henry VIII, 1512-13,
        no. 1512

1513   By 1513, Skelton was re-
        ferred to by Henry
        Bradshaw in his lives
        of St. Werburge and St.
        Radegunde, nos. 1513
        and 1513.1

1514   Skelton possibly referred
        to by Alexander Barclay
        in his "Fourth Eclogue"
        c. 1514, no. 1514

1515   Skelton possibly referred
        to by Alexander Barclay
        in his life of St.
        George c. 1515, no.
        1515

1518   Westminster Abbey Muni-
        ments, Register II, 8
        August 1518, indenture
        for Skelton's tenement
        in sanctuary, no. 1518.1

1519   Two Latin poems dedicated
        to and written about
        Skelton by Robert Whit-
        tinton, 1519, no. 1519

1520   Skelton the object of a
        satirical poem by Wil-
        liam Lily, c. 1520, no.
        1520

1528   Strype, Ecclesiastical
        Memorials (1822), Skel-
        ton a witness at the ab-
        juration of Thomas Bow-
        gas, 4 May 1528, no.
        1528

1529   Churchwardens' Accounts,

St. Margaret's Westmin-
        ster, receipts for buri-
        al, obits and lights for
        Skelton's burial [21
        June 1529], no. 1529

1529   Norwich Institution Book:
        17 July 1529. Thomas
        Clerk succeeds John
        Skelton as rector of
        Diss, no. 1529.2

1529   Comm. Ct. Westm. (Somer-
        set House): 6 Bracy,
        16 Nov. 1529, re admin-
        istration of Skelton's
        estate, no. 1529.1

1529   Burial Inscription, no.
        1529.3

BIOGRAPHY: LIFE AND WORKS

Carpenter, Nan Cooke, 1967
Edwards, H. L. R., 1934.2, 1949
Gordon, I[an] A[listair], 1936.7,
  1943.1
Green, Peter M[orris], 1960.3
Lloyd, L[eslie] J., 1938.3
Nelson, William, 1939.8
Pollet, Maurice, 1955.5, 1962.5,
  1971.6 (trans.)
Schulte, Edvige, 1963.6

CANONICAL AND NON-CANONICAL WORKS

Ardagh, J., 1933
Baine, Rodney M., 1970
Birch, W. de Gray, 1873
Brie, F[riederich], 1907, 1919
Carpenter, Nan Cooke, 1970.2
Edwards, H. L. R., 1934.3
Gordon, I[an] A., 1934.7
Kinsman, Robert S., 1966.6
Kinsman, Robert S. and Theodore
  Yonge, 1967.2
Lloyd, L[eslie] J., 1929.3
McManaway, James G., 1951.2
Maxwell, J[ohn] C[oatts], 1950.3
Salter, F[rederick] M., 1935.5
Scammell, G. V. and H. L. Rogers,
  1957.4

CRITICISM: GENERAL

Berdan, J[ohn] M[ilton], 1920

Blunden, Edmund C., 1929
Browning, Elizabeth Barrett, 1842
Budgey, Norman F., 1953
Chambers, Robert (comp.), 1843
Common, Robert Magill, 1968.2
Courthope, W. J., 1895
Crisp, Delmas, 1975
D'Israeli, Isaac, 1840
Dublin Univ. Mag., 1866, 1877
Dunbabin, R[obert] L[eslie], 1917
Edwards, H. L. R., 1938.1, 1939.3
Evans, Maurice, 1955.1
Fish, Stanley E[ugene], 1962.2, 1965
Forster, E[dmund] M[organ], 1951
Foss, Michael, 1963.2
Fraser, G. S., 1936.6
Golding, Louis, 1922
Gordon, Gary D., 1966.3
Graves, Robert, 1955.2, 1961
Hall, William C., 1933.5
Harvey, H., 1912
Henry, C. J., 1966.5
Holloway, John, 1959.3, 1960.5
Jusserand, J[ean] A. A., 1894
Kandaswami, S., 1965.3
Koelbing, A[rthur], 1908.1
Krapp, George Phillip, 1915.3
Lewis, [Clive] S[tapleton], 1954.1
Lloyd, L[eslie] J., 1925.2, 1929.2
MacDonald, Marjorie Grace Madeleine, 1967.4
Minto, William, 1889
Morley, Henry, 1891
Salter, Frederick M., 1922.3
Schulte, Edvige, 1961.4
Skelton, Robin, 1973.7
Southern, H., 1822.1
Thümmel, Arno, 1905.2
Tillemans, Th., 1946.1
Tucker, S[amuel] M[arion], 1908.4
West, Michael, 1971.7
Wills, Floreid, 1956.3
Wolfe, Humbert, 1929.4

CRITICISM: INFLUENCES ON SKELTON'S POETRY OR COMPARATIVE

STUDIES (see also "CRITICISM: PROSODIC")

Berdan, J[ohn] M[ilton], 1915
Cook, Albert S[tanhope], 1916
Farnham, Willard, 1936.5
Gordon, I[an] A[listair], 1934.8
Harrington, Karl Pomeroy, 1923.1
Harris, William O., 1965.1
Heiserman, Arthur R., 1959.1, 1961.1
Herford, Charles H[arold], 1886
Howarth, R. G., 1948.1
Kerr, William, 1934.12
Kinsman, Robert S., 1949.2
Kipling, Gordon, 1974
Koelbing, Arthur, 1904
Kozikowski, Stanley J., 1977
Lahiri-Choudhury, D. K., 1965.4
MacPeek, James A. S., 1939.6
Marc'hadour, Germain, 1972.2
Musson, J. W., 1939.7
Myers, Oliver T., 1964.1
Phillips, Norma Anne, 1958.1, 1966.9
Proppé, Katherine Miller, 1974.1
Rey, Albert, 1899
Salter, F[rederick] M. and H. L. R. Edwards (eds.), 1959.4

CRITICISM: LINGUISTIC AND PHILOLOGICAL

Atkins, J[ohn] W[illiam] H[ey], 1943
Jalava, Hilkka, 1965.2
Salter, F[rederick] M., 1945.2
Schöneberg, G[eorg], 1888

CRITICISM: PROSODIC

Auden, W[ystan] H[ugh], 1935
Bernard, J[ules] E[ugene], 1939
Evans, Robert A., 1954
Kendle, Burton Stuart, 1961.3
Kinsman, Robert S., 1953.3
Kipling, Gordon, 1974
Lee, Sir Sidney, 1910.2
Lynn, Karen, 1973.3
Norton-Smith, John, 1973.5

Pyle, Fitzroy, 1936.11
Robinson, Ian, 1971.5
Spina, Elaine, 1965.6, 1967.6
Swallow, Alan, 1941.3, 1950.6
Thümmel, Arno, 1905.2

CRITICISM: TECHNIQUES AND TOPICS
  OF COMPOSITION

Brownlow, F[rank] W[alsh],
  1968.1
Fish, Stanley E., 1962.1
Harris, William O., 1957.1,
  1963.3
Hawkins, Richard, 1968.3
Heiserman, A[rthur] R., 1959.1,
  1961.1
Kinsman, Robert S., 1963.4
McGrath, Lynette Fay, 1968.7
McQuiston, James R., 1951.3
Rubel, Veré L[aura], 1941.2
[Sale], Helen Stearns, 1937.1
Swallow, Alan, 1941.3, 1953.6
Workman, Samuel K., 1941.4

CRITICISM: SPECIFIC WORKS AND
  PASSAGES

Agaynste a Comely Coystrowne

Carpenter, Nan Cooke, 1955
Heartz, Daniel, 1966.4
Hollander, John, 1961.2
Kinsman, Robert S., 1953.2
Naylor, Edward W., 1928.1

Agenst Garnesche

Edwards, H. L. R., 1934.5,
  1934.6
Gordon, I[an] A[listair],
  1934.10
Kinsman, Robert S., 1968.5
Redstone, B., 1934.15
[Sale], Helen Stearns, 1928.3

Ballade of the Scottysshe Kynge

Ashton, John (ed.), 1882
Marc'hadour, Abbé Germain, 1972.2

Bowge of Courte

Herford, Charles H., 1886
Kozikowski, Stanley J., 1968.6,
  1977
Larson, Judith S[weetzer], 1962.4
Psilos, Paul D., 1976.1
Rey, Albert, 1899
[Sale], Helen Stearns, 1937.2
Scattergood, V. J., 1974.2
Spearing, A[nthony] C., 1976.3
Tucker, Melvin J., 1970.7
Winser, Leigh, 1976.5

Collyn Cloute

Atchity, Kenneth John, 1973
Edwards, H. L. R. (v. 297),
  1936.2; (Lat. ep.), 1936.4
Kinsman, Robert S., 1950.2,
  1963.4
McLane, Paul E., 1972.3, 1973.4
Nelson, William, 1936.9

Diodorus Siculus

Carpenter, Nan Cooke, 1970.1
Edwards, H. L. R., 1938.1
Workman, Samuel K., 1941.1

"Edward IV" [Doubtful]

Kinsman, Robert S., 1966.6

Garlande of Laurell

Apperson, G. L. (vv. 1430-31),
  1934
Bensley, Edward (vv. 1430-31),
  1934.1
Bradley, Henry (vv. 751-2), 1896
Colley, John Scott, 1973.1
Cook, Albert S., 1916
Gingerich, Owen and Melvin J.
  Tucker, 1969.1
Graves, Robert (v. 1430), 1934.11
Maring, Donald, 1966.8
Nelson, William (opening, vv. 586-
  601), 1936.9
[Sale], Helen Stearns, 1928.2
Schulte, Edvige, 1962.6

Chalker, John, 1960.2
Edwards, H. L. R. (v. 37),
  1934.4; (v. 185), 1936.3
Fisher, A. S. T., 1945
Gordon, I[an] A[listair], 1934.9
Howarth, R. G. (v. 18), 1948.1
McGrath, Lynette F[ay], 1969.4
Nelson, William, 1936.10
Skeat, W. W., 1945.3
Sutton, G. P. C. (v. 185),
  1936.13

Tunnyng of Elynour Rummyng, The

Harvey, J[ohn] H., 1946
Hawkins, Richard, 1968.3
Kinsman, Robert S., 1955.3
Phillips, Norma, 1966.9
Spina, Elaine, 1965.6, 1967.6

"Uppon a Deedmans Hed"

Kinsman, Robert S., 1953.3

Why Come Ye Nat to Courte?

Andrews, H. C. (v. 953), 1942
Dunbabin, R. L. (v. 954), 1917
Edwards, H. L. R. (vv. 915–17),
  1937
Kinsman, Robert S. (vv. 118–19),
  1952

Ware the Hauke

Bradley, Henry (vv. 238–9),
  1896
Howarth, R. G. (vv. 239–40),
  1948.1
Thornton, Richard H. (vv. 239–
  40), 1899.1

DATING OF EDITIONS AND OF POEMS

Dating of Editions

Ashton, John, 1882
Bateson, F[rederick] W. (general
  ed.), 1940, 1957
Jackson, William A. and Emma
  Ungar, 1940.1
Jackson, W[illiam] A., F. S.
  Ferguson and Katherine Pantzer,
  1976.2
Kinsman, Robert S., 1953.2, 1955.3
Kinsman, Robert S. and Theodore
  Yonge, 1967.2
Pollard, A[lfred] W. and G. R.
  Redgrave, 1926.1
[Sale], Helen Stearns, 1937.2
Schulte, Edvige, 1961.4

Dating of Poems

Berdan, John M., 1914
Brown, Carleton (ed.), 1939.1
Edwards, H. L. R. and William
  Nelson, 1938.2
Gingerich, Owen and Melvin J.
  Tucker, 1969.1
Gordon, I[an] A., 1934.9
McLane, Paul E., 1972.3
Nelson, William, 1936.10
[Sale], Helen Stearns, 1928.2,
  1937.2
Stahlman, W. D. and Owen
  Gingerich, 1963.7
Tucker, Melvin J., 1964.4,
  1967.7, 1969.7, 1970.7

EDITIONS, PRINTED: COLLECTED
AND/OR COMPLETE WORKS

Agaynste a Comely Coystrowne,
  1527
Certayne Bokes Compyled by Mayster
  Skelton Poet Laureat..., 1545,
  1554, 1560.4
The Complete Poems of John Skelton, Laureate (Henderson),
  1931, 1948, 1959.2, 1964

Dyuers Balletys and Dyties
  Solacyous, 1527.1
Pithy, Pleasaunt and Profitable
  Workes of Maister Skelton,
  Poete Laureate; Nowe Collected
  and Newly Published, Anno.
  1568, 1568, 1736.1, 1810,
  1970.5
The Poetical Works of John Skel-
  ton (Dyce), 1843.1, 1856,1864
The Poetical Works of Skelton
  and Donne, with a Memoir of
  Each, 1855, 1881.1

EDITIONS AND REPRINTS, COMPLETE,
  OF INDIVIDUAL POEMS OR PIECES
  OF PROSE

"A Ballade of the Scottysshe
  Kynge," 1513.4, 1881.2, 1882,
  1887, 1957.3, 1969 [poem not in
  PPPW, 1568 or Dyce, 1843]
The Bibliotheca Historia of Dio-
  dorus Siculus Translated by
  John Skelton, 1938.1, 1956.2+,
  1959.4 [not included in PPPW,
  1568 or Dyce, 1843]; see also
  "Manuscript Versions or Photo-
  graphic Facsimiles"
Bowge of Courte, 1499.2, 1510.3
Collyn Clout, 1531.2, 1545.1,
  1553.1, 1560.5, 1831.1, 1966.2
  (typescript, with WCY)
Garlande of Laurell, 1523.3;
  from manuscript, by HAMMOND,
  1927.5, and LEE, no. 1976
"Lawde," 1914.5, 1973.2
Magnyfycence: a Goodly Interlude
  and a Mery Deuysed and Made by
  Mayster Skelton, Poet Laureate
  Late Deceasyd, 1530.3, 1821.1,
  1908.2, 1910.1, 1925.3
Phyllyp Sparowe, 1545.2, 1553.2,
  1560.6, 1831.1
Replycacion, 1528.2
Speculum Principis, 1934.16 [not
  in PPPW, 1568, or Dyce, 1843.1]
The Tunnyng of Elynour Rummyng,
  1521, 1624, 1718, 1744, 1808,
  1928.1, 1930.1, 1953.5
Why Come Ye Nat to Courte?,

1545.3, 1553.3, 1560.7 [in-
  cluded in GLASSCO, no. 1966.2
  (typescript, with CC)]

EDITIONS: SELECTED POEMS

"John Skelton," in Select Works
  of the British Poets, from
  Chaucer to Jonson, with Biog-
  raphical Sketches, 1831.1
  (Southey)
John Skelton (Laureate) 1460?-
  1529, 1927 (Graves)
John Skelton, Poems, 1924
  (Hughes)
John Skelton, Poems, 1969.3
  (Kinsman)
John Skelton: A Selection from
  his Poems, 1950.4 (Pinto)
Poems by John Skelton, 1949.1
  (Gant)
"Select Poems of John Skelton,
  with a Life of the Author," in
  The Works of the British Poets,
  1819.1 (Sanford and Welch)
A Selection from the Poetical
  Works of John Skelton, 1902.1
  (Williams)

EDITIONS: SOME ANTHOLOGIES CON-
  TAINING SELECTIONS FROM SKEL-
  TON'S POETRY (of 5 pages or
  more)

The Anchor Anthology of Sixteenth
  Century Verse, 1974.3
Chief British Poets of the Four-
  teenth and Fifteenth Centuries,
  1916.3
Early English Poetry, 1887.2
English Poetry 1400-1580, 1970.8
The English Poets. Selections
  with Critical Introductions by
  Various Writers and a General
  Introduction by Matthew Arnold,
  1880.1
English Renaissance Poetry,
  1963.9
The Golden Hind, 1955.4

MICROFILM REPRODUCTIONS OF
SKELTON EDITIONS

Agaynste a Comely Coystrowne;
   see under entry 1527
"A Ballade of the Scottysshe
   Kynge"; see under entry
   1513.4
Bowge of Courte; see under
   entry 1499.2
Certayne Bokes; see under 1545,
   1554, 1560.4
Collyn Clout; see under 1545.1,
   1553.1, 1560.5
Dyuers Balettys and Dyties
   Solacyous; see under entry
   1527.1
Magnyfycence; see under entry
   1530.3
Phyllyp Sparowe; see under
   1545.2, 1553.2, 1560.6
Pithy, Plesaunt and Profitable
   Workes; see under entry 1568
Why Come Ye Nat to Courte?;
   see under 1545.3, 1560.7

MUSICAL SETTINGS AND RECORDINGS
OF SKELTON'S POETRY

Five Tudor Portraits...; see
   under main entry 1936.14 for
   recordings
John Skelton and Early Lyric,
   1971.4 [recording]
Magnyfycence, Part I, 1970.4
   [recording]
Prayer to the Father of Heaven,
   Motet, 1948.2
Skelton Poems: for Mixed Chorus,
   Baritone Solo and Piano (Organ)
   Accompaniment, 1966

"PORTRAITS" OF SKELTON

[Portrait of "Skelton"], 1797,
   Type 1
[Portrait of "Skelton"], 1814,
   Type 3
[Portrait of "Skelton"], 1821,
   Type 2

[Portrait of "Skelton"], 1831,
   Type 3
O'Donoghue, Freeman, 1914.4

REPUTATION AND INFLUENCE OF SKEL-
TON (References to, and Imitations or Adaptations of)

Algar, F., 1944
Alsoppe, Thomas, 1525, 1976.5
[Anstey, Christopher], 1776
Auden, W[ystan] H[ugh], 1930,
   1932, 1933.1, 1935
Avale, Lemeke, 1569
Baldwin, William, 1553
Banquet of Jests, 1639
Barclay, Alexander, 1509, 1514,
   1515
Barnes, _____, 1548.1
Baskervill, Charles R[ead], 1910,
   1911
Bischoffberger, E[lise], 1914.1
Bolton, Edmund, 1618
Bradford, John, 1555
Bradshaw, Henry, 1513, 1513.1
Breton, Nicholas, 1597
Brink, Bernhard ten, 1893
Brome, Richard, 1632
Browne, William, of Tavistock,
   1614
Browning, Elizabeth Barrett, 1842
Bullein, William, 1564
Bunyan, John, 1686
The Burial of the Mass, 1528.1
"Buried Poets: John Skelton,"
   1877
Buttes, Thomas, 1578
Carruth, Haydn, 1958
Cartwright, William, 1651
Caxton, William, 1490
Chamber, John, 1601
Charnock, Thomas, 1557
Chasles, Philarète, 1842.1
"Chateaubriand on the Culture
   of England," 1837
Churchyard, Thomas; see under
   1568, "Contents" (2)
The Cobler of Canterburie, 1590
Coleridge, Samuel Taylor, 1827

Marc'hadour, Abbé Germain, reviews POLLET, 1962.5

Merton, Thomas, reviews NELSON,
1939.8

Milligan, Burton, reviews FISH,
1965; reviews POLLET, 1962.5

MLR, reviews PINTO, 1950.4

Mustanoja, Tauno, reviews SALTER
& EDWARDS, 1956.2+

N & Q, reviews NELSON, 1939.8

Nelson, William, reviews FISH,
1965; reviews HARRIS, 1965.1;
reviews HEISERMAN, 1961.1;
reviews KINSMAN, 1969.3; reviews POLLET, 1962.5; reviews
SALTER & EDWARDS, 1956.2+

Pafford, J. H. P., reviews
GORDON, 1943.1

Pinto, V. de Sola, reviews
POLLET, 1962.5

Pollard, A. F., reviews NELSON,
1939.8

Pollet, Maurice, reviews FISH,
1965; reviews HARRIS, 1965.1;
reviews HEISERMAN, 1961.1

Reiss, Edmund, reviews FISH,
1965

Robbins, R. H., reviews POLLET,
1962.5

Salter, F. M., reviews LLOYD,
1938.3; reviews NELSON,
1939.8

Schirmer, W. F., reviews HEISER-
MAN, 1961.1

Schneider, I., reviews HENDERSON,
1931

Scovell, E. J., reviews HENDER-
SON, 1931

Smith, A. J., reviews FISH, 1965

Southey, Robert, reviews
CHALMERS (1810); see 1814.1

Spectator, reviews HUGHES, 1924

Spencer, T. J. B., reviews
SALTER & EDWARDS, 1956.2+

Spivack, Bernard, reviews
HARRIS, 1965.1

Thomas, R. George, reviews
KINSMAN, 1969.3

Thomson, Patricia, reviews FISH,
1965; reviews KINSMAN, 1969.3

TLS, reviews EDWARDS, 1949; reviews ELYNOUR RUMMYNGE (illus.
Claire Jones), 1930.1; reviews
FISH, 1965; reviews GORDON,
1943.1; reviews HENDERSON, 1931;
reviews HUGHES, 1924; reviews
LLOYD, 1938.3; reviews NELSON,
1939.8; reviews PINTO, 1950.4;
reviews POLLET, 1962.5, and
WARRINGTON's trans. of, 1971.6

Warren, C. H., reviews HENDERSON,
1931

Warren, L. C., reviews NELSON,
1939.8

Watson, Curtis Brown, reviews
POLLET, 1962.5

White, Beatrice, reviews EDWARDS,
1949 and PINTO, 1950.4

Wright, Louis B., reviews NELSON,
1939.8

Zandervoort, R. W., reviews
GREEN, 1960.3; reviews HEISER-
MAN, 1961.1

TRANSLATIONS

"Elegia in serenissemae principis
et dominae, Dominae Margaretae,"
1752

"De Kroeg van Noortje Neut,"
[TER], 1968.4

Title Index

The Academy, 1896, 1903, see
  under 1902.1
Adagia, 1499.1
Adelphi, 1936.6
"Against Venemous Tongues," 1516
"Against Wolsey: A Critical
  Edition of John Skelton's Why
  Come Ye Nat to Courte and Colyn
  Cloute" [diss.], 1966.2
Agaynste a Comely Coystrowne,
  1527
"Agaynst the Scottes," 1513.6
"Agenst Garnesch," 1514.1
"Agitato ma non troppo" (Ransom),
  1969.5
All the Workes of John Taylor,
  the Water-Poet, 1630
"Alsop's Fair Custance: Chaucer
  in Tudor Dress," 1525, 1976.4
Amenities of Literature, 1840
American Church Review, 1873.1
American Notes and Queries, 1977
Among My Books, 1876
"An Amouret Anacreontick" in
  Drayton's Poemes, 1606+
"The Ancestry and Character of
  the Skeltonic" [diss.], 1961.3
The Anchor Anthology of Sixteenth
  Century Verse, 1974.3
Ancient Fvnerall Monvments Within
  The Vnited Monarchie of Great
  Britain, Ireland and the Is-
  lands Adiacent, 1631
Anglia (1962), see under 1961.1
Animaduersions uppon the Annota-
  cions and Corrections of Some
  Imperfections of Impressiones
  of Chaucer's Workes, 1598.3

Annali Istituto Universitario
  Orientale - Napoli, Sezione
  Germanica, 1961.4, 1962.6
"Anne with her birds..."
  (Ransom), 1927.3
Antiquitatis Academie Oxoniensis
  Apologia, 1608
"Anxiety" (Carruth), 1958
"Apollyon" (Hamilton), 1941.1
Archiv, 1890.1, 1919
The Arte of English Poesie, 1589
The Arundel Harington Manuscript
  of Tudor Poetry, 1536, 1560.2,
  1566, 1960.6
"A's Song" (Auden) in Dance of
  Death, 1933.1
"Aspects of Rhetorical Analysis:
  Skelton's Philip Sparrow,"
  1962.1
"The Astronomical Dating of Skel-
  ton's Garland of Laurel," 1969.1
Astrophel and Stella, 1583
Athenae Britannicae, sive Icon
  Libellorum or, A Critical His-
  tory of Pamphlets, 1716
Athenae Oxonienses, 1691
Athenae Oxonienses...a New Edition
  with Additions, 1813
Athenaeum, 1842; 1873; 1881.2;
  (1903), see under 1902.1; 1914.5
Autograph Poetry in the English
  Language, 1973.2
Bacchus Bountie, 1593
"Baldock, Herts., and John
  Skelton," 1942
Ballad Society, 1868, see 1534.1;
  1871, see 1575.1; 1876, see
  1547.3

Folengo, Luther" (from Revue
des deux mondes), 1842.1
Dublin University Magazine, 1866,
1877
"'Dulle' Drede and the Limits of
Prudential Knowledge in Skel-
ton's Bowge of Courte," 1976.1
Dyuers Balettys and Dyties so-
lacyous deuysyd by Master
Skelton Laureat, 1527.1
The Early English Carols, 1935.4
Early English Text Society, 1865,
see 1598.3; 1870, see 1548.1;
1887, see 1513; 1888, see
1564; 1908, 1925, see 1908.2,
1925.3; 1955, see 1515; 1956
and 1959 see 1956.2+ and
1959.4
"Early Poetical Plays," 1913
Early Tudor Poetry, 1920
Edinburgh Review, 1837
"Editions of Skelton" (Dale),
1939.2
"Editions of Skelton" (Hawkins),
1939.4
An Editor's Essays of Two De-
cades (1962) see under 1953.6
Der Einfluss John Skelton auf
die Englische Literatur, 1914.1
"Eleanor Rumming," 1946
"Eleanora Rediviva," 1794.1
"Eleanora Rediviva: Fragment of
an Edition of Skelton's
Elynour Rumming, ca. 1521,"
1955.3
"Elegia in serenissimae princi-
pis et domine, domine Margar-
ete," 1516.1, 1600
"An Elegy on Henry, Fourth Earl
of Northumberland" in Reliques
of Ancient English Poetry,
1765, 1794
"An Elegy on Henry VII," 1957.4
Elynour Rummin, The Famous Ale-
Wife of England, Written by
Mr. Skelton, Poet Laureat to
King Henry the Egihth [sic],
1624, 1744, 1808
Elynoure Rumminge, 1928 (illus.
Binder), 1930.1 (illus. Jones)
"Encina and Skelton," 1964.1

Encounter, 1961
Eneydos, 1490
England Reclaimed, 1927.4
Englische Studien, 1907
The English Drama (1485-1585),
1969.8
English Drama from Early Times to
the Elizabethans, 1950.5
English Elements in Jonson's
Early Comedy, 1911
"English Epigrams" (Apperson),
1934
"English Epigrams" (Bensley),
1934.1
"English Epigrams" (Graves),
1934.11
English Language Notes, 1967.7,
1970.1, 1970.7, 1972.3
English Literary Criticism: The
Medieval Phase, 1943
English Literary Renaissance,
1971.1, 1971.3, 1976.4, 1976.5
English Literature in the Six-
teenth Century Excluding Drama,
1954.1
English Miracle Plays, Moralities
and Interludes, 1890
English Miscellany, 1954.2
The English Moral Plays, 1910.3
The English Morality Play, 1975.1
English Poetry: A Descriptive
Catalogue, 1947
English Poetry 1400-1580, 1970.8
English Poetry in the Sixteenth
Century, 1955.1
The English Poets. Selections
with Critical Introductions by
Various Writers and a General
Introduction by Matthew Arnold,
1880.1
English Renaissance Poetry,
1963.9
English Review, 1925.2
The English Secretorie, 1586
English Studies, 1946.1
English Verse between Chaucer and
Surrey; see under Garlande of
Laurell, 1927.5
English Writers, 1891
Epistolae Ho-Elianae, 1655

Nation, 1910; 1933, see under
  1931 Henderson
"Native Literary Problems (con-
  tinued): Caxton, Hawes, Skel-
  ton," 1943
Neophilologus, 1960.2
Neuenglisches Lesebuch, 1895.1
The New Bath Guide, or Memoirs of
  the B–R–D Family, 1776
The New Cambridge Bibliography of
  English Literature, 1974.5
A New Canon of English Poetry,
  1967.5
A New Enterlude Called Thersytes,
  1537
"New Light on Skelton," 1934.3,
  1934.7, 1934.13
New Oxford Book of English Verse,
  1972
New Republic, 1932; see under
  1931 Henderson
New Statesman, 1932; see under
  1931 Henderson
A Newe Interlude of Impacyente
  Pouertie, 1560.3
News from Bartholomew Fayre,
  1606.1
No Retreat, 1933.4
The Northern Lasse, 1632
Norwich Consistory Court Act Book,
  1509.1, 1510, 1510.2
Norwich Consistory Court Regis-
  try, 1504
Norwich Institution Book XIV,
  1511
"A Note on Skelton," 1929.3
Notes and Queries, 1899.1, 1905,
  1933, 1936.11, 1938, 1939.5,
  1942, 1944, 1945, 1948.1,
  1951.1, 1951.2, 1953.4,
  1960.7, 1963.1, 1964.2,
  1969.4, 1971.1, 1971.2,
  1974.2
Notes on English Verse Satire,
  1929.4
"Notes on Skelton" (Dunbabin),
  1917
"Notes on Skelton" (Howarth),
  1948.1
"Observations on the Derivative
  Method of Skelton's Realism,"
  1966.9

"Old Christmas, or Good Order,
  A Fragment of a Morality
  Play...," 1956
"The Old Gill," 1660.1
On English Poetry..., 1922.1
On Poetry: Collected Talks and
  Essays, 1969.2
Opusculum Roberti Whittintoni,
  1519
The Orators, 1932
"The Origins of 'Skeltonics,'"
  1973.5
"The Origins of the Skeltonic,"
  1936.11
"The Ornamental Compartment of
  Magnyfycence, 1530," 1976.6
"Our Two Worthies" (Ransom),
  1927.3
Over the Brazier, 1916.1
Oxford Addresses on Poetry,
  1962.3
"Palinode," 1511.1
Palladis Tamia, Wit's Treasure,
  1598.1
Pantagruel's Prognostication,
  1660.2
Papers on the Manchester Literary
  Club, 1933.5
Pathose, or an Inward Passion of
  the Pope for the Loss of His
  Daughter the Masse, 1548.3
The Penguin Book of Satirical
  Verse, 1967.3
"The Pentameter Lines in Skelton
  and Wyatt," 1950.6
"Pereles Pomegarnet," 1934.4
"Peteuelly Constrayned" (non-
  canonical), 1873
Pforzheimer...Library, English
  Literature 1474–1700; see The
  Carl H. Pforzheimer Library,
  English Literature 1475–1700,
  1940.1
"Philatelist Royal" (Graves),
  1927.2
"Philip Sparrow," 1951.1
"Philip Sparrow's Elegy," 1934.17
Philological Quarterly, 1952,
  1953.6, 1970, 1971.7, 1973
Phyllyp Sparowe, 1505.1, 1545.2,
  1553.2, 1560.6, 1831.1

Ireland...1475-1640, 1926.1;
1976.2 (2nd edn., 2nd vol.)
"Short Title Catalog 22606: A
Bibliographical Ghost!", 1971
"_____ " [a
correction], 1971.2
The Shyp of Folys, 1509
"Skelton," 1959.3
"Skelton and Aristotle" [diss.],
1965.4
"Skelton and Music: A Gloss on
Hippates," 1970.1
"Skelton and Music: Roty Bully
Joys," 1955
"Skelton and Oxford," 1936.8
"Skelton and Politian," 1934.12
Skelton and Satire, 1961.1
"Skelton and Sheriff Hutton,"
1967.7
"Skelton and the Dignity of
Poetry," 1936.6
"Skelton and the Epilogue to
Marlowe's Doctor Faustus,"
1963.1
"Skelton and the Metaphysicals,"
1965.3
"Skelton and the Renaissance Theme
of Folly," 1971.7
"A Skelton Ascription," 1950.3
"Skelton at Diss," 1937.1
"A Skelton Emendation," 1936.4
"Skelton et le Yorkshire," 1952.2
"Skelton, Hawes and Barclay,"
1941.2
"Skelton in Westminster," 1921.1
"Skelton, John (1460?-1529),"
1897
"Skelton, John (Sceltonus,
Schelton, Skeltonides, Skel-
tonus, Skelkonus)," 1959
"Skelton, Laureate," 1897
Skelton Laureate Agaynste a
Comely Coystrowne, 1527.1
"Skelton, Petrarca e l'amore
della gloria nel The Garland
of Laurel," 1962.6
"A Skelton Poem in Sloane MS 747,
f88b," 1933
Skelton Poems: for Mixed Chorus
... [musical setting], 1966
"A Skelton Query," 1934.10

"A Skelton Reference c. 1510,"
1960.7
"Skelton-Studien," 1907
Skelton: The Life and Times of
an Early Tudor Poet, 1949
"A Skeltoniad" in Drayton's
Poems, 1619; see under Drayton,
1606+
"Skeltonic Meter in Elynour
Rummyng," 1967.6
"A Skeltonic Passage in Ben
Jonson," 1953.4
"A Skeltonical Salutation...,"
1589.1, 1880
"Skeltonicall Observations of
Bishops Visitations...," 1604
"Skelton's Achievement in the
Tunnyng of Elynour Rummyng"
[M.A. thesis], 1965.6
"Skelton's Artistry: The Early
Lyrics" [M.A. thesis], 1968.2
"Skelton's Cipher," 1899.1
"Skelton's Collyn Clout," 1973
"Skelton's 'Colyn Cloute': The
Mask of 'Vox Populi,'" 1950.2
"Skelton's Colyn Cloute and
Spenser's Shepheardes Calen-
der," 1973.4
"Skelton's Garland of Laurel and
Chaucer's House of Fame," 1916
"Skelton's Hand in William
Cornish's Musical Parable,"
1970.2
"Skelton's Heare after Foloweth
Certain Bokes," 1939.9
"Skelton's Magnyfycence," 1970.4
"Skelton's Magnyfycence and Car-
dinal Wolsey," 1901
Skelton's 'Magnyfycence' and the
Cardinal Virtue Tradition,
1965.1
"Skelton's Magnyfycence and the
Morality Tradition" [diss.],
1969.9
"Skelton's Magnyfycence and the
Strategy of the 'Olde Sayde
Sawe,'" 1966.7
"Skelton's Magnificence Recon-
sidered" [M.A. thesis], 1960
"Skelton's 'Manerly Margery Mylk
and Ale,'" 1967.1

Whipperginny, 1923
Whips and Scorpions, 1932.2
"Who Killed Cock Robin?", 1944.2
Why Come Ye Nat to Courte?, 1522;
  1545.3, 1553.3, 1560.7, 1890.1;
  1966.2
"The Will of Wit, Wits Wil, or
  Wils Wit," 1597
"William Dunbar and John Skelton"
  [M.A. thesis], 1939.7
The Wisdome of Dr. Dodypoll,
  1600.7
The Wise-Woman of Hogsdon, a
  Comedie, 1638
Wit and Fancy in a Maze, 1656
Wit and Science, 1531.1
"With Ships the sea was sprinkled
  far and nigh" (Wordsworth),
  1804

"Wolsey and Skelton's Magnyfy-
  cence: A Re-evaluation,"
  1960.4
"Wolsey's Forced Loans and the
  Dating of Skelton's Colyn
  Cloute," 1972.3
The Works of Ben Jonson, 1816.1
The Works of the British Poets,
  1819.1
The Works of the English Poets
  from Chaucer to Cowper, 1810
The Wounds of Civil War, 1594.2
Yale University Library Gazette,
  1939.9
Zur Charakteristik John Skeltons,
  1904
"Zwei verlorene dichtungen von
  John Skelton," 1919